MW00479068

Praise for *Between the Gates*

"Mark Stavish has managed what few in the postmodern age can even conceive. He introduces here a methodology that instructs us in the art of conscious living, and more startlingly, in that of conscious dying. The Body of Light, included here, is an extraordinary concept that will enrich our years while wrapped in skin, while also providing a means of self-determination as we transition out of this mortal coil. *Between the Gates* is a masterpiece of esotericism and Stavish's finest work to date."

—Colleen Deatsman, author of *Inner Power: Six Techniques for Increased Energy & Self-Healing* and *Energy For Life: Connect with the Source*

"Never before has such a body of practices on lucid dreaming, astral projection, spirit vision, rising on the planes, pathworking, scrying, and the Body of Light been presented in a single volume, nor so seamlessly as to guide students step-by-step through their stages of progress and interrelationship. Mark Stavish has written what may be the best practical guide to inner journeying in the realm of Western esotericism."

—Russell House, author of *The Portal—A Story of Love, Immortality, and the Philosopher's Stone* and past President of The Philosophers of Nature (PON)

BETWEEN
the GATES

Lucid Dreaming, Astral Projection, and the
Body of Light in Western Esotericism

MARK STAVISH
Founder of The Institute for Hermetic Studies

Introduction by John Michael Greer,
Author of *Learning Ritual Magic*

WEISERBOOKS
San Francisco, CA / Newburyport, MA

This book is dedicated to Andrea, Luke, and Nathaniel, and to all who seek to remove fear of death and thereby show us how to live.

First published in 2008 by
Red Wheel/Weiser, LLC
With offices at:
500 Third Street, Suite 230
San Francisco, CA 94107
www.redwheelweiser.com

Copyright © 2008 by Mark Stavish.
All rights reserved. No part of this publication may be reproduced or transmitted in any form
or by any means, electronic or mechanical, including photocopying, recording, or by any information storage and retrieval system, without permission in writing from Red Wheel/Weiser,
LLC. Reviewers may quote brief passages.

ISBN: 978-1-57863-396-8
Library of Congress Cataloging-in-Publication Data available upon request.

Cover and interior design by Maija Tollefson
Typeset in Grajon
Cover photograph © abpeo0030618/inmagine.com
Interior art on pages 30, 35, and 40 by Marc Thorner, Thornergraphics

Printed in Canada
TCP
10 9 8 7 6 5 4 3 2 1

The paper used in this publication meets the minimum requirements of the American National
Standard for Information Sciences—Permanence of Paper for Printed Library Materials
Z39.48-1992 (R1997).

Contents

Acknowledgments

Special thanks to the following who without their generous assistance in time, talent, and treasure, this book would not have been possible: Christopher Bilardi, Paul Bowersox, Joseph C. Lisiewski, Ph.D., Donald L. Melchior, Ph.D., Flinn Mueller, Andrea M. Nerozzi, Ph.D., and Marc Thorner. And thanks to all of the students, adepts, and masters of the traditions, who have each added in their own special way to the continual advancement of the Great Work.

Foreword

One of the most overused phrases in the English language these days is "I just don't have the time." It's particularly familiar to those of us who teach spiritual traditions that place regular practice and the development of the self's hidden potentials at center stage. If you'd like to get a rueful laugh wherever teachers of spirituality gather, just ask how many students utter those words when asked to put even so little as ten minutes a day into some form of inner work.

Granted, leisure time can be in short supply these days, and an industrial society that thrives on the manufacture of artificial desires has no shortage of distractions to throw in the way of the novice in any spiritual path. Yet it's equally true that much of what passes for a shortage of spare time can be solved by figuring out one's real priorities and paying attention to where time actually goes. Plenty of people who are convinced that they have no time for an inner life spend time every evening staring blankly at TV shows that don't really interest them, or fidget away an hour or more on a commuter train every workday. And, of course, nearly every one of us spends six or eight hours coursing through the realms of dream every night, only to brush aside the fading memories of our inner adventures as we stumble from bed to shower to breakfast table to front door.

Dreams are simply the most common route into a realm of experience that has been central to spiritual traditions all around the world for thousands of years. What Henri Corbin called the *imaginal world*, the realm of symbols and similitudes accessed in dreams, visions, and out-of-body experience, forms a crucial element in the wider world of human experience recognized by spiritual traditions, and practices that open the door to that world are among the core disciplines of most branches of esoteric spirituality. The otherworld trance journeys of shamans, the dream yoga of Tibetan Buddhism, and the visionary flights of the Abrahamic religions, to name only three branches from the exuberant tree of the earth's spiritual traditions, all access the same dimension of experience.

Western esoteric traditions have their own disciplines for entering the imaginal realm, but factors woven into the structure of contemporary Western society have made those disciplines and their associated practices difficult for many people nowadays to access. Caught between a mainstream culture obsessed with the pursuit of material wealth and power and an alternative culture convinced that spirituality has to be imported from the far side of the world to be valid, much of the Western world's own esoteric traditions have suffered serious neglect in recent centuries. Certain aspects of imaginal work have seen much discussion in recent literature, but the wider context of this aspect of our Western inner way—to say nothing of entire branches of practice such as dream-work—have remained obscure even to initiates of those traditions, much less to a wider audience.

This book may well change that. Mark Stavish, one of the handful of creative teachers and writers who have helped bring many less widely known branches of Western esoteric spirituality into the light of day, has penned a practical, comprehensive, and user-friendly guide to the practices of imaginal experience in the Western tradition—the first such guide to see print in centuries. *Between the Gates: Lucid Dreaming, Astral Projection, and the Body of Light in Western Esotericism* presents the core theories and practices of the arts of inner journeying and puts them in the context of more than two thousand years of Western esoteric teachings about the subtle body and its role in spiritual development. It's a bravura performance and one that deserves a wide readership among students and practitioners of the world's spiritual traditions.

Since the time of the scientific revolution three centuries ago, people in the Western world have prided themselves on being wide awake to the realities of life. The irony in this claim is that for thousands of years before our time, the wisest of our species have described the obsession with material reality that haunts us nowadays as a dream, one from which we all awake sooner or later, whether in sleep, in trance, in the heights of spiritual attainment, or in death. To venture out of the dream of matter and into the imaginal realms, by way of lucid dreaming, astral projection, the discipline of the body of light, or any other means, marks a step into a wider world. In that world, though our physical eyes are closed, it becomes possible not only to awaken ourselves, but also to dream the whole world awake.

John Michael Greer
Ashland, Oregon

Introduction

Over the last few decades there has been an abundance of books on near-death experiences, prompting the development of an entirely new domain of scientific research and popular publishing. In fact, research into death, survival, and communication with "the other side" has been the main focus of much parapsychological research since the inception of the various societies and institutes for psychic research. The greatest amount of this kind of research seems to occur during times of intense social and political upheaval, making it no surprise that the period before, during, and after World War I saw the explosive growth of Spiritualism as well as a host of occult and mystical organizations.

Modern Research, Ancient Practices

Most recently several prominent members of the Roman Catholic Church have engaged in research on the nature of the afterlife, survival of a sense of self or ego, and its relation to what in Tibet is called the Rainbow Body or the Body of Light. The Jewish and Christian scriptures are filled with direct comments or allusions to such a thing but do not present a comprehensive teaching on what it is and how or if it could be developed.

News of the research being done by Benedictine monk David Steindl-Rast and Father Francis Tiso first appeared in an article by Gail Holland in the March-May, 2002, issue of *Institute of Noetic Sciences Review*, and the article has been reprinted several times. According to the author, Steindl-Rast proposed an investigation of the so-called Rainbow Body (named such because of the colored light the body emits during its creation), and "a phenomenon in which the corpses of highly developed spiritual individuals reputedly vanish within days of death." The research was supported by the Institute for Noetic Sciences as well as the Esalen Institute, as a means of exploring the limits of human potential.

Steindl-Rast became interested in the Rainbow Body after hearing stories of Tibetan Buddhists who were able to manifest it through specific practices and a high degree of inner development, resulting in an intense degree of wisdom and compassion for themselves and others. According to the stories, little was left of these great souls upon their death, except their hair and fingernails, and sometimes nothing at all. This phenomenon caused Steindl-Rast to consider the Gospel accounts of the resurrection of Jesus Christ in a similar light. To assist him in his research, Steindl-Rast contacted Father Francis Tiso, a Roman Catholic priest, whose knowledge of Tibetan language and culture would prove invaluable. Tiso holds the Office of Canon in the Cathedral of St. Peter, Isernia, Italy, and is a frequent traveler to Tibet.

Both men wanted to discover, or possibly rediscover, the nature of this phenomenon and the methods whereby it was achieved. They also wanted to show that the phenomenon was not an anthropological oddity, but should be placed in the context of generalized human development.

News of the Rainbow Body is not limited to Tibetan yogis or Christian saints; even one modern American alchemist is reputed to have left very little in the way of remains after his death in the late 1980s.

While reading the initial draft of this book, Christopher Bilardi, a specialist in European folk and Christian magical practices, pointed out that there is a distinct similarity between the process of Assumption of the Godform and mainstream Orthodox teachings. While there is a distinct doctrinal difference in the how and the why, it is important to note that even in this era, when many are throwing the baby out with the bathwater as far as mainstream religions are concerned, there may still be some hope that mainstream religions can develop a more mystical approach for their adherents.

Just as hermeticism teaches that we can identify with God and in so doing express its essential being, Orthodoxy teaches that through the process of deification, or *theosis*, humanity can be uplifted and become its divine nature.

In theosis, each of us can experience the energies of God, even if we are incapable of experiencing God's essence. This teaching is similar to how some schools of qabala understand the Tree of Life. While we can experience the spheres of Being, we are incapable of experiencing the Nothingness (*Ain Soph Aur*) from which it came. Just as in qabala we come to understand ourselves, creation, and God through the levels of the Tree, in Orthodoxy we can understand God through the energies experienced by the development of a spiritual life. It is no wonder that among the three main Christian groupings—Protestant, Roman Catholic, and Eastern Orthodox—Orthodoxy is considered the most mystical and truly personal of them all. Students of qabala and hermeticism will notice distinct similarities between their doctrines in the following:

The Greek word for God (*theos*) comes from the verb meaning "run," "see," or "burn." These are "energy" words. God's essence (Gr. *ousia*) is beyond our knowing when we consider that this essence is beyond both being and nonbeing. Just as the ancient qabalists described God through what He is not, and therefore derived the Three Negative Veils of Existence, or the Ain Soph Aur, in Orthodoxy God is described in part by what He is not—a created being, and such, incapable of nonbeing. In his densely packed work *The Mystical Theology of the Eastern Church*, Orthodox theologian Vladimir Lossky quotes St. Gregory Palamas in regard to the unknowable nature of the divine essence:

> "The super-essential nature of God is not a subject for speech or thought or even contemplation, for it is far removed from all that exists and more than unknowable, being founded upon the uncircumscribed might of the celestial spirits—incomprehensible and ineffable to all forever."

Yet God's energies are something that we *can* know. Out of God's essence radiates His uncreated energies, or "grace," which allow us to enter into a direct relationship with Him. These energies are His cosmic sustaining power, His love, compassion, guidance, and transforming presence that give us the ability to become *more*.

In John 10:34 Jesus quotes Psalm 82:6, repeating "Ye are gods." We are gods in the sense that we bear His *image* (Gr. *ikon*—i.e., "icon"). Here we encounter the meaning and purpose of human life: to become *more* of what one is meant to be by nature through purification (Gr. *katharsis*) in the divine fire.

It should be clear now that the process of deification does not mean that we become "divine" in ourselves. This is not like the pagan idea of *apotheosis*, where one becomes a *de facto* divinity in essence. In Christianity there is only one God, one ultimate source or root to all things. There are no other Gods, if by "God" we mean the ultimate source, meaning, and Truth of all things.

The link for Christians between God's energies and His essence is the person of Christ. In Orthodox Christian belief, Christ is of the same essence as that of the Father (Gr. *homoousios*), but also of the same essence of humanity. Thereby the transcendent Godhead makes a direct link with our creaturehood. Bishop Kallistos Ware in his work *The Orthodox Way* speaks of God's energies as being pan _en_ theistic, meaning that His energies are immanent in creation (i.e., God is in all things and is everywhere—omniscience/omnipresence—but, is *not* all things as the Godhead is transcendent). This is similar to the qabalistic concept of the Ain Soph Aur retaining some of its unique nature while still emanating the Tree of Life. We become more God-like through the action of these divine energies. Yet like the Virgin Mary, each of us must give God permission to transform our souls (Luke 1:38–56). This is similar to the process of transformation initiates into the Mysteries underwent as they willingly entered into the process of awakening by opening up to celestial unknown.

When we undergo deification, we can make the analogy to that of a sword thrust into a roaring fire, glowing red in response to the fire's heat. Another analogy is that of the planet Mercury in proximity to the Sun. While Mercury glows like a baby sun reflecting/absorbing the Sun's intense energies, Mercury is neither a sun, much less is it *the* Sun— but it is very sun-like. This is not unlike when one assumes the Godform of a deity in Hermeticism. One does not become the historical Hermes, but one takes on some of the energies, the qualities, and expressions of Hermes. They are a lesser-Hermes if you will.

In both Eastern Orthodoxy and Roman Catholicism, the Blessed Virgin Mary (know in Orthodoxy as the Holy Theotokos—i.e., "the God-bearer") is a prime example of what happens to one who undergoes deification. As Theotokos she is a perfect reflector of God's Light and Beauty because she completely and wholly consented to the transforming fire of Divine Will, the Chiah or Fire of Wisdom of the qabalists. She is indeed the very first of Christians.

Modern Challenges

Despite tremendous gains in proving the existence of extrasensory perception and related abilities—by famed facilities such as the Rhine Center for Psychic Research at Duke University, or even older mass telepathy experiments in the 1930s hosted by the BBC and Zenith Broadcasting Corporation—established means of education have done little to promote the acceptance and practical application of these ideas in daily life. While highly educated, spiritual, and well-trained individuals are doing foundation-supported research, mainstream religions and educational institutions as a whole continue to dismiss the existence of extrasensory perception as superstition or condemn it as the works of dark forces. In the end, it is individuals who are making the Herculean effort to read, digest, and distill sufficient information in order to maybe, and just maybe, figure out what it means to be human and does any part of that humanness extend beyond the end of physical life.

Fortunately, despite the crushing polarities of a repressive spiritual environment for over 1,500 years, and a powerfully attractive and addictive scientific model as a counterweight to that condition for the last 300 years, the means and methods of personal spiritual research have survived. Between the pillars of extremes, it is possible to find the keys to personal inner truth if one is just willing to grasp them, insert them into the lock, and turn the handle.

But therein lies the real test. It is easy to be a heretic against church or modernism. At the beginning of the twenty-first century it is even safe and fashionable to pretend to know better than both while offering nothing substantial as a substitute. Sophist theorizing is the hallmark of overeducation and too little life experience. In the end, this book is about life and experiencing life in its entirety. Not just physical life, but psychological and genuine spiritual life as well. If we are afraid of death, we certainly don't live to our fullest any more than if we are afraid of living lest we endanger our crude concept of an immortal soul.

Once someone has genuinely encountered the spiritual dimensions of life, the physical ones take on greater vibrancy and, at the same time, less importance. A balance is struck between the importance of experience and the ultimate experience of Being.

This balance can only be achieved on a personal level. Spirituality is a personal journey of Becoming, and requires commitment and dedication—and a good dose of courage. The methods described in this book have survived under the heels of repressive religious and political institutions for well over a thousand years. In this century alone, National Socialism and communism (Soviet as well as Maoist style) have done more to endanger the spiritual health of the world than Roman Catholic inquisitors or Protestant witch hunters ever did. Even now we are faced with the ultimate fruit of religious teachings that strip the individual of the responsibility of creating a meaningful personal, progressive, interior experience for themselves. Fundamentalism in various forms seeks to turn back the clock in nations around the world. Some of them want a return to the sixth century, and advance their goal through ruthless violence, others through more subtle tact of school boards and soup-kitchen proselytizing. Lesser cults confine themselves to simply buying entire towns in the northwest United States or building bunkers for the end of days. In the end it will not be politics or force of arms that wins the day, but the individual who is unafraid of death, not because of unquestioned teachings, but from direct experience.

To our readers, let me apologize for the necessity of repeating, in chapters one and two of this work, a small amount of material that appears in chapters one and two of my book *Kabbalah for Health and Wellness*. It is a small amount of material limited to several pages in these two sections only.

It is the nature of modern publishing that each book must be written to stand alone, as well as tie-in to related titles without being a part of a numbered series of books, like an encyclopedia. Unfortunately this requires that a small amount of material often be repeated to make sure that both new and more experienced readers have the same basic level of knowledge. If you have not read *Kabbalah for Health and Wellness* or another of my books, *The Path of Alchemy—Energetic Healing and the World of Natural Magic*, please do so. *Kabbalah for Health and Wellness* contains a great deal of information on the use of Hebrew for activating energy centers in the astral body as well as detailed information on the etheric body and its function in psychic development. *The Path of Alchemy* contains complementary information on the psychic centers, means of activating them, purification of the psychic pathways, and the effects of planetary cycles on psychic experiences.

Many readers will recognize some of the material in *Between the Gates* from when it was first published in a series of articles appearing in John Michael Greer and Al Billing's quarterly journal *Caduceus* and in *The Stone*, the journal for The Philosophers of Nature. While the original articles can be read online at www.hermeticinstitute.org, it will be clear that the presentation and language of the material as it appears in this book is significantly friendlier to the new student of esotericism. The original articles were written as part of the Occult Research and Applications Project (ORA) of the Philosophers of Nature and reflect a significant amount of research of many individuals into the nature and function of lucid dreaming, astral projection, and the creation of the Body of Light.

This book contains all you need to have the direct experience of lucid dreaming, astral projection, and the Body of Light, and rather quickly as well. Focused and dedicated practice will unlock the doors of perception to a series of individual and collective nonmaterial realities within a few months. From these experiences, confidence will be built and sustained, which, with concentrated effort, can lead to deep and profound revelations through direct experience about the very nature of life, consciousness, matter—reality—itself.

Be aware! What you hold in your hand is a treasure passed down to you through generations, in secret, and now made public in a clear, comprehensive, and easy-to-understand form with instructions anyone can follow. Do not simply read this book and casually put it down. To do so is an insult and disgrace to all those who went before you in secret and danger so that what was once deeply guarded could now so easily see the light of day and be obtained for less than the price of dinner at an average restaurant.

This book is about, and details the methods of, the Great Work of human Becoming as they apply to consciousness. Study them, apply them, and then one day you will be able to give all your books away, because you will have found an inner teacher that is more wise and powerful than the greatest library ever built.

How to Use This Book

What follows is an introductory and intermediary text on specific hermetic practices for students desiring direct experience of nonmaterial reality. Like any text on experiential mysticism or consciousness studies, this book contains explicit, detailed, and practical exercises that are simple to perform, transforming ideas into experiences. While it is possible to achieve results from each of the techniques independent of the others, it is neither desirable nor suggested that such a practice be undertaken. Each of the techniques presented in *Between the Gates* builds upon the ones preceding it.

For too long qabala and the hermetic traditions have been top heavy with extensive and baroque rituals under the false guise that complexity was the same as meaning, and that the effectiveness of a ritual could be measured in proportion to how long it took to perform or the number of props needed. An argument can be made for the exact opposite, that difficult rituals are simply the constructs of insecure minds seeking assurances in a profusion of symbols to compensate for their lack of confidence. All of the exercises, rituals, practices, and techniques presented in this book are user friendly and can be performed by anyone after one or two readings. Their effectiveness is based on traditional symbols, key ideas, and regular practice by students—unlike some systems, which involve complex thought forms, egregores, or a multitude of devices and, while designed to build confidence in students, also create dependency on external agencies or organizations.

The practices herein will demonstrate the importance of the five key steps of both healing and spiritual awakening or illumination: (1) purification, (2) imprinting, (3) activating, (4) transmuting, and (5) direct experience.

Purification: Preparing the mind and body for new experiences and that are creating emotional, mental, or physical blockages to experiencing lucid dreaming, astral projection, and eventually the formation of the Body of Light.

Imprinting: Consciously imprinting new ideas, images, symbols, sounds, and other useful devices into the etheric and psychic bodies so that the desired states of consciousness can be facilitated.

Activating: Consciously, methodically, and confidently turning on the new imprints so that they may work towards the desired end. This, along with imprinting, is critical to any genuine esoteric initiation.

Transmuting: Working directly with destructive or negative energies to use them in a new context or to modify them so that they are no longer an obstacle in your spiritual path or that of another. This phase does not mean "purifying" negative energies by getting rid of them and replacing them with new energy, but instead working directly with them and literally changing them into something more desirable. This is done primarily in the formation of the Body of Light.

Direct experience: This phase is a synthesis of the previous phases and involves direct experiences of consciousness without the intermediary steps of either purification or transmutation. It also involves experiencing the new states as they arise or consciously creating them, and simply resting or sitting in the experience while holding it as long as possible.

The premise of this book is to be a technical overview of the key methods of exteriorizing consciousness used in Western esotericism that is actually *user friendly and complete*. Fifteen minutes a day is all that is required to turn the information it contains from theory into personal knowledge, power, and experience.

Start with each technique as it is presented. Perform it for the period suggested—often fifteen minutes a day for one or two weeks—and then move on to the next exercise. It is unimportant that you feel as if you have had any "success" with each exercise. Each person responds differently to psycho-spiritual work, particularly if it is in a new area for him or her. Many of the practices will cover the same ideas but from different perspectives, and a person may respond more strongly to one practice than to another. It is impossible to tell what practices you will respond to until you have performed them all. Think of it as a kind of hermetic buffet where you get to taste all of the offerings before going back for more of your favorite food.

Another reason for performing all of the exercises is that many of them build upon one another. While it is still possible to have success if some exercises are skipped, greater success and satisfaction will come from having performed all of them, thereby experiencing the intimate relationships discussed in the text.

Students new to Western esotericism or who have struggled with other texts in the past will notice that *Between the Gates* is written to be as nontechnical as possible and is based on two basic assumptions:

- Western esotericism can be discussed in a clear, simple, and straightforward manner and still retain its validity and authenticity.
- For any esoteric tradition to have meaning it must be accessible, understandable, and practical.

As a result, *Between the Gates* is designed to be an optimal text for both new and experienced students of spirituality for the following reasons:

- A great deal of emphasis is on the actual performance of the exercises, thereby creating an experiential context for learning.
- All of the text is written in *English first*, with secondary references to the Hebrew, Latin, or Greek terms. This makes it easier to memorize and absorb the terms and technical information, and minimizes the need to constantly look up definitions. This is intended to be a major step forward in the process used to teach contemporary esotericism.
- Many of the techniques are often considered very advanced, but they are presented in a manner that makes them easy to learn and apply. Regular use and practice will allow students to quickly identify their strong points, which, when combined with additional exercises in the text, can provide an even and balanced development of skills and technique.
- To help readers clearly identify and use the practical material, it has been divided into the following types.

Exercises: methods designed to strengthen specific mental or psychic functions, or to reinforce a theoretical point;

Techniques: methods that have a specific use and function alone or in combination;

Practices: specific techniques designed to enhance spiritual awakening;

Core practices: practices that form part of a student's daily and weekly practice schedule.

Ideally, these techniques would be used in connection with a regular study group or as part of the Institute for Hermetic Studies courses. However, personal instruction is not always possible, nor is it necessary if the simple and easy-to-follow instructions are carried out, and sufficient time is given to intellectually and psychically assimilate the ideas presented. Nothing can speed up this process; only constant, steady, and heartfelt practice can move it along.

It is important to state that modern esotericism is radically different from its predecessors. It is practiced for the most part out of its cultural context, and information is transmitted in manners undreamed of by earlier students and adepts. The closely guarded and tightly knit relationship between students and teacher-initiator no longer exists. This has led many to believe that a teacher is not necessary, as they have the "Inner Master" to guide them. This is true, but only in so far as each student has the personal discipline, self-reflection, and honesty to listen to the words of their Inner Master. Until that time, an outer teacher will be needed. It is hoped that this book will act in some fashion as that outer teacher.

If at this point you are thinking there must be an easier way, let me state firmly and unequivocally that there is not. If psychic development, alchemical transformation, or cosmic consciousness were easy, the world would be a paradise, and illumination a common experience. The Path of Becoming is the Great Work. It is the single greatest challenge and undertaking anyone can pursue. Its rewards come daily in small, mostly unnoticed ways, all culminating in that moment when the Great Awakening will occur. If you wish the quick and easy road, then stop looking, for none exists except the road of sorrow and disappointment.

Magic, alchemy, and spiritual healing are not for the lazy, but for the brave. While it may seem that it is all up to you, and you do not know what you are doing, where you are going, or what to expect, know that there are invisible aids helping you all along. Friends, strangers, books like this will come to you in times of need, until you are able to listen to the voice of the Inner Master and need to read no more.

No matter what, remember this: by the very fact that you call upon God, the archangels, the invisible ones of Creation, they respond and are present with you. They are always there, and in our petition, we become aware of them.

Establishing a Program

Here are a few tips for enhancing your learning and your experience.

1. **Daily practice is essential.** Establish a regular daily schedule for fifteen minutes a day. If you have the opportunity to spend a few minutes during the day working on a particular visualization or meditation in addition to your regular program, all the better. But it is better to have three or four short sessions a day for ten or fifteen minutes than to try and cram everything into one long session. The brain and the stomach like their food in small, digestible doses, several times a day rather than in one sitting. The more time you spend on the techniques, the more proficient you will become in them, the easier it will be to apply qabala, and the more enjoyable it will be.

2. **Keep a notebook of your experiences.** This is important for self-review and for understanding your dream life and the activation of symbols within your psyche.

3. **If possible, set aside a special place just for this work.** If that is not possible, use a regular opening and closing ritual, such as the one given, to set the proper atmosphere for the work to be performed.

4. **Be regular in your time of practice.** By creating healthy habits of time and place we make our study period something we look forward to and enjoy.

5. **"Make haste slowly."** Spend the proper amount of time on each exercise, move on to the next, and complete each phase of practice in order with a calm, relaxed confidence that everything is working inside you just as it should. You will surprise yourself at the power and ability you posses. It is there when you need it, even if you are not always conscious of it.

6. **Take notes as you read.** Write down the key ideas as they are presented so that you are better able to remember and apply them. To assist in this, words in Hebrew, Latin, Greek, or any language other than English follow their modern equivalent in parentheses. Get the core ideas down first, then go back and learn the vocabulary.

7. **Take time to learn the technical terms.** This book contains a glossary of all of the non-English words used in the text. To make reading and using the material presented easier, only a limited amount of non-English words have been used. But it is important that you learn these non-English words, because they are the technical language of qabala. Knowing them will make it easier to read other qabala texts, which are often not as user friendly as this one.

8. **Study with a friend or two if possible.** The power of collective work to spark individual insights and transformations is well documented. The New Testament says it simply: "Where two or more are gathered together in my Name, I will be in the midst of them." Two or three students working regularly have often produced marvelous results, and historically small groups have been the basis for some of the most important esoteric (as well as exoteric) organizations in history.

CHAPTER 1

Mansions of the Soul

The projection of consciousness has always been an integral part of Hermetic teachings. From the *Merkavah* (Chariot) Riders and their journeys to the starry *Hekelot* (Palaces) of the invisible world in primitive qabala, to the teachings of the *Corpus Hermeticum*—"Think of a place and you are there" of the early Christian era—to the practice of Traveling in Spirit Visions undertaken by the adepts of the Hermetic Order of the Golden Dawn in the nineteenth and early twentieth centuries, it would appear that the desire to experience the invisible world while still living in the material is an overwhelming human desire.

While a wide variety of approaches has been formulated to assist the disciples of these diverse schools, many of their techniques require an extensive amount of preparatory teachings, initiations, and ritual assistance. However, while the world has changed, human beings still want to "know"—to experience for themselves—and not just believe in the spiritual realms they were taught about as children—realms that have always been so slightly out of reach. Modern life, however, is much different than the life of our predecessors, even if our instinctual spiritual desires are the same. Time is divided into smaller and smaller units, and people are expected to achieve ever more and more in those microsections of time.

Many people say they have little time for spiritual studies, let alone to dedicate to a specific discipline. Others say that many of the traditional

Western disciplines are too abstract and difficult to understand, let alone apply. Yet for those who have little or no knowledge of traditional tenth- to twelfth-century Merkavah doctrines, or no interest in learning the necessary signs, symbols, and invocations for Golden Dawn-style techniques and their "spin offs," yet who still want a Hermetic approach to their inner world, this book is the solution. The material presented is simple, direct, and does not require an extensive amount of visualization or creative imaging.

The methods herein are especially suitable for those who would like to have an "out-of-body experience" but who lack either the necessary visualization skills required for so many of the present techniques, or for those who have had violent experiences leaving their body and would like a gentler approach to the astral planes. The methods described in this treatise can be performed either by an experienced traveler or by a beginner with equal ease and similar results. If the techniques in this book are practiced regularly there is every reason to believe that everyone will be able to achieve some level of conscious experience of the invisible world. However, to accomplish this successfully and meaningfully, it is important that we first understand why we have this instinctual need for spiritual experiences in the first place—what it is that we are after, and why do we want, and seemingly *need*, to go there.

Consciousness exists on several levels, and it is the work of the occultist (one who practices esoteric methods) to experience all possible levels of consciousness, integrate them, and ultimately realize his or her oneness with the source of Being. To assist in this task, a variety of models or paradigms, as they are often called in material and social sciences, are constructed out of experiences of those who have traveled the road before us. These models are subject to a fair degree of change and even challenge as time goes on, but they are effective and necessary tools to get us where we want to be. They are, in effect, maps of consciousness, and like a road or topographical map, they are not the territory itself. Maps help us understand where we are and what lies before, behind, and around us, but no amount of studying a map can substitute for the experience of actually traveling the terrain. The map is a tool, not the territory. This important fact is often lost on students of contemporary and modern hermeticism, who come across extensive and detailed accounts of spiritual experiences under such headings as traveling in Spirit Vision, Rising on the Planes, astral projection, the Body of Light, pathworking, and skrying. To help clarify the work outlined in this book, it is helpful to understand the basic qabalistic-Hermetic cosmology and physiology and the various methods used to integrate them into a comprehensive and practical experience.

The Tree of Life and Levels of Being

The theoretical background behind the practices described herein are primarily qabalistic, and it is applicable to either the traditional Tree of Life (Golden Dawn) or the Palaces outlined in the Sepher Zohar. In short, any systematic outline of the interior body-world of humanity can be applied, as long as it has concise, easy-to-visualize symbols for the various planes of consciousness. This includes the numerous cosmological images produced during the Renaissance, particularly those dealing with alchemy.

The working assumption behind contemporary and modern Hermetico-qabalistic practices is that we as conscious beings originate in the Ain Soph Aur, or Limitless Mind of God. We incarnate through various stages of increasing density and matter into the present world in order to gain the experiences that will allow us to go from potential beings to self-actualized or self-created beings. In our journey of development we take on characteristics and "bodies" of various vibrations, and on our "return" we shed these bodies in exchange for increasingly subtle bodies and worlds of Light.

These worlds are categorized in the Gnostic, qabalistic, hermetic, and alchemical texts under different names and numbers, but share the same essential qualities and functions. That is, they go from the dense world of material earth to the subtle realms of Infinity, or the point of our origin, the Mind of the Creator.

Within our physical body we have various organs of psychic perception, called psycho-spiritual centers in modern Western esoteric nomenclature and *chakras* in Sanskrit. These centers correspond to several aspect of our physiology; one aspect is our nervous system and plexuses and another is our endocrine system of hormone secreting glands. Other correspondences exist as well, but for our purposes these are the ones most commonly and efficiently used.

Astral projection is often suggested by way of the psychic center located near the solar plexus, a major nerve center in the human body, but for many this can be an unnerving and unsettling experience. Other sources suggest visualizing your soul (or spirit) rising out of your body like a mist or appearing as a secondary body "of light" next to your physical body. It is said that advanced practitioners can project their consciousness at the time of their death through the upper psycho-spiritual centers, thus "dying consciously." The upper centers are those at the top and front of the head, or the crown and Third Eye centers, respectively, associated with the pineal and pituitary glands. Some even use the psychic center at the back of the head, the medulla oblongata, or brain stem.

In the Indian texts, each chakra is associated with a particular power (*siddha*), which is awakened in the aspirant and allows the student to then project his or her consciousness through the different psychic centers in increasing complexity and subtlety, until finally, the crown center is reached. In alchemy, these powers, or *charism* as they are referred to in the New Testament, are demonstrated and thereby proved through specific kinds of alchemical transmutations. The same is true in qabala, where, as each level of consciousness is experienced and integrated, various powers are awakened in the psyche as a result. In qabalistic practices, however, the centers are rarely used directly, but instead intense visualization of the ethereal worlds is undertaken, until these various worlds are progressively realized. Rituals combined with more generalized energizing of the psychic body are often used, alone or in conjunction with these visualized worlds. The modern variation of this practice of visualization involves the use of Tarot cards and is called pathworking, or the use of Hebrew letters. Eastern Orthodox monks have used intense visualization, in which the solar plexus is seen as a small sun, as a method of achieving exteriorization, and some schools use the heart center as a center of displacement. However, the previously mentioned methods are the most commonly used ones to date.

Alchemists use tinctures, or medicines, to assist in the projection of consciousness, but these should not be confused with hallucinogenic or psycho-active drugs. The effects of alchemical medicines generally occur when their user is relaxed, sleeping, or in meditation. They, in effect, assist the projection of consciousness—that is, the expansion of awareness—rather than induce or cause it directly. It is possible to take an alchemical medicine and drive a car unimpeded.[1]

Astrology is not directly used as a means of achieving contact with spiritual dimensions; rather it is used as a means of recognizing the most optimum time for various operations, be it creation of an alchemical product or ritual for astral projection. It is no surprise that the moon plays a significant part in many of these experiences, and lunar cycles (along with planetary hours) are the main astrological tools that are used.

The Hermetic Path and Its Practices

Three Major Areas of Study in Western Esotericism

Alchemy: for understanding the relation of energy and consciousness to matter. This relationship is most easily understood within, but not limited to, modern schools of homeopathy, herbalism, and spagyrics.

Qabala: for understanding the relation of symbols to consciousness and matter. Today, this relation is most evident in, but not limited to, the modern schools of transpersonal psychology, psychosynthesis, and even medical hypnosis. Moreover, schools of practical occultism, particularly those derived from the Hermetic Order of the Golden Dawn, Martinism, and Rosicrucianism, utilize qabala-based symbols in ritual formats for healing, manipulation of material events, and the expansion of consciousness into the spiritual realms.

Astrology: for understanding the relation of cycles to consciousness and matter. This is most easily understood in terms of, but not limited to, seasonal changes and biorhythms, as well as specialized areas of medical and horary astrology.

Combined, these three study areas form the primary disciplines of the hermetic arts and sciences. Astrology tells us who we are, qabala tells us where we are going, and alchemy provides us with the method of realization.

5

In this book the main focus is consciousness from the viewpoint of energy and symbolism, but to make it concrete we will weave in some of the more practical areas of alchemy and astrology that cross over with qabala. The techniques presented can also be seen as a form of inner alchemy, wherein the process of *solve et coagula*, or separating and recombining, is utilized as the chief tool.

The school of qabala we are discussing falls under the domain of the hermetic qabala. This is because it most closely resembles the qabalistic doctrines and practices that came out of the Renaissance, which were resurrected en force during the nineteenth and twentieth centuries' occult revival periods. During the renaissance, hermeticism brought a sense of Classical dignity to qabalistic studies that elevated them from being a purely Jewish subject, as well as making them more philosophical and less religious in appearance. In turn, qabala brought a Biblical basis, even if a Jewish one, to hermeticism, as well as practical methods of working that were still understood, respected, and even feared, in a hostile, anti-Jewish, Catholic Europe. Thus, it is important to have an understanding of both traditional hermetic and qabalistic philosophy if we are to put it into practice.

Hermetic Philosophy

Hermeticism is the study of the body of Greek texts appearing in Alexandria, Egypt, between the first and third centuries A.D. and attributed to Hermes Trismegistos, as well as variations of these writings, adaptations of them, and commentaries upon them written in all periods up to and including the current era. These commentaries include Alexandrian as well as neo-Alexandrian traditions. The traditions comprise core texts, commentaries on these texts, and specific practices designed to integrate the ideas into the practitioner's life. It is clear from the texts that communities were formed where members held communal meals, the kiss of peace was exchanged, and initiation into the sacred mysteries was performed.[2] These traditions include a variety of Gnostic, Christian, Rosicrucian, and even Masonic writings grouped from the first century A.D., across the Renaissance, into and including orders and societies rising out of several modern and contemporary occult revivals.

Named after their attributed author, Hermes Trismegistos or "Hermes the Thrice Great," these writings are collectively called the "Hermetica." This body of texts is small and has been translated several times in recent decades. Its main themes are the creation of the material world and the soul's journey, ascent, and regeneration as it progresses through the celestial spheres.

It is important to note that the hermetic texts were composed in different time periods by different authors from different traditions. The influence of Egyptian, Greek, Jewish, and Gnostic thought is clearly present. What makes hermeticism unique is that despite these diverse influences, it manages to synthesize the ideas presented and create a distinct school of thought that goes beyond each of them individually. Names and ideas of one tradition are seamlessly intermingled and interpreted according to the ideas of another.

Alexandrian hermeticism and modern hermetic practices share four key points in common, including a synthetic philosophy that while utilizing the mythology of "fall and regeneration" avoids the pitfalls of dualism, and emphasizes concrete and common sense approaches to solving mundane as well as cosmological issues.[3] Hermeticism encourages and embraces the notion of humanity and the divine existing harmoniously in and through the world. It is an exceedingly optimistic philosophy and, in this regard, very different from certain strains of Gnosticism, or even Vendantic studies, which see the world as an essential evil for the soul's growth or as a prison house and punishment for some distant and long forgotten transgression.

The eclectic nature of hermeticism is found in its fundamental premise that the desire for knowledge can be satisfied by consulting a variety of sources that find their roots in the *philosophia perennis*, or perennial philosophy. It is synthetic in that these diverse ideas are not only tolerated, *but unified into a seamless whole.*

Nous is "mind," and Hermes is informed by Nous (his Higher Self) to meditate on the nature of the universe being reflected in his own being, to extract the divine powers of nature and unite them with the powers of this soul. The universe is a text to be read—it is "the Book of Nature"—and through our divine intellect, we are able to unite with it and understand it.

The physical world is a good place and is essential to the unfolding of human consciousness. Hermeticism reaches the abstract through the concrete. The universe is met in the mineral salts of an herbal (spagyric) tincture; the psychic centers or "stars" are experienced through the influence of the planets on ones personal horoscope.[4] Heremeticism is very specific, personal, and experiential, and yet it is continually transcending the limits of material life. This natural magic gives rise to natural philosophy, and the divine is seen incarnate everywhere and in everyone.

Son is the father, Mother the moon. The wind carries
it in its belly, the Earth is the Nurse thereof.

The Emerald Tablet of Hermes

True, without error, certain and most true;

That which is above is that which is below, and that which is below is that which is above, for performing the miracle of the One Thing; and as all things were from one, by the mediation of the one, so all things arose from this one by adaptation; the father of it is the Sun, the Mother of it is the Moon; the wind carries it in its belly; the nurse thereof is the Earth.

This is the father of all perfection, of consummation of the whole world.

The power of it is integral, if it be turned into earth.

Thou shalt separate the earth from the fire, the subtle from the gross, gently with much wisdom;

It ascends from earth to heaven, and again descends to earth; and received strength of the superiors and of the inferiors—so though has the glory of the whole world;

Therefore let all obscurity flee before thee.

This is the strong fortitude of all fortitudes, overcoming every subtle and penetrating every solid thing.

So the world was created.

Hence were all wonderful adaptations of which this is the manner.

Therefore am I called "Thrice Great Hermes," have Three Parts of the philosophy of the whole world.

That which I have written is consummated concerning the oper- ation of the Sun.

The *Emerald Tablet of Hermes*, along with the *Corpus Hermeticum* and various qabalistic and alchemical manuscripts outline the general phi- losophy, cosmology, and metaphysics of hermeticism. It is important to know this because in any system designed to deliver results, the philosoph- ical basis is the basis for all practical methods. To make these methods work, each system based upon its basic philosophy requires the proper philosoph- ical view of themselves, the universe, and others. Through the application of method, this view is actualized and the philosophy demonstrates its usefulness in human life. Without the right attitude and motivation, all so-called spiritual methods are little more than a distraction at best. To treat esoteric practices as if they are a psychological or mental technology devoid of moral and ethic precepts is to reinforce the negative habits that keep us rooted in ignorance and suffering.

Our True Will

Esoteric techniques are a method, not a technology. Their success is dependent on our motivation and inner desire, or our True Will as it is sometimes called. If our True Will is genuine, it will be positive, productive, and helpful to others. If we are mistaken and what we think is our True Will is really just a justification for further materialism, then our success will be short lived, if actualized at all. In truth there is really only one True Will, that is the Will of the Creator, the Will of the First Cause, or Being from which all things come and are united. This Will is a single, pointed desire to Become, and each of us, as an aspect of that, shares in this desire, this Will to Be. However Being is linked to illumination, or cosmic consciousness. Only by experiencing our place in the universe, even if just once, do we really understand what it means to Be and to Become. In esoteric practices there are only two motivations that are genuinely acceptable if permanent lasting progress is to be made on the Path of Return:

The single pointed Will to become Illumined that personal ignorance and suffering are no more, or;

The single pointed Will to become Illumined and in doing so we become a means of helping others dispel their ignorance and suffering.

To undertake the Path with a motivation other than one of those listed above is tricky at best. The desire for power, wealth, more stuff, psychic experiences without purpose, or as entertainment is catastrophic to spiritual development. To undertake the practice of methods that allow one to enter into the invisible worlds there must be strong desire to actually go there. The journey to invisible worlds cannot be half-hearted or simply be carried out from curiosity. One must be firmly rooted in a strong foundation built on the proper intention or failure is guaranteed. This comes not from some force exterior to ourselves, but from our own meeting with the Guardian of the Threshhold.

The Guardian of the Threshold

Within each of us, deep in our subconscious, is the summation of everything we have ever thought, felt, or done. This locus of energy creates within us a sense of conscience, which becomes translated into moral and ethical codes of conduct based upon the culture we live in. While it is difficult to make absolute statements about right and wrong or good and evil, it is clear that if we are to progress spiritually there must be some general code of conduct that we can use to help us get started. When this code of conduct is broken, we may feel guilt or remorse and make efforts to amend our actions. If we do not, we run the risk of creating future conditions in which it will be easier to undertake such an action again. While we can hide from our actions while incarnate, we cannot hide from them forever. Anxiety, neurotic behavior, and nightmares are all a result of some actual or perceived breaking of an ethical or moral code. If our violation was severe in its injury to another, thereby inhibiting their progress in life or their spiritual studies, we will experience a tremendous sense of fear and apprehension at the moment of death. This fear and apprehension is known as the Terror of the Threshold.

The Terror is induced by our coming face to face with the Guardian of the Threshold, or the collective energies of our subconscious, the summation of our past experiences in this life and all others, in a single form. This form is our creation and is our personal "devil." It is our judge and jury and also the means by which we understand the purpose of our life. It is this internal, emotional incongruity that is the source of all failure in occult practices and in material circumstances.

Confidence or an overwhelming positive certitude is required for occult practice to succeed. If we are mentally positive, but emotionally conflicted, then we will fail. Emotions win over ideas every time. It is necessary to build strong and positive emotional neural connections between the ideas we are presenting and the outcomes we desire. This can only be done when we allow ourselves to feel joyful and worthy of success. To do this we must make the Guardian into our friend and ally. We fear death because we fear our encounter with the Guardian. In this encounter all of our ideas of self give way to what truly is, what we have made of our life and lifetimes. Cultivating the emotions of gratitude, mercy, and humility go a long way to creating the proper inner conditions for success in both our inner and outer life, for in reality, they are one and the same.

Humility, Mercy, and Gratitude

If we want to avoid any shock in our encounter with the Guardian of the Threshold we should undertake a sincere daily reflection upon our thoughts, words, and deeds. In Tibetan iconography and Tantra it is common to imagine one's teacher before them in midair as a perfectly enlightened being, emanating three rays of light: white from the head, red from the throat, and blue from the heart. The disciple visualizes these rays of light as entering into their head, throat, and heart respectively, and cleansing it of all errors in thought, speech, and conduct. In Roman Catholic iconography it is common to see pictures of Jesus with his hand pointing to his heart and the same three colored rays of light extending outward.

It is important that at the end of the day we undertake a period of reflection, prayer, and meditation to cleanse ourselves of any harmful habits or new actions we may have undertaken so that we can better experience out periods of sleep, dreaming, and projection of consciousness without the disruption of unresolved issues or negative emotional habits. Each person is free to formulate their own methods of reflection, prayer, and meditation, as long as they are sincere about the desire to improve their life and relations with others. One need not beat themselves up over things nor feel as though they are hopeless. Heartfelt honesty, the sincere desire to improve, and the courage to continue are what matters the most.

In doing this, the terrifying aspects of the Guardian of the Threshold are modified and transformed into active powers and potencies that we can access as we proceed along the Path.

The Guardian is sometimes portrayed as a dragon or serpent with seven heads or wrapped around a jewel or great treasure. The dragon is the deep powers and forces of the universe that we possess but have yet to fully understand, and use unconsciously and instinctually. The jewel is the Red Stone, Philosopher's Stone, or the light of illuminated consciousness within us, and its power to transform our life on all levels. As we learn to make friends with these various levels of our inner world, of our psyche, the dragon becomes a powerful source of energy in the material and psychic worlds.

While some may see this approach as too religious sounding, it is important to step back for a moment and reevaluate your ideas on this matter, for if your previous notions and methods had proven fruitful, you most likely would not be reading this book.

Exercise: Simple Purification Practice

Preparation

Sit comfortably with your back straight, feet flat on the floor, palms of your hands flat on your thighs and close to your hips (to take stress off your shoulders and elbows), and chin slightly tucked. Breathe deeply several times, holding your breath in for as long as is comfortable, exhaling slowly, and holding your breath out for as long as is comfortable. Feel yourself relax mentally, emotionally, and physically as you do this. Say the following prayer (or something similar): "Divine Mind, source of all, assist me in this work of purification of thought, word, and deed, so that I will awaken to the innermost depths of my being and achieve perfection in my creation of the Body of Light."

Affirmations or prayers to our inner self, our Holy Guardian Angel, such as the above are powerful tools for jump-starting and maintaining our practice and success.

Explanation

This practice prepares the mind and psychic body of the practitioner for experiencing increased psychic and mystical states by decreasing the amount of resistance within them. This focus on decreasing unconscious, internal resistance prior to additional practices makes this a purification, as well as a preliminary practice.

Type of Practice

This is a preliminary practice designed to be used prior to meditation, prayer, or healing intervention. It can also be done alone in the evening or prior to sleep.

Method

1. While still seated, visualize the sun and moon above you. The sun is on your right, and the moon is on your left. Imagine their powerful energies drawn together, as the sun brings life energy and the moon absorbs that energy into itself, giving form. The two energies mix and project a point of energy, forming an invisible triangle that sits on the top of your head, with one point pointing downward. This energy enters into your body, filling it with brilliant vibrant light. Imagine that all of the negative energies are pushed out your lower openings and absorbed by the earth.

2. Imagine the fiery heat and energy of the earth (the Secret Fire) purifying the emotional, psychic, and mental refuse that you have ejected.

3. Imagine this brilliant and dynamic energy of the sun and the moon filling you, radiating outward from you, and the purification, happiness, and stability that it brings. Rest in this feeling.

4. Close your meditation with a prayer of gratitude for what you have experienced and dedicate any benefits from it to your path of Becoming and to that of others.

Incorporation into Daily Practice

This practice should take ten to fifteen minutes at most and be done once or twice a day for a month to get some grounded experience in the importance of purification practices in all spiritual work. Failure to undertake purification practices is tantamount to pouring fresh water into a dirty vessel. Over time the vessel will eventually get clean, but the cleaning will take much longer and be more difficult than if a little soap and elbow grease had been used in the beginning. If you have a strong attraction to alchemical symbolism, you can use the Solar King and Lunar Queen in place of the sun and moon symbols.[5] Purification practices are especially important when undertaking the practices involving the formation and use of the Body of Light, astral projection, and similar advanced practices.

The practice of purification can be performed by and taught to anyone who seeks to proceed on the spiritual path and, more importantly, on a hermetic, qabalistic, or alchemical one. This exercise is very important and is the foundation upon which all the following practices in this book are built.

Methods of Experiencing the Invisible Worlds

There are a variety of methods for experiencing the invisible worlds, the various dimensions of the Tree of Life. These methods can be divided into two categories: subjective and objective. Subjective methods allow only the practitioner to experience the invisible worlds and bring back information, which then must be verified through experience or historical record. Objective methods allow individuals other than the principal practitioner to experience an aspect of the invisible world—particularly as it enters into or modifies the material world. These experiences, while often amazing and encouraging in the area of after-death survival, do little to actually give the kind of experience that one could call initiatic or significantly transformational on the spiritual level. However, objective phenomena is important as a means of understanding our relationship to the universe, as well as of preventing self-delusion from entering into our path. In recent years it has been significantly discarded in favor of the fuzzier and less discernable psychological approach to spirituality.

This alone may be the most significant point for many readers of this book. While there is a high degree of similarity and continuity between modern (late nineteenth into the twentieth century) and Renaissance practices through their use of visualization, meditation, prayer, correspondences, and ritual, there is also a considerable divergence of conceptual view and practice. The primary break is this point of objective and subjective phenomena as a result of occult practices. Even a cursory look at Classical, Medieval, or Renaissance occult literature will show that practical material effects were the main concern of the operator. Modern literature is mainly concerned with subjective, transpersonal, and more abstract concerns. In general, religion was the domain of "spiritual" concerns and the community, and "occultism" (be it magic or alchemy) was the domain of demonstrating spiritual ideas on a practical level in daily life and often an individual pursuit. Occultism was, it must be remembered, the science of the age and were allied with the study of mathematics, optics, geometry, linguistics, and a host of other disciplines whose study has fallen to secular education.

It is easy to see why such a break would occur between the practical and the transpersonal if we allow history and pragmatism to be our guide. Until recently life has been very difficult even in the most technologically developed nations. Only with the onset of the industrial revolution did Europe and the United States see the growth of a leisure and ultimately a middle class that does not depend on slavery, serfdom, or cheap domestic staffs to maintain a household. Washing machines and dryers for clothes, dishwashers, gas and electric stoves, even curbside pickup of refuse and indoor plumbing all allowed a tremendous amount of time that had been dedicated to daily survival to be freed up for education and entertainment on a mass level never before experienced.

Medicines prevented or cured many simple diseases that previously killed the young, old, and physically weakened. The rule of law was increasingly enforced, and justice systems that functioned as expressions of law and operated under public scrutiny replaced corrupt systems. This list goes on. As a result, the need for operations dealing with day-to-day concerns diminished, and greater emphasis could be placed on self-development and self-awareness, areas being explored in the emerging fields of psychology and psychiatry. While the "spell-book" phenomenon would continue to exist, offering for many their gateway into practical occultism, and occult ideas would be modified to fit the mold of "positive thinking" for marketing to the sports and professional fields, the premise that a magician could open up the invisible worlds, and bring through its energies and even inhabitants into the material, faded into the background. Angels and demons were reduced to subjective Jungian archetypes as the they changed from being God's servants into projections of humanity's hopes and fears—and with that change made magic safe, but often impotent.

We have seen that esotericism is the study of the cosmos and humanity's place in it, and occultism is the practical application of esoteric philosophy. We have also seen that Western occult practices generally fall into three categories: qabala, or magical practices based on qabala for the study of symbols; alchemy, or the study of matter; and astrology for the study of cycles. It is also possible to say there are three main paths to esotericism: the Path of the Mystic, the Path of the Magus, and the Path of the Sage.

The mystic is concerned with his or her direct relationship to Deity through the heart and devotion; the magus is concerned with his or her relationship to Deity through the intellect and understanding power as it is expressed in and through creation; the sage is concerned about his or her relationship to Deity as an expression of cosmic wisdom or total harmony, and holds some resemblance to the idea of the village wise man or wise woman.

Each path is a path we must walk and integrate into our life. We are complete only when we have experienced and mastered what each path has to teach us. The great Renaissance hermeticist Guidorno Bruno stated true hermeticists must express themselves in three ways: (1) first as a physician and healed the physical and psychological wounds of the individual; (2) as a prophet in line with the prophets of the Old Testament, who spoke out to warn the community of possible problems and hardships if continued courses of action were taken, and in doing so helped heal the community and keep it in harmony with divine laws; (3) as a magus, or master of the occult arts, and co-creator with the Divine. In modern esoteric terms we might see these three roles as the shaman, the priest/priestess, and the magus/magician.

TRADITIONAL	BRUNO	MODERN
Mystic	Physician	Shaman
Sage	Prophet	Priest/Priestess
Magus	Magus	Magus/Magician

While this is not a book on objective occult phenomena, it is important to recognize this side of all occult methods and the role it plays in the different expressions of esoteric practices, be they alchemical or qabalistic. The most common objective methods are:

Miraculous Healings: While a so-called miraculous healing is a very personal experience, it is one that is verifiable by a third party, or even science, which can determine that physical limitations were overcome by an unknown means or source. This kind of tangible phenomena can be emotionally powerful enough to profoundly affect the spiritual views of those caregivers and medical personal who experience and/or witness it.

Paranormal Phenomena: While scientifically verifiable, most paranormal phenomena occur on a personal level and are never subject to outside (or third-party) scrutiny. However, paranormal experiences by children or adolescents are often the cause of people entering into religious vocations or spiritual searches later in life.

Evocation to Visible Appearance: This is by far the single most dangerous, technically demanding, and little explored area of occult practices. In evocation, instead of the operator entering into a trance and either skrying or astrally projecting into a specific realm of being to converse with beings who may be there, the operator constrains and brings a preselected and specific entity into the material world through ritual means. The reality of alternate dimensions is definitely made clear to those who experience this kind of ritual; however, unless the evocation is done to full manifestation in physical form, there is always the possibility of self-delusion on the part of the operator. For this reason, many evocations are seen as dealing with little integrated areas of one's own psyche rather than a truly separate entity.

Transmutations: In a transmutation, a piece of physical matter is changed from one state to another. This phenomenon is most commonly associated with alchemy, wherein one metal is changed into another (most commonly mercury, lead, or antimony into silver or gold) through an application of the Philosopher's Stone. Transmutation is a means whereby an individual's inner state of consciousness is manifested in the material world by his or her ability to create an object of a nature sympathetic to their interior initiation.

The most common subjective methods are:

Skrying and Seership: Skrying and seership utilize crystal bowls, balls of water, ink pools, or other devices to enable the operator to enter into a trance whereby the mind is able to sense, see, and in some instances experience potential events coalescing in the astral matrix. In most instances the consciousness of the operator or experimenter does not leave the body, but instead becomes aware of the particular details around a preselected topic. The key to successful skrying is the ability to enter into the collective consciousness and to discern the meaning of the information obtained.

Pathworking—Guided Visualization: This is the most common method of entering into the astral planes. The operator uses images and characters in storybook fashion (with a beginning, middle, and end) and visualizes in the imagination the story presented. If the method is done properly, the operator may have an experience immediately during the pathworking session or later during sleep or meditation.

Normal Dreaming: Dreams are the most common, fragmented, and unreliable means of experiencing inner worlds because they depend on inner energies working to the surface of the operator's consciousness and then the operator remembering them in some meaningful way on awakening. Normal dreams, however, are a valuable tool for taking the next step, directed dreaming, for reaching the inner worlds. Inner dreaming, in fact, may be passed over entirely, and lucid dreaming directly experienced in some instances.

Directed Dreaming: Directed dreaming is nearly identical to pathworking, only the story is not described in detail. Instead, the dreamer imagines a particular setting, or possibly a scene from an unfinished previous dream, while going to sleep. At the same time, the dreamer gives verbal affirmations of the intention to dream about this particular subject. This is a very useful method for use in problem solving.

Lucid Dreaming: Lucid dreaming is when the dreamer "wakes up" inside of a dream and knows he or she is dreaming. Initially this will cause a rupture in the required concentration needed for the dream to continue, and the dreamer will involuntarily wake up. With experience and practice, the dreamer will develop greater control over the dream, as well as the ability to do physically impossible acts in the dream state as proof that what is happening is not material reality. Access to higher levels of consciousness, interior initiation, and the death experience are available once this ability has been achieved.

Astral Projection: Astral projection is an extension of the lucid dreaming experience, only the operator is fully aware of being conscious in a nonmaterial state. From this point, it is possible to access various levels of consciousness, as well as physical locations on the earth and the Archives of Nature. It is also possible to view events that have occurred in the deep past, are occurring (clairvoyance), or may occur in the future (precognition). Astral projection and the remaining subjective methods are the only means whereby one can free themselves from the fear of death and experience while incarnate the reality of post-mortem survival and spiritual illumination.

Rising on the Planes: Rising on the Planes is a method whereby the consciousness is directed towards a specific level of awareness through the use of symbols and associations—similar to pathworking—and takes on a living, vital awareness of that level. After developing sufficient experience with Rising on the Planes, it is possible that one can experience any level of consciousness of the Tree of Life without undertaking extensive ritualistic work or having to journey through the intermediary levels. The Body of Light can be utilized in this method as well.

Experiencing the Body of Light: The Body of Light is unique and distinct from the astral body in that it has profound tangibility to it and can be made visible, under proper conditions, to the naked eye. It is a means of using the etheric energies of the material body and subconscious to create a form or shell that can experience extremely high levels of consciousness, maintain consciousness after death, and take on a variety of shapes and forms. The Body of Light is technically simple, but in practice is not without its dangers, as the essence from which it is constructed is often vitalized with powerful psychic residue from our subconscious, giving a sort of potential semiautonomous consciousness to the Body of Light. The Body of Light must never be allowed to operate independent of its creator.

Death: For the average person, outside of the occasional lucid dream or possible sudden insight or psychic experience, death is the the first real experience with the invisible world. However, unlike with the other methods, in death the physical body is abandoned completely, the energy withdrawn, and opportunities to integrate the experience into the entire spectrum of life experiences is partially lost, because death is not limited to the dissolution of the physical body, but the material persona or ego and to the astral sheaths built up around it as well. Experiences are stripped down to their bare-essential minimum and absorbed into the eternal memory that composes Self. However, those who have experienced death consciously during their incarnation are capable of dying consciously, with full awareness, and entering into a variety of spiritual domains after leaving physical life. They are also capable of choosing their "death path," as well as their next life path, in the form of reincarnation, while still in this life. These choices are easy and simple to make; it is simply a matter of making the decision and committing to it rather than regarding it as a special privilege reserved for so-called high initiates.

All of the above methods are based on the fundamental truths presented in the Emerald Tablet. The methods covered in this book—lucid dreaming, astral projection, the Body of Light, Rising on the Planes, and preparations for death and dying—are clearly from the subjective category, but are described in a manner that encourages objective testing of results whenever possible.

Key Points

- Hermeticism is the principal expression of esotericism in the West.
- The Emerald Tablet of Hermes forms the basis for hermetic theory and practice.
- Alchemy, qabala, and astrology are the three principal expressions of the occult arts and sciences.
- The occult practices that form the practical expression of esoteric philosophy are not technical devices that operate devoid of moral and ethical requirements. Humility, mercy, and gratitude are important moral and ethical qualities that we must develop and express if we are to make an ally of the Guardian of the Threshold.
- Methods of contacting the invisible world can be divided into two categories: subjective and objective methods. There are roughly nine subjective methods and four objective methods that can be used. All methods are based on the fundamental truth found in the Emerald Tablet of Hermes.

Assignments for Chapter One

1. Copy the text of the Emerald Tablet on a piece of paper and read it daily, making it the basis of your meditations for at least two weeks.

2. Perform a nightly review prior to going to bed or as you fall asleep. Working your way backwards, examine each of your actions across the day and determine if you could have acted in a more productive manner and what that manner would be if you had the opportunity to relive the experience. Imagine yourself going through the experience again, this time, changing your actions to the desired ones.

3. At least once a day, more if possible, offer a heartfelt prayer of gratitude for all that you have, are, and will be, and all that you have experienced, so that you may discover its meaning in your life.

4. Begin keeping a nightly log of your dreams.

CHAPTER 2

Maps of Eternity: The Invisible in Western Esotericism

In contemporary esotericism the most common map used to describe the invisible worlds is the Tree of Life. While there are several versions of the Tree of Life, they are all in agreement about the number and placement of the *sepherah*, or spheres that represent the various levels of consciousness we are working at directly experiencing. Variations between the different models of the Tree consist in the placement of the paths, or interconnecting lines that demonstrate the primary means by which we interact between these levels of consciousness and move from one to another. For the sake of instruction, the standard Lurianic Tree as used by modern magical groups will be utilized.

The Tree of Life described here is rooted in Jewish mysticism, but has been highly modified by the later addition of non-Jewish elements and interpretations. Its extensive use by various authors and societies in Renaissance and later occult revivals has qualified its use as being specific to the hermetic schools of those periods. These methods still apply to any cosmological model students wish to use. It is important to remember that cosmological models such as the Tree of Life are maps of eternity, and the map is not the territory. Only by direct and personal experience in these domains do we understand the profound limits we have in expressing them in concrete terms, as well as the inspired creativity many have had in their successful efforts to do so, so that others might follow after them.

In addition, there is the Neoplatonic model of the universe, used during the Renaissance and later periods, in which the various levels of creation were arranged in concentric circles, rather than in the linear model of the Tree of Life. This concentric-circle model is seen extensively in the writings of Robert Fludd.

It is easy to ask, "Why so many versions of the same universe?" Historical and cultural reasons aside, the answer is pretty simple: each model reflects a different *starting* perspective. While all models will take you from the relative to the absolute, from the concrete to the abstract, from the material to spiritual, each does it from a slightly different starting emphasis. Qabala is concerned with the big picture, with cosmology from the start. Alchemy is concerned with unlocking the energy that makes up matter and experiencing the spiritual in the material. The Egyptian cosmology, as related in *The Book of the Dead*, is concerned with the invisible, but starts from the view of the recently deceased as they find themselves in their tomb and experiencing the Lower and Upper Worlds. Like the Tibetans, the Egyptians saw physical life, and initiation in particular, as a dress rehearsal for what happens after death.

Modeling the universe then becomes further complicated by the attempt to make individual experiences meaningful and understood by the collective group, be it religious, esoteric, or society as a whole. Known symbols are used, or new ones are placed in relation to known ones to show similarity. In turning the abstract into the concrete, the words "like" or "as" are used, and metaphor becomes the medium of the day. Historical events become teaching tools of cosmic significance, and teaching stories are taken as literal events. New symbols, words, and myths are created to express what was previously unexpressed in a specific cultural context resulting from previous iconic, linguistic, or folk limitations.

For this reason it is important to learn a tradition from someone who has gone down the road before us whenever possible. It is also the reason why a system must be picked and adhered to exclusively for at least eighteen to twenty-four months if one expects to make serious advancement along the path. Remember, intellectual development is quick in comparison to psychic and emotional integration. Persistent and repeated practice enables one to develop the necessary positive habits that make success a reality. The inner mysteries of a system can be transmitted in weekend seminar, a book, or even in a moment of receptivity, but to fully understand and articulate them takes years of steady effort. This effort is all the more important if we are not under the tutelage of an experienced senior student or genuine adept.

Creation: An Overview

When the universe came into being, humanity, or the "human seed," that aspect of consciousness that was to grow into realization of godhood, descended from primal unity. This unity is symbolized in qabala by the divine world of Atzilooth, and the Holy Upper Trinity in the Tree of Life, consisting of the three highest spheres or levels: Kether, Hockmah, and Binah. These levels are so subtle and intense in the purity of their singular natures that contact with them permanently alters our self-awareness. Technically speaking, it is only on these levels that true and genuine spiritual development takes place—that is, experiences we carry with us for eternity and not just as a phase of our Becoming.

When consciousness experiences increasing levels of density as matter is created, duality forms and continues to the material world. This first descent from unity to duality is the so-called Fall, and to prevent a premature return to unity—that is, before all of creation could be encountered—a barrier, referred to in the qabalistic literature as the Abyss, appears. This separation from the unitive experience is the "first day of creation," or appearance of time and space as we can understand them.

As the descent continued, the human seed experiences progressive levels of sexual polarization as well as further removal from its memory of unified consciousness—unified not only in the sense of an interior state, but also in terms of unity with the rest of creation. As the human seed takes on denser levels of awareness, its psychic connection is reduced, and its ability to exert an occult influence in the natural world is diminished to a point of being nonexistent.

After the level of Divine Harmony in creation, or Tiphareth, the center of humanity's sense of self, an additional barrier was created: the Veil, or Paroketh. Here is the appearance of individuality free of the Divine spark.

Finally, a third barrier is encountered, and that barrier is what separates material creation from the psychic and spiritual worlds. Here, humanity has no memory of its Divine origin and has complete free will to seek what it desires. But it also no longer has any occult powers and is purely materialistic in its actions and effects. All that remains is a faint memory of what was and could be again. It is this subtle memory that drives humanity back up the Tree and on the Path of Return to its primordial estate. This dim ember of spiritual consciousness and the power it contains is the driving force that has led to the creation of every known philosophical, esoteric, religious, and occult practice.

Levels of Being

The reduction of the human seed's unity with creation parallels a similar fragmentation within itself, or at least there is the appearance of a fragmentation, for if there were no sense of separation and free will, there would be no reason to undertake the work of Becoming. The Great Work of self-creation must be a choice, and while assistance is available, it must be asked for, as an act of will—it is not forced upon anyone. To help us understand our options, the various levels of consciousness within us voice their opinions of what "we" should do, and in turn, each human being functions more as a collection of competing interests and desires rather than as a rational and functional being. It is by recognizing, addressing, sorting out, and satisfying in a constructive manner these competing forces—and getting them to cooperate—that we become whole again. It is in our experiencing of wholeness that we experience our natural state of holiness, or unity.

In qabala the soul or consciousness is seen as existing on four levels, each corresponding to a letter in the divine name of God—YHVH—as well as to one of the ancient Elements of Fire, Air, Water, and Earth. These Elements are energetic states that are expressed through their named counterparts; as such, all things solid are said to be Earth, liquids belong to Water, gasses to Air, and intense energy, heat, or radiations to Fire. Since humanity is said to be made in the image and likeness of the Creator, it is no surprise that we find focal points in ourselves that correspond to these Elements or qualities. The physical body is given to Earth, the emotions and astral body to Water, the rational and organizing self (also the ego or limited sense of self) to Air, and our immortal awareness and absolute potential to Fire. It is these four selves or levels of awareness that we must integrate into a single and effective working unit to be successful on the esoteric path. To do otherwise is to undertake occult operations for the wrong purpose and reasons and to risk further fragmenting of our being.

What is convenient about this organizational structure of the human being is that it is not limited to qabala, but also finds direct parallels (or outright use) in alchemy, many schools of general esotericism, and specialized areas such as Enochian magic. Modern schools of esotericism, particularly those in the New Age movement, have adopted it wholesale when they refer to the four levels of Being: physical, emotional, mental, and spiritual. As a result, none of these ideas will be particularly new even to the inexperienced reader. But the root and more subtle aspects presented here may be, and it is in this deeper knowledge of the origin of ideas and the details that they are composed of that we can achieve a meaningful and useful relationship with them.

What is important to keep in mind is that each of these levels, while interacting in a continuous manner with one another, also constitutes its own complete environment or world. These worlds (*olam*), are an important part of practical qabala, as well as alchemy, in that they are a vital, living example of how nature repeats itself over and over again from the subtle to the dense, and in that repetition creates environments that, when they are being experienced, give the impression of being a universe unto themselves. This is easy to understand if we simply take a look at our own life. How often do we not get so engrossed in our own actions of the moment that we lose sight of the bigger picture? A single moment of lust, rage, altruism, or distraction can lead to a series of events that affect us for months, years, or our entire lives. It is a common remark that many people are so focused on the singular nature of their work that they are ignorant of the most basic events in the world around them, or even of the people they may be working with.

This kind of myopic obsession is no different in some aspects of the psychic and spiritual domains, particularly when we keep in mind that the energies and intelligences we are dealing with are more instinctual than rational. They absorb and digest ideas, emotions, thoughts, acts, and so on, and create a unified whole—but that whole is centered around a single or primary theme. This primary theme colors everything that happens in that level of consciousness (*sepherah*) or even the larger worlds (*olam*).

For example, experiences in the sphere or cosmic level known as Netzach will always be focused around beauty, harmony, sexual love and romance, art, music, and natural magic. A profound sense of nature, refined instinctual power, and personal joy will be present. The astrological energies of Venus would dominate and stimulate the corresponding psychic center in our physical, etheric, and psychic anatomy.

The same experience, if we could call it that, in the sphere known as Tiphareth would be focused around the self in harmony with the Cosmic rather than the more social oriented harmonies of Netzach. Love would be more impersonal, even devotional in a spiritual sense, and the creative-sexual drive to union would be directed towards deity, Cosmic Consciousness, or one's Higher Self rather than personified into physical sex and projected onto another human being. A sense of being at the center of the universe, or in harmony with all of creation—visible and invisible—might preside, as the astrological energies of the Sun would dominate and stimulate the corresponding psychic center in our physical, etheric, and psychic anatomy.

In Hod, one would have the sense of union as an idea, an intellectual form symbolically represented and given expression by making the abstract concrete, but still impersonal in mind. Here union—be it sexual, social-emotional, or mystical—would be translated into words, forms, and images that convey an idea rather than directly experience it in the more conventional sense. Here, the astrological energies of the planet

Mercury would dominate, stimulating the corresponding psychic center in our physical, etheric, and psychic anatomy.

This is just an example of how three of the ten levels of Being filter, or tincts, as they say in alchemy, our perceptions of an experience, thereby creating or setting in motion new and additional experiences. Each cause has an effect, which in turn is a new cause, pushing us further on our chosen Path.

The same experience would also be altered by the world it is experienced in. Powerful experiences of Netzach in the physical world (Earth) would lead to physical sex, artistic creations, and a love of nature. In the psychic world (Water) the experience would be highly emotional and sensation centered. In the mental world of the ego and self (Air) it would be more idealistic, archetypal. In the true and genuine spiritual world (Fire) it would be pure energy and concepts experienced directly, without separation or sense of "otherness."

It is critical to keep in mind that as we experience something, we develop a consciousness of it. Even if that thing or "it" is an aspect of our physical body, emotions, or subconscious, the more we experience it, the more comfortable we become in that experience, the more mastery we gain with the challenges it presents. Until we have an experience, consciousness is latent and existing only as a potential in seed form. It is from experience that we develop *self-awareness* and become *self-created beings*.

The scheme of Western esotericism, based on the Tree of Life, gives us four worlds and ten levels of consciousness, for a total of forty potential specific areas of consciousness, in which to experience a greater degree of complexity and unity of life. Some schools even say it is fifty, in reference to the Fifty Gates of Wisdom. There are at least seven hundred psychic centers in the human body that can be developed to assist us in our journey. From this it is easy to see where incongruities between how an idea is imagined or idealized in the mental world, and how it is actually experienced in the material world, can lead to emotional knots or obstructions that present themselves as psychological complexes. These complexes are the root of all human suffering, and untying them is a major aspect of the Great Work. When they are released, a wave of energy, insight, and emotional satisfaction and joy fills our life, even when we are faced with seemingly unconquerable obstacles.

For students serious about their progress on the spiritual path, it is critical that these obstructions or emotional knots, these complexes of the psyche, be addressed in an orderly and timely manner. Psychotherapy can be of great assistance, especially if it is combined with the use of an astrological birth or natal chart to identify them, and if therapeutic suggestions are grounded in daily living.[1]

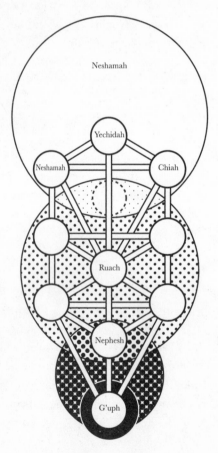

The Divisions of the Soul

The Higher Self: the Soul of Fire

The Higher Self is a confusing topic; since it is something we really know little about, we need to take other people's words for it, hoping that they have enough experience to know what they are talking about. Such experiences and their codification become the basis for religious, philosophical, and esoteric movements. Rituals are then used to dramatically enact the process, phases, and results of one or more individual paths of awakening made accessible to the broader public. In Western esoteric circles it has become fashionable to talk about one's Holy Guardian Angel. For some, the Holy Guardian Angel, or HGA for short, is an individual's Higher Self, their spiritual spark (*Yechidah*) made accessible to them, or in some instances merging with them into a single being. This access is often referred to as Knowledge and Conversation—a literal dialogue in which Self (*Neshamah*) speaks unto self (ego/*Ruach*), and the little self is increasingly brought into a union with the Higher Self. This unbreakable union is known as the alchemical marriage and is the first major milestone of the spiritual path. There is still more work to be done, but at this point on the spiritual path, we are adults in the universe—we are emancipated.

Others say that our Holy Guardian Angel is not our Higher Self, but is a completely separate entity or being that is assigned to us at birth, follows us for our life, and, if we undertake the proper methods, can unite with and we become "more than human."

A possible reason for perceiving the Higher Self as "other" is that it is the nature of our subconscious to objectify inner as well as outer experiences, to clothe experience in human form, to make them more "like us." The Higher Self in qabala is said to have three main expressions: Divine Self (*Yechidah*), True Will (*Chiah*), and Intuition (*Neshamah*). was used to refer to The Divine Self that we think of as our Higher Self or Holy Guardian Angel has a tendency to be *initially* experienced as a blinding light, an angelic figure, or simply a luminous human form. Our True Will is our *divine discontent*: our instinctual urge, even need, to become more than we presently are. It is our creative energies at their most basic and profound level. Intuition is the "Voice of the God" speaking to us, connecting us, and making us aware that we are more than flesh and blood, fleeting emotions, or grand ideas—that we are all these things and more.

Regardless of which theory about the higher guardian angel or about the Higher Self you believe, they are both only theories until they are experienced, and they have been mentioned only to put the methods discussed in this book in their proper context. In the end, we must elevate our awareness of the Higher Self within ourselves through our own efforts and actions. Visible and invisible assistance is always available for us; all we need to do is ask for it, and before our petition is even complete, the aid will have been granted. Simply by thinking about our Higher Self for even a moment elevates us and places us in communion with the seed and the fruit of our Becoming. This is the most direct practice and is the path of prayer.

What both theories have in common is that the energies experienced when the Higher Self/HGA and the little self/ego join are like fire. Pure, intense, pulsating, active, and dynamic, they quicken everything they come into contact with, making it complete, integrated and pure; this purity is of a singular nature, without incongruities or aberrations—a veritable expression of an archetype, even if just for a moment or two.

The Middle Self: the Soul of Air

In qabala the Middle Self or ego is referred to as Ruach, which literally means "air." This Middle Self is what we experience in day-to-day, moment-to-moment life. It is our sense of mind or awareness, our reasoning capacity, and is very much directed at interpreting information, stimulation, and sensation coming to it from the physical world. Despite its hair's breath proximity to both the Higher and Lower Selves, it tends to ignore both of them except during times of extreme crises. It is here that our free will is centered and we can choose what we want to do, experience, become, or create. It is here that all ethical decisions regarding right and wrong are made, based upon the impulses we receive from the Higher and Lower Selves, as well as external training and social habituations.

To unlearn habits that have become no longer useful and, as a result, a detriment to our self-expression, the tools of psychotherapy and magic are often employed. Both share similar methods, overlap in areas, and, as stated, should be pursued concurrently during initial training. Much of this work is expressed ritualistically and forms a path suited to the mind, as it is organizational in nature—it brings order to the chaos of our psyche. This is often the ceremonial path and finds its compliments in ritual magic, as well as formal ritualized religious worship.

The Lower Self: the Soul of Water and Earth

This is the most complex, least understood, and often most ignored of all the levels of Self. Known as the *Nefesh*, it is directly connected to our physical world, material instincts, and hereditary issues, and it is present at birth, with the first breath, before the arrival of the already-perfect Higher Self and yet-to-be-formed Middle Self. The Lower Self is the power base of physical and psychic life, and without it, nothing can happen in this world. Through its first letter, *Nun (N)* it is directly tied to the Hebrew concepts of the serpent, creative energy, sexual power, light, brilliance, and magic.

The Lower Self is sometimes referred to in Jungian terms as the shadow because of the dark, powerful, potentially violent energies that reside there. It is important to point out that the Middle Self is primarily ideas, thoughts, and organized processes that have very little energy in their own right, whereas the Lower Self is mainly emotions, energy, and actions that have little intelligence behind them and no rational capacity. The Middle Self thinks and plans, but the Lower Self simply acts on what it is told. It is synthetic in function. However, without the energy of the Lower Self all the good ideas of the Middle Self are worthless. Plans collect dust, and dreams fade into the darkness of death. Only with the skilled direction and cultivation of the raw emotions of the Lower Self is anything accomplished in the material or psychic domains.

Through proper training, suggestion, and specific practices, the Lower Self will accept the directions of the Middle Self, thereby opening up awareness of the world of miracles.

These emotions can rise up when stimulated by material conditions and create an urge or idea within the Middle Self, which in turn opens up a connection to the Higher Self. The Higher Self can also directly communicate with the Lower Self, bypassing the ego, if the health of the body is at risk or if even injury or death threaten it. There are numerous instances of this kind of phenomenon where an individual takes action without any conscious thought or reason—such as changing directions, sleeping in late, or turning back to pick up a forgotten item—only to avoid an accident, traffic jam, or catastrophe.

Bringing the energies of the Lower Self into full cooperation and direction of the Middle Self, so that an effective channel to the Higher Self can be opened, is the work of various schools of ritual magic, Tantra, and alchemy. It is important to note that the Lower Self is directly tied to the physical body (*Guph*). While some will say the physical body is a separate entity, this is false. The physical body is a direct extension, or densification, of the etheric energies of the Lower Self. They are one and the same, but with an extensive and little understood range of operations. It is the inherent energy in matter that alchemists use to make vegetable and mineral products that purify and strengthen their etheric energies, thereby providing health to the body and energy to the mind. Tantra uses the energies of the body, particularly stimulation of the physical sensations to stimulate emotions that in turn are directed by the ego to open a pathway for the superconsciousness of the Higher Self to pour through. It is as the alchemical manuscript that the Golden Chain of Homer refers to it, "a great chain of being." In the Lower Self, the Great Chain is complete within us, all we need to do is recognize its links.

While we are constantly forced to think in terms of small pieces to make the vast array of consciousness digestible, the domain of energy-matter-consciousness from the most subtle to the most dense is, in reality, one thing. We divide the One Thing to work with it and understand it, but in the end it is still One Thing.

The Tree of Life : "You Are Here"

In qabalistic (and hermetic-alchemical) terms, Creation is seen to have taken place in the following process.

The Divine Mind of God, the Absolute Nothingness (also known as the Limitless Light), through a series of expansions and contractions, establishes the boundaries of Creation. The first world, *Atzilooth*, is the most subtle and closest to the original state of nonexistence. This is called the world of Fire, because of the lively, undefined, and almost uncontrollable

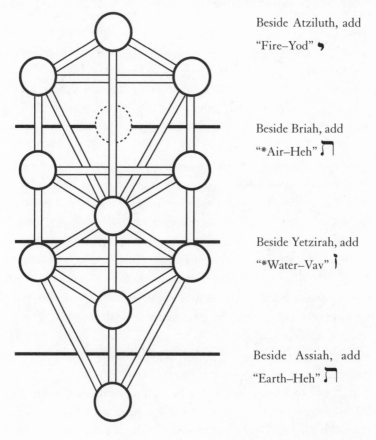

Beside Atziluth, add

"Fire–Yod" ׳

Beside Briah, add

"*Air–Heh" ה

Beside Yetzirah, add

"*Water–Vav" ו

Beside Assiah, add

"Earth–Heh" ה

The Elemental associations given here are in accordance with alchemy. Modern schools of magic will often place Water in Briah and Air in Yetzirah.

nature of fire. Next is *Briah*, or the world of archetypes, which forms as our human mind grasps these archetypes. It is symbolized as the world of Air, and, as a result, it is a barrier world that is formed by the creation of the next world, *Yetzirah*, or Water. This is the highly psychic and emotionally charged world immediately behind the veil of material existence, or *Assiah* (action). *Assiah* is also known as the world of Earth, because of the solid, concrete nature of material life.[2]

One Tree, Four Worlds

The doctrine of involution and evolution is important to hermetic thought, but a detailed explanation of the doctrine as it relates to specific practices will be given in later chapters. In summary, this doctrine states that the energy-matter-consciousness nucleus grows denser, and less powerful, as it moves from unity (*Kether*) to materialization (*Malkuth*), and that the various stages involved create the intermediary spheres of the Tree of Life. It is the purpose of each being (Adam) to go from blissful ignorance (Paradise) into ignorance (the Fall), and, through the experiences found in material existence, return to his or her primordial state (New Jerusalem), but with total knowledge, wisdom, and power. It is the story of the Prodigal Son as told in the New Testament.

As unity emanates and creates the various levels of energy-matter-consciousness we call the Tree of Life, it also creates several reflections of it, each with its own unique expression of those energies. The first Tree, if we could call it that, is mostly energy, little mind, and virtually no form and no matter (at least as we would understand it). This is the Tree of Atzilooth, of the spiritual world, and because of its energetic nature it is often associated with Fire, or the letter *Yod*, in the Tetragrammaton, or the four-lettered name of God.

The second Tree, also known as the Tree of Briah, emanated from the completion of the first, imitates this process and creates another Tree. This second Tree takes the minute, highly discrete, and distinct energy pulses that create the seed sepheroth in the first Tree and turns them into distinct and discrete ideas. These ideas are still broad and encompass many subsets, and are abstract in that they are more arche-types than facts. Platonic solids and geometric forms are a perfect expression of the spheres as they relate to this Tree. This Tree is process and organizational in nature, and is often associated with Air and the first *Heh* in the Tetragrammaton.

A third Tree, also known as the Tree of Yetzirah, is created in the same fashion as the second. It takes abstract ideas of the shape and thought, be they collective or individual, and turns them into powerful emotions, feelings, instincts, and concrete images. This Tree is associated with the domain of Water, for water is what gives life and physical form to creation, and the letter *Vau* of the Tetragrammaton.

The fourth and final Tree is created in identical fashion as the previous ones, only it is dense, hard, material, and concrete. It gives rise to and is tangible to the physical senses. This world moves from its own point of near nonexistence, the first swirlings, to the universe as we know it. This physical universe is the world of Assiah, action, and associated with the final *Heh* of the Tetragrammaton. It is here, in the material world, that the abstract ideas and ideals of consciousness are worked out and made manifest.

Each human being has their own Tree within their aura. This Tree connects them to the larger Tree, or Trees, and holds the seed energies of our evolution. The awakening, directing, and expression of these seed energies in harmony with their spiritual source, is the Great Work of each qabalist. These energies also express themselves in a unique fashion, in that our physical body (Guph) connects us to the physical earth (Malkuth), and it is Malkuth that connects us to the broader physical universe (Assiah).

As stated above, the etheric energies that compose our physical body are shared by our nervous system, instinctual need to create (libido), and subconscious mind. Just as our nervous system connects our consciousness to the material world, and our libido connects us to another human beings (to continue the species), our subconscious connects us to the emotions, instincts, and thoughts in our immediate environment, and if developed, to other people, places, and dimensions, or spheres (and eventually worlds), on the Tree of Life. This is how psychic phenomena are possible.

The energies of the Tree, as they manifest in our aura, appear in ideal archetypal form, but as they enter into the physical body they shift, change, and express themselves in accordance with the needs of physical, not spiritual, life. One need only recognize that the orbital pattern of the solar system is distinct and different from the stacked, linear hierarchy of powers presented on the Tree.

Just as the energies of the astral, or Watery, world of Creation make their way into material existence through the planets and their etheric energies (creating the doctrines of astrology in the process), the same energies are manifested in the physical earth through mineral and plant life. The earth acts as a container for the total expression of all of the etheric and material energies of each of the individual planets. The human body also acts as a container for their same expression, first through the archetypes of the Tree in the aura, then by the psychic centers relating to the planets and Elements in the etheric body, and finally through specific and distinct expression in the actual physical body and the organs related to those planets. The planets derive their existence and energy from the spheres of the Tree of Life, but are not identical with them. The energies of the planets are primarily material, etheric (Lower Self/Nefesh), and to some degree astral in nature, but they are not concerned with extremely abstract concepts or pure energy as are the worlds of Briah (Middle Self) and Atzilooth (Higher Self).

For this reason, it is possible for someone to become a very powerful qabalist, able to create seeming miracles in the material world, yet not be very developed in the spiritual sense. Through focusing on the relationship of the etheric energies of the planets, and the interaction of those energies with the earth and, in turn, our individual physical body and subconscious, we can release profound and powerful energies. This is the secret of practical alchemy and talismanic magic.

The purpose of this scheme is to show that creation occurs through subtle changes in the levels of energy-matter, from the most subtle (Fire) to the most dense (Earth). Within this context of increasing density, there also arises a series of ten planes or levels of consciousness that combine with energy-matter; these planes or levels are known as sepheroth, or spheres of Being. (*Sepherah* can be translated as "sphere," "emanation," or "number," and its root, *seph*, is used in forming the Hebrew word for "book.") They occur in a threefold pattern, three times: unity, polarity, synthesis, and finally materialization. This basic idea of unity, polarity, and reharmonizing is the basis of qabalistic (and hermetic) practices, and is derived from the observation of nature.

Each world is a reflection to a denser or subtler degree of the one before or after it. Each sphere is a reflection, in part, of what proceeds or follows it. However, since each reflection is only partial, or slightly distorted, each sphere takes on its own unique characteristics. For this reason the ten levels of the Tree of Life can also be visualized as round, luminous spheres of energy-consciousness-matter, each with its own characteristic, which is related but not identical to those spheres that follow or came before it.

This zigzag of creation is called *mezla*, and is also referred to as the Lightning Flash. The return of energy from matter, back through the various stages of Creation is known as the Path of the Serpent because of its reverse, or complimentary zigzag nature back up this diagram called the Tree of Life. It is also called the Path of Return.

The Ten Levels of Creation

The goal of the mystic is to experience union with the Divine. This is an interior journey of repair or healing that brings our entire being into fullness. However, before we undertake a journey it is important to have a map to guide us. For qabalists, this map is the Tree of Life. It is important to remember that each sphere or level has a variety of qualities associated with it, in particular, matter, energy, and consciousness. Different experiences belong to different worlds. Day-to-day life is in the world of matter (Assiah), associated with the Element Earth. Yet in our dreams, inner fantasies, and periods of creative thought, we are more deeply involved with the world of emotions (Yetzirah), associated with the world of Water. Periods and flashes of terrific insight, synthesis, great intuitive clarity, profound experiences of light beyond form or emotion (other

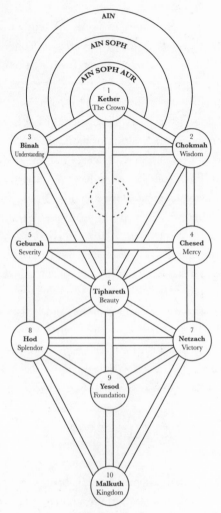

The Tree of Life

than exaltation and joy) are from the world of the mind (Briah), associated with the world of Air. The world of spirit (Atzilooth) is associated with the world of Fire and is beyond the scope of any description other than a sense of complete unity with the essence of a particular sphere.

The work of this book is to cultivate the necessary skills and techniques to progressively experience the ten different levels of the Tree of Life in each of the worlds, either through direct effort or as a spontaneous reaction to it.

The ten spheres of the cosmos emanating from the undifferentiated source, or Limitless Light (Ain Soph Aur), are as follows. Note that each sphere has an energy and a set of ideas associated with it, as well as a location in our psychic body that allows us to access those ideas and that energy on a personal level. This energy is generally related to an area of the physical body, but it is not limited to that location and has other, more direct means of affecting the physical structure.

Crown—(Kether) is unity. Kether contains all that potentially will be, and all that has been. It is the godhead and font of creation. Its physical location is the top of head and the brain as a whole. The imagery associated with Kether is pure brilliance, a point of light, or similar abstract concepts.

Wisdom—(Hokmah) is thinking, a clear concept of what is and the proper relationship between all of the aspects involved. Its physical location is the left temple and the left side of the brain. The imagery associated with Hokmah is that of the zodiacal belt, vast interiors of space embracing the cosmos.

For practical purposes, these two spheres or levels of Being are only tangentially addressed with the techniques mentioned in this book. Anyone who faithfully practices the methods described herein will be able to figure out how to address them in a more detailed fashion.

Understanding—(Binah) is the ability to know as symbolized by Wisdom, plus the ability to act and the courage to do so. It is stability, focus, and power. Its physical location is the right side of the brain and the right temple. The imagery associated with Binah is cold, silent, and embraces an aspect of the Path of Return known described as the "Contact with Eternity," as it can involve a sense of timelessness. Imagery associated with it include a pyramid or temple with a single spire. Also, when placed in context, Hokmah can give the experience of spacelessness, or everything being crushed into one point. (Kether, of course, is also the experience of that point to some degree.)

These first three spheres form the Holy Upper Trinity and are deeply interconnected; they act more as a unified entity than as singular levels. One could say that this world is unity, and to digest its totality we experience it in one of three ways: timelessness, spacelessness, and the point.[3]

Mercy—(Chesed) is compassion and, more importantly, purity. Mercy provides us with the energy to be in the world but not of it—to be a morally and ethically upright, but not an uptight, person. Mercy connects heaven and earth, and, in its influence, the divine plan is understood and expressed. Selflessness is the current manifest here. Its physical location is the left shoulder. Imagery associated with Chesed includes vast temples and buildings of great culture, philosophy, and worship.

Strength—(Geburah) is self-discipline, the ability to get to work on what needs to be done and the courage to follow it through. Here we mean the work of self-actualization, as well as the work of quieting the mind and getting down to business. Its physical location is the right shoulder. Imagery associated with Geburah is stoic, spartan, and militaristic, or at least geared towards action.

Beauty—(Tiphareth) is the experience of self or "I." Here we exist as an independent being, but also feel the subtle and not-so-subtle connections to others and, more importantly, to our divine origins. This experience offers us the highest levels of subjectivity, or "selfness." The higher we go on the Tree, the more selfless we become and the clearer our perception of our self, others, and the universe is. The lower we go, the more selfish and marred in our perspective of people, things, and experiences we are. Tiphareth's physical location is the heart and solar plexus. Imagery associated with Tiphareth is usually bright and brilliant and includes beautiful architecture, overviews of gardens, and openness to bright blue skies. It is regal, royal, and very elaborate at times.

Victory—(Netzach) is the interface between self and the material world. It is the domain of the emotions and, more importantly, the instincts to be, have, and do. Its physical location is the left hip. The imagery associated with Netzach is very natural, green, and vast. Trees can be huge, with dwellings in them. A deep connection to the natural world is expressed here, and it feels like an eternal late spring or early summer.

Splendor—(Hod) is the intellect, but also the highest level of human reason that, if turned inward, can help us sense our connectedness to the Divine. Its physical location is the right hip. The imagery associated with Hod is often confusing and filled with mental tricks or illusions. Castles containing libraries, magical chambers, and alchemical laboratories predominate.

Foundation—(Yesod) is the realm of the psyche, or soul, in the sea of creation, with all of its many parts, images, dreams, and aspirations. It is the power of the godhead driving downward to create the material world, and the pull of the godhead on each of us to go inward, upward, and back to oneness with the Being of all. It is the basis for all creation and experiences in the material and psychic realms. Its physical location is the sexual organs. The imagery associated with Yesod is eternal night, with a full moon always in view no matter where you look. There can also be a library, or "Archives of Nature"—the astral record that can be accessed. Gardens, water, and threshold areas such as doors, crossroads, and cemeteries will dominate. One can meet the deceased most easily on this level.

Kingdom—(Malkuth) is the place of action, our body, and the material world. Kingdom is the strong pull of emotional desire (Victory) in action in and around us, through our flesh, and in the experiences of daily living. These powerful desires can be used to link us even deeper into material life, to the Divine, or to a host of psychic subtleties between the two. Its physical location is the feet, as well as the perineum (when the body is seated on the ground) and the organs of excretion/bowels. The imagery of Malkuth is dual—part of it is the subtle energy behind the material world and the other part is the actual material world from the view of the invisible. One can encounter a host of other beings and people on this level, as well as deceased persons who are bound to the material or who do not know they are dead. A vast array of potential exists in this area for those working alchemical operations or attempting to understand how earth energies manifest.

Each of the spheres acts a kind of rest station, as well as a focal point along the way. They are, in turn, connected to each other by a series of paths, which help us to take the concepts they individually represent and combine them with each other in a systematic synthesis. There are ten sepheroth and twenty-two paths.[4] It is through meditation on the different levels of the Tree of Life, and the paths that unite them, that we sharpen our awareness, increase our expression of divine potential, and bring healing to our body and mind.

To summarize qabalistic theories on Creation, we could say that the visible and invisible worlds are interrelated and are, in fact, various projections of one another. Focal points of energy concentration exist, and these have specific functions in modifying the way we experience and perceive the relationship between energy, matter, and consciousness. Links between these focal points create new expressions of energy-matter-consciousness, as they represent a synthesis of the different focal points involved. We could say, simplistically, that Creation is a giant hologram over which we have far more influence than is generally understood or believed. Through proper training, each human being has the potential to be an active creator within this holographic structure (even to the degree that their very thoughts can materialize), thereby increasing their physical, emotional, and mental wholeness.

Rings of Power: Worlds of the Renaissance Magi

The Renaissance was the highpoint in the development of Western esotericism, primarily in the form of hermeticism, Rosicrucianism, and even primitive Freemasonry. It was during this time that the seeds of qabala as we now know it were grown to fruition; alchemy was practiced by kings and emperors, astrology by princes, and magic by popes. Nearly all of the material referred to by the great modern authorities and used during the European occult revival of the late nineteenth and early twentieth centuries can be traced back to the Renaissance. So widespread was the influence of men like Cornelius Agrippa, Paracelsus, and John Dee that without them not only would modern magic be radically different, but even folk practices, including the Pow-Wow of the Pennsylvania Germans, and the core beliefs of the early Mormons

(Church of Jesus Christ of Latter Day Saints) would not exist. The summation of Western culture can be found in the Renaissance, and the Renaissance was defined by magic.[5]

To understand Renaissance occult practices, it is important to recognize that from the fifteenth century to the first decades of the seventeenth century Western civilization stood at a crossroads. It, and the rest of the world, has yet to fully realize the importance of the decisions made along the path it picked, particularly as those decisions relate to our ideas of science, mysticism, and physical life.

During the Middle Ages the worldview of both Christian and non-Christian Europe was essentially magical, but devoid of critical understanding. Despite the church's aversion to pre-Christian beliefs, many pre-Christian practices were synthesized into church holidays and local practices, and many clergy willingly or out of necessity turned a blind eye to local folk practices that showed a continuation of early beliefs. The magical practices of late antiquity survived the barbarian onslaught and collapse of a rotting civilization by following along several distinct lines of transmission. It is only later in the Late Middle Ages, with writings of two of its most famous magicians, Albertus Magnus and Thomas Aquinas, that we see the early development of modern scientific theory in an attempt to understand how the physical world worked. However, both men proposed and supported the idea of natural magic and the early theory that through the power of imagination or active fantasy the spiritual and material worlds could be united and the magician could assume his role as cocreator in harmony with the natural forces of the universe as established by God. It is this mingling of reason, scientific study, and active imagination with the practices of astrology, magic, and alchemy that makes the Renaissance the most fruitful period of occult development Europe has ever seen.

While the writings of Johannes Trithemius, Agrippa, Paracelsus, Marsilio Ficino, Giordano Bruno, Giulio Camillo Delminio, Fabio Paolini, Athanansius Kircher, and others would cross the timeline of the Renaissance, it is Robert Fludd that we will turn to as one of the last great Renaissance Men who sought to understand and synthesize the totality of human learning.[6]

Fludd's major work, *History of the Macrocosm and the Microcosm*, was more a compilation of encyclopedia articles than a linear history of the topics it covered. Fludd's works embraced every topic then known, and because they stayed clear of controversial theology, they were widely accepted by the many emerging Protestant sects. However, even this acceptance and Fludd's hearty dedication to King James I could not keep him from being suspected of witchcraft and have to politely defend himself in person against such dangerous accusations. During Fludd's European travels a group of Jesuits discovered that he was skilled in divination and reported him to the papal vice legate in an effort to have him arrested. Instead, the local vice legate, who was interested in Fludd's specialty of geomancy, invited him for an evening of fine food and discussion of the mysterious art.

What makes Fludd important is not only the fact that he stands at the end of the Renaissance and thereby encapsulates its victories and failures, but also the fact that that his great gift appears to have been the ability to summarize highly complex ideas and doctrines in diagrams, thereby visually making the philosophy comprehensible in a manner that words alone cannot do. Fludd praises nature, and much of his work is focused on "the Soul of the World" (*Anima Mundi*), represented by the naked woman, or Venus, and humanity's relationship to this ever-present power of God. His diagram entitled *The Mirror of the Whole of Nature and the Image of Art* is his most comprehensive representation of the cosmos, visible and invisible, in a single diagram.[7]

The Soul of the World

The cosmos of the Renaissance magi was often depicted in vast circular engravings, of which Fludd's *Image of Art* is among the most well known, commonly reproduced, and complete in every detail. While knowledge of alchemy, qabala, and astrology—the principal hermetic practices—is required to interpret the images, what makes it and similar diagrams stand out is its circular form. Instead of the linear diagrams of qabala or architectural representations of the Great Work, diagrams such as *Image of Art* draw upon Neo-platonic philosophy to shape their form and contents.

Nature has three kingdoms—animal, vegetable, and mineral—which also function as the three areas of work in laboratory alchemy. While Fludd states that the beautiful virgin in the center of the image is not a goddess, but an agent of God who governs the material and psychic

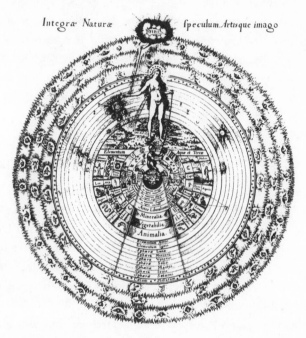

Fludd's "The Mirror of the Whole of Nature and the Image of Art"

worlds, it is clear that she acts in a similar fashion to the *Shekinah* of qabala, or Venus unveiled of Rosicrucian alchemy. She is the Soul of the World, who nourishes all of creation from her breast, and is the secret fire that gives life to all of creation. She is the feminine creative power—the Salt of alchemy—without which nothing could happen, for without material form, there is no means of consciousness, no ultimate expression of divine power. Just as she is chained to the Divine represented by the Tetragrammaton, so is the Divine chained to her. She stands upon the Water and Earth while her head is in the celestial realm of the angels. Chained to her other hand is the Ape of Nature, the attempt of humanity to imitate and understand nature's methods through reason or science. These liberal arts are depicted in the images surrounding the ape, just as the powers of the planets surround the body of nature above, and the Fire and Air of the spiritual realms framing the entire scene.

Within the body of nature, and in every aspect of these engraving, we see the fundamental ideas of harmony, polarity, or tension necessary for creation, and the interconnection of the most subtle realms of heaven and the densest of material form; constructive human activity is the focal point that unites the two in a conscious manner. Fludd, like his contemporaries, was a monotheist who saw the Divine as not only unifying creation, but also imminent and present in material form and human life.

The Enochian Aethyrs : Visions of Ancient Things

There are few students of contemporary esotericism who are not at least superficially familiar with Enochian magic and its role in the lives of Dr. John Dee, Edward Kelly, McGregor Mathers, and Aleister Crowley. Like its qabalistic and Gnostic predecessors, Enochian magic is a revealed cosmology that developed into an operative system of magic for those who, not being privy to the initial revelations, wanted to experience the described worlds first hand.

Enochian magic is often viewed as an extremely fluid and adaptable system that responds to the intention and true inner desire of the operator in a manner that becomes extremely clear after even the slightest experience with it. In many ways this makes Enochian unique not only in modern magical practices, but also in its original context. Renaissance magic is highly technical, and yet when Enochian was revealed to Dee and Kelly, none of the expected trappings of the period were present in the directions they were given. When introduced into the teachings of the Hermetic Order of the Golden Dawn, Enochian was transformed into something very different than what had been transmitted to Dee. Further modifications have occurred over the decades, as the writings of Aleister Crowley and Israel Regardie revealed the mass of the Golden Dawn Enochian material to the world. For many people, the Golden Dawn's teachings on Enochian are their first and most important introduction to the material.

There are, in fact, several areas of Enochian magic, including the Elemental Tablets and the Aethyrs, and several other forms of Enochian magic that were revealed to (or devised by) Dee and Kelly. These include, but are not limited to, working with the forces inscribed upon the *Sigillum Dei Aemeth*; opening the Twelve Gates, the planetary

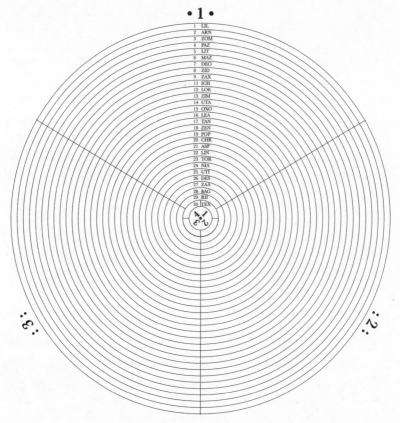

The Thirty Aethers
Each Aether has Three Guardians or Governors, Save Tex, Which has Four

Angels of the Bonorum, or the *Heptarchia Mystica*; and using the *Tabula Sancta*, or Holy Table, described in Dee's *Heptarchia Mystica*. Each of these areas of operation would constitute an area of intense study in its own right. However, when most students think of Enochian magic, they are referring to working with the Elemental Tablets and the Thirty Aeythers.

This ability for Enochian to be combined with other systems, particularly qabala, or to be used alone has made it very popular over the last few decades and has led many to believe that in many ways it is comparable to a kind of high-octane fuel, or high-voltage energy source, that can be layered onto an existing magical system.

The Elemental Tablets: a Journey Outward

The Elemental Tablets and the Tablet of Union are the most well known and easily recognized of the Enochian tools. They depict in chart form, using a series of letters and a unique alphabet, the various divine names, kings, seniors, angels, and demons that compose the Enochian universe, at least as it relates to etheric energy and life on earth. There is one tablet for each of the ancient elements of Fire, Air, Water, and Earth, with a fifth tablet—the tablet of Union—unifying the diverse aspects of these four into a cohesive whole. Many people have spent a great deal of time both skrying and astral projecting to these Enochian realms and recording their experiences. Others have simply viewed them more pragmatically, using them for practical magical operations, while using the Aethyrs as their principal method of spiritual development.

The Aethyrs: a Journey Inward

While working with the Tablets can be a trying and complex task for the beginning Enochian student, astral experience of the Aethyrs is by far the simplest of all practices to undertake within the Enochian system, and in many ways the most important. While the Elemental Tablets address the etheric and material energies of creation, the Aethyrs represent the influences of the subtle spiritual energies that give rise to consciousness—that, in fact, are consciousness as we understand it. It is only by ascending the planes represented by the Aethyrs that we can expand our awareness; this is similar to what is done when Rising on the Planes in qabala. While exploration of the Elemental Tablets will reveal a great deal, and manipulation of their energies can be useful or foolish depending on the maturity of the magician, it is skrying the Aethyrs that gives us the experience of Knowledge and Conversation with our Holy Guardian Angel. This experience must be the focal point of all esoteric operations if we are to grow as beings and not simply wander in an astral quagmire of self-created amusement or delusion.

Regardless of one's experience, working systematically through each Aethyr is important, as simply doing so stimulates some level of response, even if it is not as dramatic or profound as the magician might like. This is the same as working on the higher levels of the Tree of Life; not everyone will have great insights as a result of working on the Holy Upper Trinity, but all will experience the benefits of attempting to experience the pure light of unity. This aspect of Enochian is critical to the spiritual evolution of the operator and should take preference to other areas of work after the initial foundation has been built.

While Aleister Crowley's words on this topic may be a bit harsh, they stress its importance and place all occult operations, regardless of their origin or tradition, in the proper context:

The Magical Will is in its essence twofold, for it presupposes a beginning and an end; to Will to be a thing is to admit that you are not that thing. Hence to Will anything but the supreme thing [Knowledge and Conversation with one's Holy Guardian Angel], is to wander still further from it—any **Will but that to give up the self to the Beloved is Black Magic**—yet this surrender is so simple an act that to our complex minds it is the most difficult of all acts; and hence training is necessary.

He further states:

The majority of people in this world are ataxic; they cannot coordinate their mental muscles to make a purposeful movement. They have no real Will, only a set of wishes, many of which contradict others. The victim wobbles from one to the other . . . Nothing has been achieved, except the one thing the victim is not conscious of: the destruction of his own character . . . How then is Will to be trained? All the wishes, caprices, inclinations, tendencies, appetites, must be detected, examined, judged by the standard of whether they help or hinder the main purpose [attaining Knowledge and Conversation with one's Holy Guardian Angel, and treated accordingly. Vigilance and courage are obviously required.[8]

Working with the Aethyrs is also a fairly accurate litmus test of one's inner initiation. The Thirty Aethyrs and their ninety-one Governors roughly approximate the spheres on the Tree of Life and their guardians or gatekeepers. While people can get a glimpse of areas beyond their level of initiation (a fancy word for integration), they can't enter those areas. It is like being able to ride an elevator to the top of a skyscraper but not being allowed to get off when the elevator stops, and only getting to peek out as the doors open and close. On levels at which we function, we can actually get off and walk around. The Governors, as guardians of each Aethyr, also act as guides in that they can give us those keys, clues, and outright information we need to proceed into the next Aethyr.

All of the practices described in this book are ideal for use with Enochian magic, particularly with its unique alphabet, and with the Planes with their Threshold Guardians.

Other Maps of Eternity

The above three esoteric models—the qabalist Tree of Life, the Enochian Aethyrs, and Anima Mundi—are the most common maps of eternity; the Tree of Life and Enochian magic are the frontrunners. However, the techniques described in this book are easily applied to any well-described esoteric system, or aap of eternity, if you will. Several "maps" that should be studied, even if you have no intention of spending a great deal of time with them, are the Egyptian underworld and the Celtic underworld. The Gnostic aethers are also found in contemporary occult circles and very valuable in their own right.

The mystic visions of the great medieval Christian saints should be studied in the light of these methods as well. St. John of the Cross and his spiritual wife, St. Theresa, both wrote about ascending and descending into the various castles of heaven, and it is now believed that both were not only influenced by qabala, but also descendents of Jews forced to convert to Catholicism.[9] The mystical visions of Hildegard von Bingen, with their mysterious "blue man," are equally profound and deeply riveting. When studied in conjunction with her music, they evoke a near instant sense of otherworldliness and transcendence. The mystical visions of St. John of Patmos, recorded in the Book of Revelation are always a timely source for profound and deeply moving initiatic experiences as well.

What to Do If You Don't Have a Map

If you are reading this book and are intrigued by the ideas of lucid dreaming, astral projection, and the Body of Light but do not have a cosmology to wed them to, that's fine. All of the practices in this book can be done by anyone virtually anywhere. Having a working cosmology is helpful in that it allows you to integrate the experiences you will have and understand them better, but it is no reason not to begin practicing on some level. Students of nonhermetic paths, such as the various schools of Wicca and Neopaganism, will see that the following methods are easily adapted to their cosmology without doing any violence or weakening of the techniques themselves. In the end, it will be your experience that matters. So even if you don't have a map to guide you, you can still make progress on the journey if you know where you want to end up, even if you don't know where you are going. The inner world is funny that way.

Key Points

- The Higher Self, or Neshamah, in qabala is the divine and unchanging aspect of our consciousness. It is perfect and is constantly willing to make itself known to the Middle Self, or Ruach. The Higher Self is perfect in its expression of consciousness.

- The Middle Self, or Ruach, is the ego, or sense of self we create as we go through life and experience the material world. It is our vision of our self in relation to external experiences. It is the work of the Middle Self to allow the Higher Self greater influence and expression in daily affairs, thereby bringing greater harmony to life. The Middle Self is the rational and moral aspect of our being and makes all decisions, including suggestions to the Lower Self.

- The Lower Self, or Nefesh is the raw psychic power of the individual. It is the subconscious and directly related to the physical body in that it is instinctual. The Lower Self is the source of all psychic power, in particular those phenomena relating to healing, materializations, and the physical world.

- The Tree of Life is the most common of all qabalistic diagrams. It illustrates the cosmos and our place in both the visible and invisible worlds. Through it, a vast array of associations are possible, and these associations allow consciousness to experience the most subtle to the most dense realms of being.

- There are ten levels or spheres on the Tree of Life, each with its own unique function that, in turn, is related to the remaining spheres.

- Paths connect the spheres and demonstrate the flow of energy on the Tree of Life. When the energy flows into matter, or "down," it is called the Lightning Flash; when it flows from matter to spirit, or "up," it is called the Path of Return.

- There are four worlds in qabala that represent the many variations and subtle relationships between the spheres. Each of these worlds is represented by a letter of the Tetragrammaton—the four-lettered name of God—and an Element.

- Imagination is considered the key tool of the magician for connecting the material and spiritual worlds. Use of the imagination can be found in earlier medieval texts, but finds its greatest exposition in the writings of the Renaissance.

- *Anima Mundi*, the Soul of the World, is the belief that the universe is a seamless interconnection of energies, ideas, forms, and intelligences from the mind of God to the world of matter. At the heart of this creation is distinctly feminine force of Anima Mundi, guiding, nurturing, and maintaining creation.

- Enochian is a series of magical systems revealed to Dr. John Dee and his assistant Edward Kelly during the sixteenth century. The system has been extremely influential in the modern occult revivals, particularly those stemming from the Hermetic Order of the Golden Dawn. Enochian is an extremely fluid method of working that is often linked to qabala or other systems of working, but can be used alone.

- Elemental Tablets are the most well-known aspect of Enochian. There are four tablets used in conjunction with a fifth tablet, the Tablet of Union, in controlling the flow of energy into the material world.

- The Thirty Aethyrs in Enochian are used in a similar fashion as Rising on the Planes is used in qabala, and have the potential to be the most spiritual aspect of Enochian magic.

Assignments for Chapter Two

1. Read a book on psychology from the Reading List. Take notes for future reference.

2. Read a book from the Reading List on one of the cosmological models presented in this chapter. Take notes for future reference.

CHAPTER 3

Lucid Dreaming: Gateway to the Invisible

Psychic Centers: Our Connection Between the Worlds

While it is nice to say that we exist and that the universe exists and that we are reflections of one another, mirrored through the great Chain of Being and expressed in the words of microcosm and macrocosm, to demonstrate it is another thing. In each of us there is a point where our connection to the material world, as well as to the astral, the archetypal, and the spiritual worlds, begins. While we have shown how those connections take place in our consciousness thought the Higher, Middle, and Lower Selves, it is in the physical body where we spend most of our awareness and the greatest and most powerful connections are made. These connecting points we call psychic centers, or chakras.

Through the psychic centers, our nervous system is brought into harmony with the cosmic influences, primarily astrological or planetary, as a result of the daily and seasonal rhythms that occur in nature. These are the same rhythms that are consciously used in the creation of talismans, alchemical products, and astrological charts in methods often referred to as natural magic.

These psychic centers change in number and location depending on the system one is using, but there is general agreement about *key* centers. In addition, these centers have a peculiar relationship to the spheres of the Tree of Life when the Tree is projected onto the human body to create the archetypal image of the perfect being, or Adam Qadmon.

It is the five primary centers located on the Middle Pillar of the Tree of Life that concern us, and one in particular for inducing states of lucid dreaming.

In Eastern techniques, the number of psychic centers attributed to the body varies depending on the school in question. In general, it is said that we have at least seven major and five minor psychic centers. Location, color attributes, divine names, vowel sounds, and other symbols attributed to each center vary considerably.[1]

According to Sri Aurobindo, a prominent twentieth-century yogi, the throat center, or Vissudha chakra, is associated with the externalization of mental forces and is the link between the higher and lower mental spheres; the color gray is associated with this center, the same as it is in qabala.[2] In *Serpent of Fire: A Modern View of Kundalini*, Darrel Irving points out that the *Vissudha* chakra is presided over by the dual deities of Shakini and Shiva. Each deity is five faced, representing each of the five Elements of Indian Tantra (Earth, Water, Air, Fire, and Akasha or Aether), with three eyes, showing physical and psychic perception, or knowledge. Shakini is seen as Light itself, and Shiva, like the hermetic ideal, is androgynous, half white and half gold. The center is associated with the purification of intelligence, the psychic substratum or ether (*akasha*), and hearing. The color given by Irving is smoky purple. Along with Sri Aurobindo's gray, purple is also sometimes associated with the throat center in modern qabalistic works.[3]

The throat center, along with the upper psychic centers in the brain, constitute the only centers whereby *direct psychic perception* is possible.[4] This point is important, because we can perceive psychic information a variety of different ways—ways that are primarily counterparts to our physical senses (which can be seen as coarse imitations of our psychic ones)—as well as with a sixth sense of intuitive wholeness or synthesis. It is these upper centers that provide us with psychic perception that is untainted, or at least less tainted, by our personal filters.

In Western esotericism the throat center is less well defined, although it shares in all of the above named characteristics. In *Kabbalah of the Golden Dawn*, Pat Zalewski states that the throat center is associated with the thyroid gland and controls respiration. Each of the preceding centers the throat center is associated with an Element, starting with Earth, Water, Fire, and Air. While not stated by Zalewski, it might be presumed that the throat center is then the first center to be associated with Spirit, or Quintessence, as it is in yoga.

Here we run into a problem regarding the attributes associated with this area. In alchemy, the throat is ruled by Mercury, the god of Air, as well as magic, voice, and initiation. In most systems no planetary attribute is given to the throat. Instead, it is the sepherothic realm of Daath that presides over this region.

Daath is Hebrew for "knowledge" and perhaps is the best attribute for things associated with the mind, speech, and magic. However, for many qabalists, Daath is a region better left alone and feared more than the so-called Qlippoth, or demonic realms. How did Daath come to be seen with such awe? Mostly from the second-hand reports of book-learned occultists repeating what they read. Although, if we keep in mind that Daath is knowledge, then some interesting correlations can be drawn.

Israel Regardie states:

This central point between two symbolic pillars of the opposites, the place of balanced power from which the working of the opposites may correctly be viewed, is the implication of DAAS [Daath], which is the name of this shadowy Sephirah. Rightly it *is* shadowy, and the word is used advisedly for in the majority of us who have not cultivated the difficult art of avoiding the opposites, the development of this new principle has proceeded with the utmost slowness. It is a new factor of adaptation or equilibrium, especially between the two broad divisions of conscious-ness—the ego on one hand with its desire for adjustment to modern life with its refined and non-natural conditions, and on the other hand with the superficial level of the instinctual life, concerned with primitive things, of self-assertion and the unbridled gratification of its every whim and caprice.[5]

And further on Regardie says:

DAAS (sic), the shadowy Sephirah, which develops in the course of evolution as we learn the domination of our mental and emotional propensities, *is situated at the nape of the neck*. Its position is at a point on the spine just below the occiput, about *one or two inches above the larynx* [italics added], and its diameter may be imagined to be about four inches in extent. It is conceived to be a symbolic link, self-induced, and self-devised, between the higher Genius on the one hand, and on the other, the ego, the consciousness self referred to that group of characteristics clustered around TIPHARAS (sic).[6]

Regardie also refers to Daath as "The Link" between the Higher Self and the ego, or waking brain, and this is critical for the work we are seeking to undertake through lucid dreaming. It is this link that we will develop and utilize for our access to knowledge of the invisible worlds.

Gareth Knight writes:

The Daath powers in balanced function, of course, give the type of person with a mission or sense of destiny who will have sufficient detachment to cut his way through any obstruction to his aims, at no matter what cost, and who has absolutely no concern for what danger the future may have in store such is his faith in his powers and acceptance of his destiny.[7]

On a personal level the psycho-physical sphere associated with Daath allows for the highest awareness in human consciousness as it is progressively opened. When this occurs, many of the fears, obstructions, and psychological malfunctions that have previously plagued us fall away under the intense awareness of our true power and presence as beings becoming consciously divine. In many ways, the function of our dreams and nightmares is to raise these unresolved issues, conflicts, even hopes and aspirations, to the surface of consciousness so that we can address them. In this regard it is no wonder that such "knowledge," even when addressed abstractly in a dream state, could be seen as threatening to some. However, in accepting it and working with it, especially

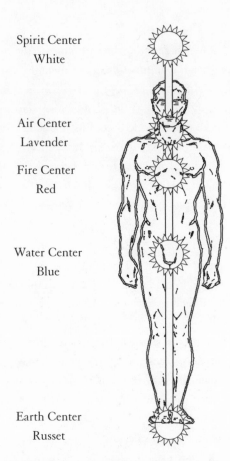

Spirit Center
White

Air Center
Lavender

Fire Center
Red

Water Center
Blue

Earth Center
Russet

in our dream state, we are able to integrate vast areas of our psyche in a shorter period of time and without the need for unpleasant psychic complexes to manifest in our material life before we recognize them. If we are to experience all that we can possibly be, then we must undertake the journey without fear or concern for the cost; we must cast our lot and accept the destiny we have created for ourselves by seeking to be more than human.

In short, what we do in our dream life reveals who and what we are and who and what we have chosen to become. What we hide during the day comes out to greet us when we sleep, just as it greets us when we die. This is the biggest fear many instinctually know and seek to avoid when they speak of the Terror of the Threshold, and Daath as the Guardian of the Threshold.

The fears presented by entry into the inner world are real, in that once we cross the bridge of knowledge, there is no turning back. Once we go from the theoretical to the experiential, we cannot return to ignorance. When innocence is lost, it is gone for good. Thus, we can cross the bridge several times: from the material world to the psychic, from the psychic to the more abstract mental realms, and from the mental to the highly spiritual, from which none is said to have returned. Most of what is reported about Daath may be in relation to this last and highest reality.

The function of lucid dreaming is to assist those who desire to cross their personal psychic bridge from the visible into the invisible with consciousness and memory.

Mercury, Hermes, and the Psychopomp

The caduceus, a symbol of the god Mercury and the psychopomp Hermes, is often used as a symbol for approaching Daath. The relationship of the throat center to Mercury must not be overlooked, for it is this very relationship that we are seeking to establish within ourselves. That is, we want to be able to enter into the psychic realms with the aid and assistance of our Higher Self, as well as our human intellect or Ruach, and to make use of the information upon return to waking consciousness. We want, in effect, to do as Hermes does: to "walk between two worlds" and unite them within our psyche.

The symbol for Mercury is the stylized caduceus in the form of the combined symbols of Luna (Moon), Sol (Sun), and Terra (Earth). Combined, they state the function of this part of our psychic anatomy, the throat center. The upturned lunar symbol represents our brain, nervous system, and psychic functioning, resting upon the solar symbol beneath it. The Sun is our spiritual powers, life force, and intuition. It sits astride the symbol for matter: the equal armed cross. This Cross of the Four Elements is the symbol of material existence, and is our physical bodies as well as the material world we live in.

In the symbol for Mercury, we see that the terrestrial energies are dominated by the solar forces of the Sun and soul. However, these spiritual forces are, in turn, dominated by the intellect and physical brain of man. The brain directs them or represses them, depending on the spiritual health of the aspirant.

The caduceus also illustrates a unique point: the relationship between the heart, Sun, brain, and spiritual awakening. As messenger of the gods, Mercury assists in the transfer of knowledge, but not in the creation or interpretation of that knowledge, these functions being left to the brain and psychic heart. The heart is the seat of intuition, the Voice of the Soul, and the Interior Master. Only through its awakening can we become conscious and free beings. However, the energy of the awakened heart, with all of its love, must be transferred to the physical brain for insight and understanding. In doing so, it requires the assistance of the throat center. Once in the brain, the energy must also be able to return to the heart, or send information there for spiritual consideration, via the Mercurial center.

Herein lies some confusion for some students. It is said that the heart is the center of intuition, yet it is in the pituitary body of the physical brain that intuition is realized in mundane consciousness. Is it not possible to simply awaken the pituitary body without the needed functions of the psychic heart?

The answer is yes. To understand this somewhat confusing relationship between the heart, the pituitary gland, and our spiritual awakening, we need to realize that according to esoteric tradition both of these organs are solar in nature, and as such are affected by the material and spiritual Sun. Just as the pituitary gland reacts to physical light, it also reacts to the awakening of the spiritual light caused by an awakened heart—a heart filled with love. There is also a direct physical relationship between the heartbeat and brain rhythms.

The brain in general is lunar, but certain aspects of it respond to other planetary influences in their specific functions.

This need to awaken both the heart and brain is what is required for travels through the psychic realms. An awakened heart with no brain is subject to an extreme lack of practicality; a brain with no heart can function psychically, but only in a cold and detached manner. The thinking heart and feeling brain are what Mercury helps us to establish. In doing so, the polarity of the heart and brain is overcome through union, and the material and remaining psychic forces of our body are brought into play in a harmonious manner.

The use of blues and purples is said to show the relationship between Daath and the ideas of a Higher Mind (blue/Chesed) and the subconscious (purple/Yesod). Thus, Daath, or the sphere of Knowledge that we are contacting through our meditations, is our personal connecting point, and not the transpersonal or cosmic Daath on the Tree of Life, to which so many dangers have been attributed and written about.

Daath is also the synthesis of the Holy Upper Trinity in a form we can approach and understand more easily.[8]

Also, if Yesod, or the gateway and principle sphere of the astral realm is a reflection of Daath "on a lower arch," as our British fraters and sorors are so fond of saying, then meditations on the Daath sphere in ourselves should not only sublimate the sexual creative powers of Yesod, but also allow us to enter into astral consciousness more fully and completely.

In most schools of Western esotericism the entire brain is ruled by the Moon and its peculiar monthly cycles; however, the brain also has other planetary subdivisions. The pituitary gland is solar in nature, while the brain stem, or medulla oblongata, is the most lunar of all locations. It is here in the medulla oblongata, the oldest part of our anatomy and nervous system, that automatic functioning of the body is regulated—breathing, digestions, pulse—and immediately above it sits the areas of the brain that deal with sight and sound. When we focus our attention on this area, we are, in fact, increasing the flow of blood, vital energy, and consciousness to it. This, in turn, also affects to some the degree the rest of our nervous system and physical health. The same is true if we focus on our nearby throat center. The two centers are physically close enough so that it is impossible to affect one without to some degree affecting the other. For this reason, some schools utilize the throat center, rather than the cervical center, as the first gateway for lucid dreaming.

There is a school of thought that says that the etheric energies enter the body not only through the breath, but also through the point at the nape of the neck, or this lunar center. They travel down the spine and ascend again, and during their ascent and descent they modify the other psychic centers. While the physiology of energy entering directly through the lunar center needs further investigation, it is clear that through breathing we immediately and directly affect this area of our brain and, as a result, the rest of our physical, etheric, and astral bodies. For this reason, certain forms of breathing, from the simple to complex, have been used to achieve exteriorization of consciousness, and have been coupled with the use of specific scents, in the form of incense and evaporated essential oils, to further stimulate this primitive area of our anatomy.

Some Thoughts from the East

In Chinese and Mongolian Chi Kung, meditation on the throat center is used for these purposes: (1) sublimation of the sexual force and (2) assisting in the conscious projection of consciousness and the induction of lucid dreaming.[9] The throat center is the connecting center between the heart and the brain.

According to Taoist master Mantak Chia:

Taoists who practice Dream Yoga focus on the throat point when going to sleep so as to consciously cross the bridge between the waking state and the dream state. Being able to dream lucidly helps one gain greater control of one's Chi (internal energy) and also enables one to consciously bridge the gap between life and death.[10]

Conscious dreaming is used to awaken the "Seventy-Two Magical Abilities," in order to prepare for eventual transfer of these abilities to the waking, material world. Seventy-two is an interesting number, as it matches the number of permutations of the "Great Name" of God, or *Schemhamphoresch*. Theoretically, each of these names, signs, seals, and correspondences[11] could be awakened using the technique described. Just as in Indian and Western techniques, in Taoist practices the throat is associated with Air, spirit energy, and consciousness.

Tibetan Buddhism has highly developed methods of dream yoga that give the same results as those described below. Success in dream yoga is considered among the most important markers along the Tantric path and plays an important part in higher meditations and practices.[12]

Technique: Lucid Dreaming

There are three basic methods of projecting consciousness, each of which utilizes a different aspect of consciousness. Mental projection uses the psychic center located at either the brain stem or the throat and is pivotal in inducing lucid dreaming; the dis-alignment of the physical and psychic bodies occur roughly at the level of the neck.

In order to present the subconscious with an orderly supply of symbols in a coherent and meaningful manner, either the signs for the alchemical Elements or Kerubic Signs, their magical equivalent, can be initially used. Afterwards, the signs of the seven principle planets are used in their place. This progressive use of the same symbols allows the subconscious to understand that these symbols are meaningful to the student and are the official means of transferring consciousness from one level to another. This same method will be repeated in chapter four with the Hebrew alphabet to awaken the magical voice, as well as direct the energies of the astral plane as represented in the *Sepher Yetzirah*.

If used repeatedly, the symbols will not be needed after a period of time, and if this technique is done with good heart and mind, one may potentially realize his or her level of spiritual awakening during one of the dream states provoked.

While full-scale astral projection may not immediately occur, a degree of lucid dreaming, dream memory, and even a limited increase in one's magical voice will be experienced. It is up to each aspirant to make the most of these "out-of-body" dream states and increase their level of intensity so as to realize full and controlled projection of consciousness.

Unlike other methods of projection, the method outlined here will, through regular practice, work gently and progressively—yielding increased dreaming, then lucid dreaming, and finally astral projection—in most cases, thus allowing for an acclimation of consciousness to these new states of being.

Preparation

Sit comfortably with your back straight, feet flat on the floor, palms of your hands flat on your thighs and close to your hips (to take stress of your shoulders and elbows), and chin slightly tucked. Breathe deeply several times, holding your inhaled breath for as long as is comfortable, and exhaling slowly, holding your breath out for as long as is comfortable. Feel yourself relax mentally, emotionally, and physically. (You may also do this laying down on a firm, straight bed or couch, as long as you don't fall asleep. Cover yourself with a light blanket even if the room is warm, as you may feel cold as your body begins to relax and your circulation slows down.) Say the following prayer (or something similar): "Divine Mind, source of all, assist me in this work of purification of thought, word, and deed, so that I will awaken to the innermost depths of my being and achieve perfection in lucid dreaming."

Affirmations or prayers to our inner self, our Holy Guardian Angel, such as the above are powerful tools for jumpstarting and maintaining our practice and success.

Obtain a set of symbols for the Four Elements and Spirit, as well as the seven planetary signs (see sidebar on page 69). Start with Earth, then progress to Water, Air, Fire, and Spirit as the days proceed. The basic procedure will not change, only the symbols used to attain projection. Therefore, it is best to use symbols that you can easily visualize, either in gold, phosphorescent white, or their complimentary colors.

Explanation

This practice focuses our attention on the primary psychic center used in the induction of lucid dreaming and may, as a result, allow the student to experience spontaneous projection of consciousness. This exercise assists us in becoming increasingly aware of the psychic center that deal with consciousness, memory, and our primitive nervous system and the increased the flow of energy to them for the specific purpose of inducing lucid dreaming states.

Type of Practice

This is a core practice and central to inducing lucid dreaming. It should be practiced nightly. The Simple Purification Practice in chapter one can be done prior to it as a preliminary practice to establish the proper mental and emotional framework.

Method

Step One: When going to sleep, or even just relaxing for a few minutes, turn your attention to the nape of your neck, right where your head sits on top of the spinal cord, and imagine a brilliant blue-black (or indigo/ultraviolet) sphere there, about the size of a tennis ball. Make it brilliant and translucent, as though it were illuminated from the inside. It should be large enough to envelope the medulla oblongata, or brain stem. If imagined as very large (as Regardie suggests),[13] this sphere may even have its farthest edges at the bridge of the nose, brushing the thymus gland, or heart with its radiant aura. However, the sphere itself is small and clearly defined. Some have imagined it as small as a marble, and others about the size of a tennis ball; golf-ball size is the most common.

It is important that the image is three dimensional and not just as a flat plate in front of you. Thus, the sphere and its energy field will encompass your neck and parts of your head. Your imagination is internally directed. It is all right to imagine the organs mentioned if this aids in visualization; otherwise, stay with the bright, translucent color, imagine that this sphere is all that is present, and lose yourself in it. Place yourself in its center, look around at the brilliant sphere of light you are centered in.

Step Two: After achieving familiarity with the first step, imagine your chosen symbol for Earth present with you. See it brilliant and before you, with the qualities of Earth—heaviness and density. Simply stay with the symbol for a while or until you fall asleep. Imagine the Earth symbol for seven days, then move on to the remaining symbols. After you have completed all of the Elemental symbols, including Spirit, proceed on to the planetary symbols and work with each one for seven days before moving on to the next symbol. It is important that the sphere and these symbols be distinct, clear, and either larger or smaller than physical life would present them. The mind responds very well to dramatic distinctions, particularly to induce psychic states.

Step Three: You have several choices on how to approach the planetary symbols. First, you can simply move through them, starting with the Moon and progressing up the Tree of Life. Second, you can start with Saturn and progress down. Third, you can simply alternate through them according to the ruling planet of the day. Since it is desirable to spend several cycles with each symbol, the third method offers the easiest and least tedious way of working through them without worrying about breaking off in the middle somewhere and having to start that symbol over again. Seven weeks is to be spent working with the planetary symbols.

Step Four: Note your experiences in your daily notebook and see what if any connections exist from week to week between the symbols of each planet.

It is desirable to spend at least seven cycles (nights) with each planetary symbol, or between six and seven weeks total, working with them as you fall asleep. Added to the previous four or five weeks working with the Elements, this makes nearlyh three months of nightly work. Upon rising in the morning, a minute or two can also be spent visualizing the symbol of that day.

Projecting from the Throat

The same method as above applies when using the throat as the focal point for inducing lucid dreaming or projection, only the initial color is red rather than indigo. The throat, as we have noted, is associated with Mercury, which is about both information gathering and transfer, as well as energy and motion. As a result, the throat responds very well to the color red (or even orange, but considerably less so for this specific practice).

In step one above, simply focus your attention at the level of the thyroid gland, a small butterfly-shaped gland slightly below the center point of your throat, and imagine a brilliant sphere of red light. You may wish to add some golden highlights to the edges in order to facilitate the image and to give it depth, but this is not essential. After you have stabilized this sphere, begin adding the listed symbols to it by placing them in the center of the sphere. Here again, bright white or gold works well. Other colors can be used, but they will have a modifying effect on the outcome of the experiences. Be very careful not to just imagine the sphere as if you were looking at it, but place your consciousness fully in it, as if you were looking out from the sphere or are the sphere. Do not imagine a small body for yourself, but simply be aware of the environment you have created for yourself.

Order of Elements: Earth Water Air Fire Spirit

Order of the Planets	Descending the Tree	Ascending the Tree	Planetary Rulers
1	Saturn	Moon	Saturday Saturn
2	Jupiter	Mercury	Sunday Sun
3	Mars	Venus	Monday Moon
4	Sun	Sun	Tuesday Mars
5	Venus	Mars	Wednesday Mercury
6	Mercury	Jupiter	Thursday Jupiter
7	Moon	Saturn	Friday Venus

Key Points

- There is a variety of opinions on the number and location of the psychic centers. Lucid dreaming is concerned with primary and highly agreed upon centers, their uses and functions.
- In Western esotericism, the nape of the neck, where the brain stem enters the spinal column, is a principal center associated with Daath—Knowledge—on the Tree of Life.
- Daath is sometimes assigned to the throat, where its function overlaps with the thyroid's Mercurial aspects. But this is a

minor error, and the throat and the nape of the neck should be seen as separate psychic centers.

• Daath is a construct, created during the descent and ascent of consciousness, whereas the psychic centers, or charkas, have distinct associations with the glands and plexuses of the nervous system.

• Our dream consciousness is our pure and unadulterated consciousness, and is an expression of our true state of awakening.

• Dream practices are critical to spiritual development, even more important in some ways than other practices done while awake.

• There are several ways to approach dream practices, but all are essentially the same, even across traditions.

• Recording your experiences is an important step to developing memory and dream consciousness.

• Lucid dreaming practices can trigger spontaneous astral projection, or exteriorization of consciousness.

Assignments for Chapter Three

1. Obtain a three-ring notebook and divide it into seven sections, each labeled as follows: Saturday–Sunday, Sunday–Monday, Monday–Tuesday, Tuesday–Wednesday, Wednesday–Thursday Thursday–Friday, Friday–Saturday. Record your dreams in the appropriate section. If you begin a practice on Saturday night, you will record any dreams in the section marked "Saturday–Sunday" because it will be Sunday when you awaken. However, be aware that the night hours will still be under the planetary influence of Saturn, so the notebook is designed to reflect the natural flow of planetary energies rather than artificial divisions of days.

2. Obtain a set of symbols, drawing them if necessary, to assist you in your work. They should be clear and bright.

3. Perform the technique in this chapter nightly and write down your results each morning.

CHAPTER 4

The Magical Voice and the Body of Light

The material in this chapter is designed to show practitioners how they might achieve the following:

1. Increased dream content via the Hebrew letters.

2. Creation of the magical voice.

3. Ritual awakening of the Hebrew letters within the psychic body.

While Hebrew is the language of choice for the practices in this chapter, much of the material can be easily adapted to fit Enochian, Egyptian, or similar languages that are used in an esoteric context. Students who do not wish to work with the traditional language of qabala can still derive extensive benefit from the material that follows.

At this point in your studies, a notebook of your practices and experiences should be in place. This is often referred to as a magical diary, but it is also your personal "Book of Life." It is your account of your coming of age in the universe, and it is a critical tool for further work. A notebook is required for successful understanding of the qabalistic or alchemical paths, as it reflects our personal experiences and makes concrete the volatile information we begin to receive from our inner self during receptive moments of our practices. This information is accumulated over time and must be made into a synthetic idea by each of us. If you are not keeping a notebook, begin to do so immediately. Just as any academic teacher will discontinue instruction if their lessons go unheeded, so will your interior one. If you are serious about your inner growth, then keep a record of your interior contacts. This record will later develop into a series of inner teachings, some of which will be of a universal nature and others of which will be strictly personal.

The Power of the Word

In principa erat Verbum.

In the Beginning was the Word.

JOHN 1:1

Positive thinking is the single most important key to success on the eso-teric path. In fact, we could almost call it, the "magic of Tiphareth," in that thinking is by itself a magical act. Each time we speak we invoke a host of images and associated emotions, within ourselves and within those who hear us. If those words are active, positive, and generous, we open up ourselves and others to unlimited possibilities. By focusing on the positive aspects of a given situation, no matter how despairing or hopeless it might appear, we can find a resolution that is in harmony with our inner growth.

This focusing on the positive doesn't ignore the reality of negativity and evil in the world, but simply accepts it. We realize that all things have a function even if we are not conscious of them, and that by addressing the positive we can progress along our life path.

By extending this inner attitude into the outer world, we begin to share it with others and mold a new life for our self. This is principally done through the speech, or the power of the spoken word, because speech is our principle form of creative energy in day-to-day life. Additionally, sexual energy is our most fundamental form of creative impulse. These two expressions of energy are deeply connected to one another.

Through harmonic resonance, or sound, we can create conditions that are favorable or unfavorable to us. This harmonic resonance can be on either an exoteric or esoteric level. By finding those sounds, or vibrations with which we resonate to most harmoniously, we can create conditions favorable to us. Thus, our speech becomes a tool, albeit an expression, of our inner state.

Rabbi Aryeh Kaplan in his book, *Inner Space*, describes the relationship between the cosmic Worlds and human life in the following terms:

The five universes are often explained in terms of their parallels at the human level. Man's innermost will and volition correspond to the universe of *Adam Kadmon*. The level of preconceptual or undifferentiated mind corresponds to *Atzilut*. The process of thought corresponds to the universe of *Beriyah*. Speech and communication parallel the universe of *Yetzirah* and, finally, action corresponds to *Asiyah*.[1]

He further states:

The term Yetzirah comes from the root *Yatzar*, meaning "to form." Yetzirah thus denotes the formation of something from a substance that already exists . . . something from something . . . In general, thought is said to be on the level of Beriyah-Creation, since thought is "something from nothing." Speech, on the other hand, emanates from thought—"something from something"— and is therefore on the level of Yetzirah-Formation.[2]

The thought that proceeds speech comes from our Middle Self— our rational soul, or Ruach. The will is centered in Tipareth. Whenever we act, we reinforce a mode of action to the point of forming a habit, an unconscious response. Our acts, our will, our sense of self or ego are all related, and, in fact, are one. They are expressed through the sphere of Tiphareth on the Tree of Life, and relate to our heart and solar plexus. As we will see later, the solar plexus is an important plexus for all psychic work, and, in particular, conscious astral projection. By developing a positive attitude towards life and the people, places, and things we encounter, we charge our solar plexus (and heart) with positive emotions, thereby benefiting our entire physical and psychic anatomy. The solar plexus can best be described as our individual psychic tuning fork, with which we can create the psychic and material conditions we desire—but only if we are positive, confident, and generous, just as is the sun in our solar system.

Our words are our expression of our degree of inner light, and with them we can open up portals to other worlds.

Aleph, or What Is a Glottal Stop Anyway?

When visualizing the Hebrew letters, start simple: imagine them as blazing white against an ultraviolet, or indigo, background, or as gold against a red background. Later on you can use one of the many color scales available, such as is found in the Golden Dawn. However, keeping it simple works just fine. Over a period of two or three months, you can also begin to add the Elemental qualities of Fire (hot and dry/expansive-electric), Water (cold and wet/contracting-magnetic), Air (warm and moist), and Earth (cold and hard) that are associated with each letter.

By working with each letter this way, the costly task of attempting to memorize all of the symbols at once is avoided. Instead, the diverse associations are slowly layered over a period of several weeks or months, being absorbed and synthesized in small doses. We come to have an understanding of each letter and its associations through personal experience, instead of through an exhaustive and at times confusing intellectual exercise.

In this or any esoteric work your notebook will serve as your best friend and teacher for your inner exploration. Through it, you will chart your progress and begin to see how the patterns of inner teaching develop and progress.

You may eventually add the vibration to each letter, either silent or spoken, so that you can discover for yourself the best resonance for when you intone divine names, combinations of letters, and other forms of sacred speech. In this regard, Hebrew is a little tricky. Each letter has a natural vowel, or sound associated with its being said, just as letters in the alphabet of any language do. For example, the long e sound is the natural vowel in *B* or *C* or *D*. These sounds help us to designate one letter from the other, but they also demonstrate an important point one well known in esoteric practices: it is the vowel sound that provides the energy, while the consonant provides the breaking power, or modification of the sound-energy being vibrated. While there are a variety of ways to pronounce mystic words and divine names, a general rule is that the vowel should be sounded two or three times longer than the consonant. For our work at this stage, sound is less important than being able to visualize the letters clearly and forming the proper intention to open up our psyche to their influences and being able to consciously use them as a tool on our Path of Return.

If you chose to vibrate each letter, remember that the sounds created should be deep, resonant, and cause a subtle, if not exhausting, vibration throughout your entire body. They should be imagined as being inhaled and then spoken (or shouted) to the ends of the universe and returning again to you. Sound can be added slowly and progressively, adding color and quality to each letter over time.

The Word is the vehicle of the will and of thought. That is why magicians can utter words that may seem devoid of meaning. However, we can say that these words are energized by them because they know what to expect from their vocalizations. In addition, these words, through repetition, acquire a charge which still increase their power of action.[3]

And:

In addition, the magical theory considers that the vibrations triggered by human voice have the power not only to fashion the plastic substance of the Astral Light into various forms according to frequency, amplitude, intensity and the resonance of the emission of the sound, but also to attract to our world the attention of various metaphysical entities . . . With regular practice we can rather quickly feel at will an intense tremor in the entire body under the impact of the vocalization of a single word. In addition, practice will allow the student to contain at will the vibratory effects to a specific part of his body.[4]

The Hebrew letter Aleph is of particular interest in esoteric work because it symbolizes primordial energy, unity, and divine movement to create the worlds. Yet its odd phonetic designation is a glottal stop rather than a vowel, and is a smooth exhalation, similar to the silent *h* in the English word "honor." The throat is open and energy moves without heavy sound or interruption. When pronounced with the letters in alphabet form, the natural vowel of Aleph is *a* as in the English word "father."

Aleph helps us unite seeming opposites, experience the divine energy, and experience infinite creative potential. For this reason we will use it for uniting our internal energies within ourselves, as well as with the cosmos, in both lucid dreaming and astral projection practices.

Power of the Voice

The throat is directly connected to our power of speech and creation. Through it we communicate to others, be they human, animal, or divine. Use of it is the quickest way to turn something into a reality in the material world, for sound itself is both transient and permanent. Once a word is spoken, it is gone, yet its meaning and effects remain forever. A word spoken cannot be taken back.

Words crystallize or make tangible our innermost thoughts. The more complex the thought, the more complex the word to describe it. These complexities act as verbal DNA or programming, creating a series of visible and invisible conditions that become our life.

How often haven't we said something in haste, jest, lust, or anger only wishing later that we could undo what was done?

If mortal speech is so powerful, then how much more potent is our speech when magically directed?

If man is made in the image of God, then each human being has the potential to be a creator. The Genesis account of creation states, "And God said, 'Let us make man in our own image, and after our likeness.'" The "us" is the creative energies of the universe, the active expression of divine creative power—some say it is the Elohim, making each of us an Elohim, or god, in miniature. This potential is activated by only one of two means: the slow path of evolution or the faster path of initiation and esoteric discipline. When initiation and its attendant practices are undertaken, the newly born being becomes a Being—one who can say to some degree the words that Moses heard from the burning bush: "*Ehieh asher Ehieh*," or "I am that which is Becoming."

This Becoming, or expansion of awareness, in initiates is demonstrated by their becoming a transformer of energy. When they speak sacred sound, it resonates with the higher frequencies and creates thought forms, states of awareness, even matter itself. The more one advances, the more definite and pronounced this power becomes, even transforming mundane language into a direct expression of will without the need for elaborate rituals or complex formula. Jesus said, "Believe me, if you trust and do not falter, not only will you do what I did . . . but if you say to this mountain, 'Be lifted up and thrown into the sea,' even that will happen." This section of the Book of Matthew reveals several constant and repeated themes found in the Gospels, the following points are critical to understanding them from an initiatic viewpoint:

1. Jesus tells his disciples that they must have unswerving confidence in their actions (prayer being an act) in order to accomplish anything they desire.

2. That each of them—and, in turn, each human being—has the potential to do everything Jesus did and more.

3. These "miracles" that Jesus performed were done without extensive elaboration, often with only a *word* or *simple command*, and often with an act as simple as others unexpectedly touching him or his cloak.

The word of the initiate increasingly approaches the "original language" and thereby is able to create, just as we read of Adam bringing the animals into existence by his act of naming them. Moses pronounces the word for water, and it flows from a rock in the desert. The words of the initiate vibrate forth the very thing they represent.

Silence

"If speech is silvery, then silence is golden" is an old proverb that is more true than many realize. By practicing silence we learn to conserve our energies and to direct them to other creative enterprises. Have you ever had a great idea and spent so much time talking about it to others that by the time you got around to doing it your enthusiasm was gone? The once buoyant energy you felt had escaped through your lips, and you were left literally feeling empty? This was later compounded by questions from friends and enemies alike who heard of your project and asked you about it. Sheepishly you changed the subject or went out of your way to avoid further discussion of it. The seed energy, the initial passion, was wasted, and nothing was born of it. This failure to produce then creates interior feelings of loss and embarrassment that must be removed before future developments can be made. This is the reason why so many creators, artists, writers, designers, and engineers hide their work from prying eyes. Reveal it for criticism and renovation only after it has successfully germinated into a viable product, plan, or design.[5]

Just as speaking of positive things often weakens their energy or power to materialize by directing our energy away from the doing of the project (as well as opening ourselves up to the energy of those who might oppose us, even unconsciously), constant talking of our problems only reinforces them and makes them stronger, more concrete.

It seems that those who succeed in an undertaking keep silent about it until it is manifest. Those who fail seemingly waste their energy in verbal outlets or misery mongering.

With regards to karma, keep in mind the following statement from Jean Dubuis:

> In order to neutralize and master "karma"—we could say our difficulties, our stumbling blocks—we should remember that Universal Justice is infallible . . .
>
> How can we participate in or be part of the solution? First of all, the most obvious thing is not to complicate our case and the first practice is silence. As a matter of fact, talking about our "problems" with the conscious or unconscious intention to complain about or justify our behavior certainly results in the prolongation of the situation even if the latter doesn't get worse . . . The less individuals know of your problem, the easier it is to resolve it, the easier it is to dissolve it. We should therefore avoid giving a fixed quality by crystallizing it.[6]

The reverse of this is also true. If voice can crystallize a condition, through judicious use of voice we can realize conditions that are preferred by us. When combined with the above use of Hebrew letters and the powers they manifest, we can begin to direct our inner energies in any manner we see fit.

The power of affirmation, or autosuggestion, can be combined with this process of energizing the throat and medulla centers to create a more potent technique. However, as with anything of an esoteric nature, the best affirmations are ones created by each of us. Since each letter has several qualities, the energies we seek to strengthen may be slightly different for each of us. Thus, research and review the nature of each letter and develop your affirmation from there.

The general rules of creating affirmations are the following:

1. Keep it positive and active.

2. State it in the first person possessive.

3. Keep it short.

4. Energize it with emotion, as you do the letters themselves.

For example, if one needs to reinforce the qualities of the Moon, the following affirmations could be used in conjunction with the Hebrew letter *Beth*.

I am Beth, master of Wisdom and Ignorance! Here me oh
Universe and reveal to me the House of the Lord!

I am Beth, the Moon in its glory! The powers of expansion and
decline are obedient unto me.

The Moon in its fullness I am! Reveler of hidden Wisdom and
the powers of right action.

As you can see, each of the above affirmations is similar to the other in that it places the "I" in the active and possessive part of the statement, but each expresses a slightly different quality of the Beth-lunar energy. Using the above as a model, consult the *Sepher Yetzirah*, and develop several affirmations for each of the seven double letters.[7]

Bal Shem: the Master of the Name

The *Bal Shem*, or Master of "the Name," was one of the most remarkable aspect of Medieval and Renaissance Jewish qabala. For these rabbis, nothing was impossible, and miracles are said to have been performed by them simply through the spoken expression of one or more of the names of God. Their beliefs even continued and were adopted by various folk traditions of Europe and North America.[8]

However, the pronunciation of divine names, letters, or any words of power, comes from several factors, including proper internalization of the sounds to be vibrated. The general method for their invocation is as follows:

> When vibrating divine names, the operator must first reach the highest possible notion of the idea of the white Divine Radiance of Kether, while keeping his mind at the level of the highest aspirations. If this is not achieved it is dangerous to only vibrate with the forces of the Astral world, because the vibration draws to the operator a certain force and the nature of this force depends very strongly on his state-of-mind.

> The usual way to proceed is as follows: breathe in deeply and profusely and focus your attention on your heart, which corresponds to Tiphareth. (Having first meditated on your Kether [slightly above the crown of your head], you will attempt to lower the white radiance to the innermost part of your heart before fixing your attention there.)

> Then formulate the letters of the selected name in white letters in your heart, feel them as if they were carved. Make sure to formulate these letters in a white luminous radiance and not silver-white. Then, while breathing out, pronounce the letters softly so that the sound vibrates inside you and imagine that the breath while leaving your body swells to fill the entire space. Pronounce the name as if you were emitting it throughout the entire Universe and that the sound could not stop before it had reached its ultimate limits.

Any practical successful occult work exhausts the operator or takes away some of his magnetism. That is why if you want to realize work of some magnitude you must possess a perfect magnetic balance. Otherwise you would do more harm than good.[9]

Exercise for Attunement to the Letters

For those who would like to try another method of attuning to each of the letters of the Hebrew alphabet, the following exercise is suggested. It will help to awaken, anchor, and link the concepts of the letters more firmly, while bringing your Higher, Middle, and Lower Selves into greater harmony with each other using the letters as a focal point.

In the *Sepher Yetzirah* the three mother letters in Hebrew—*Shin*, *Aleph*, and *Mem*—are attributed to the head, chest, and stomach. Students will quickly recognize these as the three main primitive psychic centers that occur across traditions. In alchemy, Mercury (life force), Sulphur (consciousness or soul), and Salt (body) are attributed to these centers, thereby giving us an additional link between these two systems.

For this practice we will use the specific locations of slightly above the head, or the crown center; the physical heart or slightly below, or the heart centers; and the naval. These, we will quickly see, represent the physical anchor points of the Higher Self (Neshamah), Middle Self (Ruach), and Lower Self (Nefesh) within us. We will progressively place the letter we are working on in each of the centers and link them together as a unit to begin the process of integration that will increase the power of our Word—or creative power expressed through our voice. This is very important, for in later practices you may undertake a series of divine names may be invoked to project to a specific sphere, planet, or Element using the attributes of the Tree of Life. Once awakened, our word or speech acts as a potent vehicle of creative will, thereby projecting and manifesting our desire in time, space, and consciousness.[10]

Preparation

Begin on a Wednesday immediately following a new moon, preferably after sunset or when the moon is above the horizon.

Explanation

This exercise reinforces our association of the three mother letters of the Hebrew alphabet with their corresponding physical locations. It also reinforces action as an interface between the psychic and physical bodies, integrates our levels of Being, and strengthens our work on the Magical Voice.

Type of Practice

This exercise both imprints new ideas into the psychic body and activates them for greater range of function and expression.

Method

1. Visualize the letter Shin slightly above your head. Be sure that it is clear and brilliant, almost phosphorescent white. Hold the image for a few minutes, and there will be a distinct pressure at your crown.

2. As you inhale, imagine the Shin is directing its energies into your body and filling it with the fiery energies of consciousness, will, and Being. You may imagine that your body is hollow or made of light, or that the energy permeates every cell of your being.

3. As you exhale, imagine that the energy activates your self-consciousness, will, and intuition.

4. After several minutes direct your attention to the center of your chest, or slightly above your heart, where oxygen enters the blood. Imagine the letter Aleph in brilliant blazing white.

5. As you inhale, feel the Aleph pull the vital energies of life into your psychic body, as well as your physical body, and concentrate in the Aleph.

6. As you exhale, imagine the energy moving from the Aleph and filling your body, penetrating every cell. You may even imagine it radiating out your pores and forming the shell of your aura around you. This imagery should all be clear and brilliant.

7. After a few minutes, move your attention to your naval and imagine the letter Mem there in clear, brilliant white.

8. As you inhale, imagine all of the energies focusing in the Mem, as if it were a powerful magnet attracting the energies of life into a powerful single point.

9. As you exhale, imagine that the Mem directs these energies of life into your blood, your cells, your flesh, and that all of the "watery" parts of your body and their psychic counter parts are brought to a higher level of functioning.

10. After several minutes, visualize each of the letters in their respective locations, and create a sense of harmony, communication, and conscious function between them.

Integration into Daily Practice

After an initial two-week period of practice, this exercise can be done at the practitioner's discretion.

Our Inner Name

Students seeking a practical experience in the various practices involving the development of the magical voice as an expression of their Holy Guardian Angel are encouraged to find a list of Hebrew names, such as the one in *The Occult Philosophy* by Agrippa; a list of Hebrew surnames; a list of the names of the Apostles, and so on, and discover one, or ones, that resonate with them on an interior level. After having cleansed and rebalanced the energies of their environment—through the Ritual of the Pentagram, a prayer, or other means—simply perform the following:[11]

Recite in a low voice the Hebrew names that you chose, one at a time, and meditate a minute or two after each name. Several things can occur. We are only interested in two of them. One of the names provokes a heart resonance: it is your spiritual mystical name; one of them provokes a cerebral resonance: it is your material occult name. Note the name, the date, the time, and the place of the revelation.

In either case, it is a rebirth and your astrological chart becomes the one of the moment of revelation. You and nobody else should interpret it. Look into the *Sepher Yetzirah*—and there only—for its real meaning. . . . You can incorporate these names into your mystical work of the descent of *Mezla*, either for the occult, spiritual or practical work without any negative Karmic repercussions.[12]

Finding Your Inner Name

Prepare yourself as usual for sleep, or even meditation. As you imagine an indigo sphere, large and luminous, at the level of your throat, vibrate one of the names on your list. Pause for two or three minutes and await a response. If none comes, move on to the next name. It will help if you can visualize the Hebrew letters of the name moving forth from within to the farthest reaches of the universe, pausing for a moment, and then returning to you as a creative vibration or force of some kind. If you are doing this prior to sleep, you may choose to use only one name a night for twelve nights.

It will help, as well, if you add an affirmation to your visualization, one that expresses your inner desire and intent of the experiment—that is, to realize your inner name of power. For example: "I call upon my inner name to reveal itself to me!" More will be said on the power of affirmations later in this chapter.

In working with the inner name keep in mind the following advice from Jean Dubuis:

Each being on Earth has an esoteric name, which starts at the time of entry into duality for the involutionary-evolutionary journey. Man receives a name which is in fact an image of the Eternal Vibration—his being. All men do not receive the same name but all names are equivalent, as a very function of the principles of Universal Justice . . . [F]or each level or plane man will receive a new name. Knowing one or several of these names is an important step for the student because the accurate vibration will create a profound resonance in him between the physical level and the inner level. The name vibrated corresponds to the inner level.

Warning: in no event whatsoever should you communicate your name(s) to anyone, should you discover them. . . . To communicate one's esoteric name to someone else is a betrayal of the Inner Being and can stop the evolution for the duration of an incarnation . . . [E]ach one of us has an esoteric name for each level of Creation. Pronouncing one of these words provokes a kind of invocation in our Inner Self at the level corresponding to the name . . . If someone cannot find his inner names on his own, he doesn't possess the wisdom to use them.[13]

If your name is revealed to you in Hebrew, remember: *Hebrew is read from right to left* and may need to be transliterated into Latin characters.

Dubuis further explains the importance of Divine Names and their use:

[T]he vocalization of divine names is one of the most important elements of ritual magic. . . The result of the vibratory vocalization of the divine name is to achieve in the higher levels of Astral Light, to the limits of the world of Briah, a harmonic response of the first invoked then secondly evoked intelligence."[14]

After having worked through the basic symbols of the lucid dreaming exercise, you can substitute Hebrew letters for the planetary signs. This will create a deeper resonance within you for not only when using the letters themselves, but also when they are combined into divine names.

Through practice, the above exercises will prove useful to you in your search for inner resonance and outer harmony. The tools have been given and are yours to use. Only by using them over a period of time do they become an interior part of us and are we capable of mastering them. The techniques described are among the simplest and most effective we know of for attaining inner resonance. As stated several times, they add little time to your daily schedule as they are performed for a few minutes at night prior to sleep and, if desired, for a minute or so in the morning upon awakening. Their purpose is to attune each of us to the specific qualities of the day—either through astrological symbols or

Hebrew letters—or to other archetypal qualities as expressed through the twelve simple and three mother letters of Hebrew.

As these forces become known and mature within us on an intimate level, they will eventually combine into more complex ideas and forces for the realization of those ideas. This will hopefully reveal to us the nature of the seven dual principles, the stages of energy density, and our interior name(s) so that we can better direct these forces within us.

Ritual for Awakening the Hebrew Letters

The origin of the following ritual is unknown, but it appears to be in current use by members of the Elus Cohen and some Martinist organizations. It may very well have its origins in the writings of the eighteenth-century theurgist Martinez Pasquelaz.[15] The ritual appears in Robert Ambelain's *Kabbalah* and has also been circulated in manuscript form.[16] The basic ritual is very simple, requires about fifteen to twenty minutes to perform, and takes about five minutes to set up and break down. Because of the extreme simplicity of the ritual, additional comments and suggestions have been added, with notions to distinguish them from the original. All of the additions are based upon the experience of students of qabala who have worked directly with the ritual and the techniques in this book and, as such, the additions form a seamless continuum of method.

The main thrust of the ritual is the utilization of the 119th Psalm and its relationship to the twenty-two letters of the Hebrew alphabet in order to stimulate our inner resonance with these letters and their various uses in practical magic. The ritual is peculiar in its simplicity and has been found to be very effective in stimulating lucid dreaming in its own right. Ambelain states that the ritual will allow the operator to experience the *Ruach Elohim* (Soul of God), or creative force better known as the Holy Spirit. It is clear from those who have performed the rite in it entirety that it is also a very condensed working of the twenty-two connecting paths of the Tree of Life.

Chart of the Hebrew Letters, Divine Names, and Verses

Hebrew Letter	The Day	Divine Name	Psalm 119	Quality
Aleph	1st (Sunday)	Elohim Ehieh	Verses 1–8	God of Becoming
Beth	2nd (Monday)	Elohim	Verses 9–16	Chosen God
Gimel	3rd (Tuesday)	Bachour	Verses 17–24	Greatness of God
Daleth	4th (Wednesday)	Elohim Gadol	Verses 25–32	Well-known God
Heh	5th (Thursday)	Elohim Dagoul	Verses 33–40	Magnificent God
Vau	6th (Friday)	Elohim Hadour	Verses 41–48	Splendorous God
Zain	7th (Saturday)	Elohim Vesio	Verses 49–56	Pure God
Cheth	8th (Sunday)	Elohim Zakai	Verses 57–64	Merciful God
Teth	9th (Monday)	Elohim Chesed	Verses 65–72	Spotless God
Yod	10th (Tuesday)	Elohim Thehor	Verses 73–80	Seed of God
Kaph	11th (Wednesday)	Elohim Yah	Verses 81–88	Powerful God
Lamed	12th (Thursday)	Elohim Kabir	Verses 89–96	Knowing God
Mem	13th (Friday)	Elohim Limmoud	Verses 97–104	God of Praise
Nun	14th (Saturday)	Elohim Maborak	Verses 105–112	Formidable God
Samek	15th (Sunday)	Elohim Norah	Verses113–120	Supporting God
Ayin	16th (Monday)	Elohim Samek	Verses 121–128	Strong God
Peh	17th (Tuesday)	Elohim Hazaz	Verses 129–136	Redeeming God
Tzaddi	18th (Wednesday)	Elohim Phodey	Verses 137–144	Just God
Qoph	19th (Thursday)	Elohim Tzedek	Verses 145–152	Holy God
Resh	20th (Friday)	Elohim Kadosh	Verses 153–160	Commanding God
Shin	21st (Saturday)	Elohim Rodah	Verses 161–168	Almighty God
Tau	22nd (Sunday)	Elohim Shaddai	Verses 169–176	Favorable God

Preparation

This ritual requires several tools that are easy to acquire and make. You will need to make a simple ritual floor cloth, preferably made out of a white or slightly off-white material that has never been used for any other purpose. You may also paint the following diagrams on plywood as long as the wood has not been previously used. The ritual carpet, as it is sometimes called, consists of one large circle, approximately three to four feet in diameter with four overlapping circles at each of its four cardinal points, or quarters. Each quarter has one of the Hebrew letters of the divine name of God, the Tetragrammaton, painted or drawn in it. In the ritualistic east, the direction you face when performing the ritual, is the letter Yod. To your right, in the ritualistic south, is Heh; behind you, in the west, is Vau; and to you left, in the north, is Heh. This is the supreme name of God in Judaism and qabala. It is also known as the lost word in many initiatic groups, as its proper pronunciation has been lost across the ages. It is the work of the magician, the alchemist, the qabalist, to recover its proper pronunciation, and in doing so, restore their inner harmony. In the center of the large circle is the Hebrew letter Shin, which stands for the Holy Spirit, or Divine Presence, also known as the Shekinah. With the other four letters, Shin creates the divine name YHShVH, or Yodheshuah, an important name in Christian mysticism, as well as in the works of the Golden Dawn, particularly the in Ritual of the Rose Cross. A small candle in a red votive holder stands on the letter Shin, or slightly above it.

You will also need to make a Triangle of Art, or focal point for the energies you are about to invoke over the twenty-two-day period of the operation. The Triangle of Art is an equilateral triangle inside of a circle. Inside of the triangle, at each point, will be placed a small candle (tea-light candles work fine), a talisman, and the divine name and letter of the day you will be working with. The Triangle can be any size you are comfortable in working with as long as it can safely hold the required candles, pantacle, and divine name.

In addition, you will need a white robe, preferably one that does not go beyond your calves, as you will be standing on the letter Shin, directly above the candle in the votive holder while performing this operation. A red mantle is traditional, although a red sash, cassock, or cordelier will suffice. Red is the color of fire, the essence of initiation, the only power that can expand our consciousness.

Frankincense will be used, preferably in tears or grains, with a live charcoal. However, if you are not experienced with this kind of incense or the appropriate burner it requires, high-quality essential oil can be used instead, along a simple joss stick of frankincense. The essential oil is used to fill the room with the required perfume, while a lesser-quality stick of frankincense incense is used to cense the quarters upon the opening and closing nights of the ritual. It is important that the odor be strong, clean, and of high quality so that the appropriate emotions in the Lower Self (Nefesh) can be called into play in the ritual. Once the ritual censing of the quarters is done, the stick incense can be snuffed out while the essential oil provides the real perfume for the ritual. This is a safe way to go if you are uncomfortable with swinging around brass burners filled with sand and hot coals.

The scripture passage this ritual utilizes is the 119th Psalm, which can be read in English, Hebrew, or Latin. The 119th Psalm is the longest of the psalms and contains specific references to each of the letters of the Hebrew alphabet. As such, it is preferable to use the Hebrew version; however, historically this ritual was done using the Latin. If you cannot read Hebrew and do not wish to use Latin, English will do. The psalm sets the context of the work and links us to tradition. The meditation on the letter and the intonations of the divine name are what awaken the energies within us and, as such, are more critical. The numbering of the Psalms, however, is not universal; those using Hebrew will notice that the numeration is 119, as it is the King James English translation, while a Latin or Catholic translation places the numeration as Psalm118. Since most will be doing this ritual in English, this discrepancy will not be a problem. Those wishing to read the original Hebrew or who are look-ing for an authoritative English translation are advised to use the *Hebrew-English Tanakh* published by the Jewish Publication Society.

A talisman or pantacle in the shape of a St. Andrew's Cross will be used across the entire ritual. It has inscribed on it the divine name

Jahdoni, or the combination of Yah (Yod-Heh) and Adonai (Aleph-Daleth-Nun-Yod). This name is considered a symbol of universal benediction and appropriate for the work of this ritual.

A candlesnuffer, matches or a lighter, and a small amount of electric light for reading will be needed.

Explanation

This ritual progressively awakens us to the creative power inherent in the letters of the Hebrew alphabet as an expression of the most fundamental energies of the universe. These building blocks of sound, light, and form are imprinted, awakened, and stimulated within our psyche, thereby linking us to the world of Yetzirah in a manner previously unknown. This ritual is also, in its own right, a form of condensed pathworking, wherein the paths of the Tree of Life are called into action via their relationships to the letters. The Ruach Elohim (Soul of God), or mysterious creative energy known as the Holy Spirit, as expressed through the Shekinah, or the female aspect of divinity with its redemptive, healing, and initiatic qualities, are called into play as well. The prominent name invoked each night is *Elohim*, a strange name that demonstrates the creative forces of the cosmos, but also is related to the energies of the sphere of Netzach. Elohim directly is concerned with the forces of earthly time through the days of the week and the creation of harmony in our daily lives. The ritual is also performed under the lunar auspices of the fall equinox, further reinforcing its astral harmonization aspects.

Type of Practice

Core. This ritual should be done annually by those who wish to work a qabalistic path and, in particular, want to develop the power of their word.

Method

Note: This ritual is to be performed on the first Sunday of a new moon after the fall equinox, between the 9 p.m. and midnight. While out of necessity it can be performed at others times of the year, the lunar phase should be strictly adhered to.

Prepare your area of working, traditionally called an oratory, or place of prayer, placing your ritual cloth on the floor and the Triangle of Art in the east as illustrated. Face geographical east, if possible. Have the pantacle of universal benediction inside the triangle. On a separate strip of paper write the name of the day in Hebrew with the letter of the day beneath it and place it beneath the pantacle, so that both are visible when you look at the triangle. Be sure there is ample illumination to read the proper psalms by and that your candles are safely placed.

Wearing only a white robe with a red cordelier, sash, or mantle, enter your oratory barefoot and free of all metal and jewelry (save for one magical ring or wedding bands) and proceed as follows:

1. Light the candle in the votive holder placed on the letter Shin. From it, if possible, light the three candles on the Triangle of Art, starting with the apex candle, then the right hand corner, and then the left hand corner.

2. Light some frankincense and allow it fill the room as you prepare yourself. Stand in the center of the circle above the letter Shin, facing east. Relax by taking several slow deep breaths. Feel the power of the perfume stimulate and awaken your inner self on a mental level—that of the Ruach—and on a psychic level—of the Lower Self, the Nefesh.

3. Light the single white candle that you will hold in your left hand for the duration of the ritual and say a prayer to your Higher Self, or Holy Guardian Angel, to assist you in this operation, that through it you may awaken the power of the word within yourself to fortify your Body of Light and, in doing so, unite now and eternally with your angel as a single being.

4. Continue facing east, cense the circle three times, and recite Psalm 19, "The heavens declare the glory . . ."

5. Turn to your right, the south, cense three times, and recite Psalm 11, "In Adonai I put my trust . . ."

6. Turn to the west, cense three times, and recite Psalm 15, "Adonai, who shall abide in thy tabernacle? . . ."

7. Turn to the north, cense three times, and recite Psalm 8, "Adonai our Lord, how excellent is thy Name . . ."

8. Turn to the east and extinguish your incense or place it at a safe place within your circle.

9. Facing the Triangle of Art, holding the candle in your left hand, extend your right palm down hand towards the Triangle and say, "Elohim Eheieh! Aleph!" Recite verses one through eight of Psalm 119.

10. When you have completed the verses say, "By this pantacle of Universal Benediction—Jahdonai—and this divine name of Elohim Ehieh, I perfectly, completely, and wholly, awaken, direct, and express the intelligence, power, and presence of the letter Aleph, now and forever more within myself and all of creation. Amen, Amen, Amen."

11. Imagine that your body is completely hollow and made up of light. Visualize the letter Aleph in the area of your heart as a brilliant white letter, tinged with gold. Intone the divine name of the day seven times, being sure to pronounce it in such a way that a vibration is felt in your solar plexus or even throughout your entire body.

12. Focus your entire consciousness in the letter. Meditate on it for a few minutes.

13. When your meditation is complete, say the following: "By this pantacle of Universal Benediction—Jahdonai—and this divine name of Elohim Ehieh, I have perfectly, completely, and wholly awakened, directed, and expressed the intelligence, power, and presence of the Letter Aleph, now and forever more within myself and all of creation, fortifying my Body of Light and bringing me into perfect union with my Holy Guardian Angel. Amen, Amen, Amen."

14. Pause. Exit the circle and extinguish your candles in the reverse order that you lit them.

15. Fold your ritual cloth and place it and your Triangle of Art where they will not be touched by anyone else for the duration of this operation.

16. As you fall asleep later that night, visualize the letter of the day in brilliant white light, tinged with gold, at the nape of your neck or in your throat as described in the lucid-dreaming technique in the previous chapter, and recite the divine name silently several times with the firm intention that you are awakening the energy-intelligence-matter of this letter within your Body of Light.

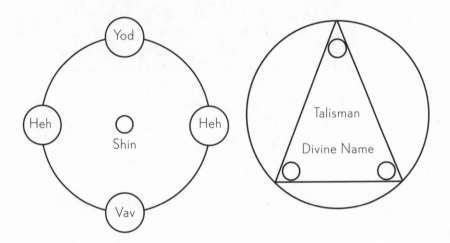

Commentary and Ritual Rubric

Part One

Shin represents the Divine Presence, the Holy Upper Trinity manifest in the material world, Shekinah, the nurturing, healing, protective power of the cosmos. It is lit first, because without it no other light would exist. The candles on the triangle are lit clockwise and later are extinguished counterclockwise.

Parts Two and Three

This preparatory phase is crucial and should be done slowly and with deep solemnity.

Part Three

The candle you hold is your personal inner light, your Higher Self, Holy Guardian Angel—whatever you chose to call it. Just as you must hold it for the entire ritual, it, in turn, holds you for the duration of your earthly existence. Just as you must make a conscious effort to hold the candle and pay attention to it while performing other acts, you must also make a conscious effort to pay attention to your intuition, messages from your Higher Self, while in the midst of your daily duties. The prayer is critical, as it is a message from the ego (Ruach) to the subconscious (Nefesh) about the purpose of this ritual—it is a veritable suggestion, affirmation, and command—to open up to the ever-present impulses of the Higher Self (Neshamah).

Parts Four through Eight

The Psalms assert the authority of the Divine Mind, the cosmos over and through all that exists. It also asserts the righteous authority of the operator to undertake this work. The divine name most often used is Adonai, which in sixteenth- and seventeenth-century Rosicrucian circles was interpreted to mean not a distance God, but the operator's own Holy Guardian Angel.

Censing is performed by swinging the censor up and forward over the area to be cleansed. Since this requires some practice, particularly if you do not want to have hot coals or incense flying about, a simple joss stick variety of frankincense should be used. The motion is large, from groin to about or above the forehead. It is not uncommon to make the sign of the cross in its place—again, making the gesture large and having the cross arm go past your shoulders. The cross is the cross of unfoldment, of light opening within matter, and not a sectarian symbol. Simply move your incense stick from the level of your heart or solar plexus to above your forehead, bring it straight down to level with your groin or slightly below, curve up and to your left, and draw a line straight across to your right; pause and bring the incense back to center. Repeat three times. When done in this manner, the cross represents the divine flow of energy into matter.[17]

Part Nine

The ritual gesture engages the Lower Self in participating in the act of authority, while cooperating with the Middle Self (ego) and Higher Self (Holy Guardian Angel). The divine name is recited to link in the subconscious with the energies of the letter to the verse from the psalm and to the name itself, so that when the conscious Middle Self recites them in the future, the Lower Self knows what energies to send into action.

Part Ten

The specific nature and function of the signs, symbols, and names being used, and for what purpose, is stated as an affirmation, invocation, or command so that all three levels of consciousness are in harmony as to their purpose. The threefold nature of an invocation is utilized as well, so that there are no gaps whereby the Lower Self can suggest doubt or qualifications as a result of previous experiences. The affirmation of "amen" is used, as it means, "So shall it be!" Again, this is affirmed three times, once for each level of consciousness, but really to bring the Lower Self into agreement through the power of suggestion and repetition.

Parts Eleven and Twelve

The physical body is light, composed of dense light, and by imagining it as such we bring our self-conception back to reality. By imagining it as empty—that is, devoid of physical organs—we further reinforce this process of awakening to our pure and unerring nature. The heart is the center of our being and the psychic focal point for all awakening. By vibrating the names we further strengthen our actual use of the sounds and bring them into manifestation. We make them material, concrete, rather than abstract. The seven repetitions are used to correspond the overall psychic influences of this ritual, and the solar plexis is used because of its role as our personal tuning fork. The period of meditation is to assimilate what we have just experienced.

Part Thirteen

The closing affirmation is used to state the success of the operation and to reinforce the first affirmation stating the nature of the ritual.

Parts Fourteen and Fifteen

Candles are routinely lit clockwise and extinguished counterclockwise, or in some similar ritualistic fashion to show order in the cosmos and the cycles of unfoldment. Candles are never blown out but extinguished with a snuffer or pinched out. The cloth will accumulate a psychic charge for this work, and that charge must not be lost through carelessness.

Part Sixteen

The work of the heart is reinforced by the work of the head. Dream practices are utilized to reinforce the ritual work of the evening. Careful notations of any dreams during the period is critical.

Key Points

- It is important to maintain a diary of your esoteric practices. This acts as a permanent record of your spiritual coming of age and helps identify specific areas of study for future work.
- Positive thinking is the single most important key to success on the esoteric path. It is the genuine and true magic of our inner self, and opens us up to unlimited possibilities, regardless of our material situation.
- Through harmonic resonance, or sound, we create conditions that are favorable or unfavorable to us. Our speech is the principal tool for the expression of our inner state and creating resonance.
- *Yetzirah* comes from the root *yatzar*, meaning "to form" and denotes the formation of "something from something." Speech is formed from thought and is "something from something."
- The solar plexus is our individual psychic tuning fork.

- Words are an expression of our individual will. A magician knows what to expect from specific vocalizations and energizes them with use, thereby increasing their power of action.
- The psychic center at the throat is a secondary sexual center and is connected to the power of speech and creation.
- The power of "the Word" is stated across various scriptures and easily demonstrated through the injunctions towards spoken prayer and invocations.
- Speech is related to silence. Silence allows us to focus our energy and protect our ambitions and projects from the destructive (even if well-meaning) attitudes of others.
- Just as speech can make an unfavorable condition more concrete, silence can be used to eliminate it. By not talking about our problems, or talking only to others who can actually assist us in their resolution, we can eliminate troubling conditions.
- The Hebrew alphabet can be used to strengthen the power of our magical voice, thereby giving greater power and effect to our occult operations.
- Our inner name is the key to our personal unfolding. Once it is discovered, it should not be disclosed to anyone.

Assignments for Chapter Four

1. Read one of the books on the Hebrew alphabet from the Reading List and create a synthesis of each letter's key ideas, reducing it to one or two words.
2. Create an affirmation for each of the letters and use them in connection with your lucid dreaming and astral projection practices.
3. Pay careful attention to your daily speech, its tone and character. Do you use positive, active language, or is it passive and negative?
4. Read one of the books on the effects of language, listed in the Reading List.
5. Perform each of the exercises in the chapter and carefully record your experiences in your notebook.

CHAPTER 5

Astral Projection in Qabala

It is important to recognize that some of the methods used to achieve astral projection, or full exteriorization of consciousness, are similar to those methods used in skrying or experiments involving clairvoyance and remote viewing. The difference is that in astral projection there is such a significant and sufficient projection of consciousness from the physical body to make physical movement or conversation impossible. Etheric projection is even more powerful when a significant amount of life force is taken from the body and used by the astral form. During skrying or clairvoyant sessions, the mind is attuned to a specific topic or idea, just as one tunes a radio to a specific frequency, and then receives information through one or more of the psychic senses. The quality of the information received depends on how well the psychic senses have been developed. This is why some psychics will "hear" better than they "see," and some will sense or intuit as a direct knowing.

In order for consciousness to be projected, the aura of the individual must be sufficiently magnified to be extremely positive or expansive in nature. With people inexperienced in psychic phenomena, this magnification and expansion of the aura or consciousness sometimes occurs as a kind of pressure on the left side of the head near the temple, or a feeling as if they were being pushed forward or to one side. It is not uncommon to see a person, or find oneself, leaning forward and to the right as a result of the increase of energy coming into the physical and psychic bodies on the left.

Projection allows for a kind of synthetic life in the various worlds, a full-fledged consciousness separate from the physical brain, which clairvoyance does not and cannot. The difference could be compared to riding in a car or train and viewing the scenery instead of walking through the scenery and experiencing it directly.

In some instances, information is obtained by blending clairvoyance and projection; a small part of one's psychic anatomy—a sensorium—is projected in the shape of a sphere or animal. This projected part can be visible to others, but is limited to observation rather than having the possibility of interaction. Herein lies one of the advantages to developing skill in astral projection. Astral projection provides a level of privacy, intimacy, and totality that other forms of psychic awareness cannot.

The greatest obstacle to success in life is lack of perseverance. This is particularly true in any esoteric study or occult practice. The reality is that most activities we undertake reach a point where they are not fun, exciting, or stimulating, and they become boring. However, if everyone gave up when things reached their most functional and laborious stage, nothing would ever be accomplished. For example, this book would not have been written, the store it was bought in never opened, or the building it sits in ever built. The list goes on and without belaboring the point, this is also true with many of the more important exercises in practical occultism. It takes dedication and focus to become an expert in any mundane area of activity—no less so when we seek to become an expert in *consciousness*.

What is nice about the methods presented here is that steady practice will give results, and it is hoped that from these results sufficient confidence will be established to continue with the process. In the end, each of us is responsible for our own Becoming. If we view these exercises as experiments in consciousness, like playing with a Ouija board or table tipping, and not part of a larger practice of spiritual culture, then we lessen our opportunities for success. Esoteric practices must be put in their proper perspective, and this is even more important with those practices described here. Success in achieving a genuine out-of-body experience, projection to an astral plane, and undertaking the creation of the Body of Light, will all remove from us the fear of death. When this is done, we are free to live our life here and now as we see fit, as we not only understand that we are immortal, but also begin to have our entire life framed by this direct experience. For many people it is therapeutic. Trivialities and mind-numbing, energy-sucking problems disappear. This does not mean that they suddenly vanish, but that one is able to put them in their proper perspective of, "Will this matter in five years? Ten years? When I am dead?"

These types of life-changing experiences are often called *initiatic*, in that they initiate or start a new phase of life for us. In esotericism ritual initiations are used by various groups to help jump-start a member's sense of the invisible worlds. More often than not these rituals impress the candidate with a sense of solemnity and symbolic splendor but fail to actually create a significant shift in consciousness. The reasons for this are many, but in the end, such rituals can be only a hint or shadow of the true spiritual initiation they imitate.

Spiritual interior initiation is the goal of all sincere students of traditional Western esotericism, for with it comes the illumination, wisdom, compassion, and freedom that esotericism offers. Therefore students are strongly urged to pick a system of study and to stay with it to understand as completely as possible its operative symbols. These symbols are not only a gateway for lucid dreaming, but they are also the tools of communication used when projecting into the astral planes. Through a structured set of symbols, such as the Tree of Life or alchemical prints, it is possible to have a series of *progressive interior experiences* or initiations.

Initiations are defined as progressive interior experiences, because that is what best describes them. They are progressive in that they lead from one step to another from a beginning to an end. They are interior in that they are part of the student's psyche and not a ritual experience— although rituals can trigger them, and they are experiences. They are a direct contact by the student and within their own psyche, with some energy, consciousness, or "other" that permanently modifies the student's consciousness and is not an intellectual abstraction. However, the grave danger students face when undertaking these practices without the guidance of someone who has traveled the path before them is the possibility of misinterpreting their experiences and giving them more significance than they deserve. Skilled and experienced teachers are rare; however, they provide an objective measure against which to assess one's undertaking. When such a teacher is not available, then anything short of a direct and verified awakening should be the litmus test of a successful initiation or experience with all other experiences as simply steps along the way.

The Palaces of the Hekelot and the Tree of Life

At a weeklong seminar sponsored by the Philosophers of Nature in September 1994, Jean Dubuis, the founder and president of the Philosophers of Nature, gave a talk on the nature of reality from a qabalistic point of view and how it interrelates with alchemical practices.

According to Dubuis, the function of all of these Qabalistic exercises and alchemical creations (in addition to clearing psychological and physical illnesses) is to allow us to be initiated into the realms of our being. These realms are both personal and impersonal in that we share a common meeting ground with others experiencing these levels of specific vibration, and yet there are aspects of the experience that are unique to us.[1] These levels exist as semi-independent worlds in which we can live fully and consciously, just as we do in this one. These worlds are referred to in the *Zohar* as the *Hekelot*, or Palaces. The intensity of living that we experience in them is reflective of our level of consciousness and how much of our awareness we can transfer to them. Thus, while on one level we may feel intensely, on another level we may only sense vaguely. In Yesod, we may experience life as fully as we do on earth, yet in Hod we may have only a sense of what is happening, and in Netzach even less. It is only through progressively transferring the bulk of our consciousness from sphere to sphere, or palace to palace, that we achieve mastery over the astral realm and enter into the sphere of Tiphareth in full power and glory.

Drawing heavily from modern Golden Dawn material, French copies of older Golden Dawn lectures, and Dubuis's extensive experiences in Rosicrucianism, Martinism, and the Elus Cohen, the procedures suggested were less original than they were a new twist on some well-known and tried techniques. Through combinations of the rituals of the pentagram and hexagram, with emphasis on personal initiation and the development of a comprehensive and corporate life in the astral spheres, the ideas presented during Dubuis's lecture were similar in fashion to those of some schools of Tibetan and Chinese Buddhism, where one literally takes corporeal life and consciousness with them into the invisible.

To assist students who have been experimenting with hermetic techniques and help each person discern where he or she might be on the Path of Return, Dubuis gave the following descriptions to help students discover which sepherah they were at as a result of either a lucid dreaming experience or astral projection. These descriptions could also help strengthening awareness and conscious power in each sphere.

Yesod is a place of pale light, often charged with the thought forms of earth. Most students of esotericism have gone beyond it, usually to Hod.

Hod is described as being a fairy-tale-like palace, complete with a magical oratory, alchemical lab, and astrological observatory. For some Hod can be frightening.

Netzach is inspired by nature, and green things predominate there. It may appear as a half tree, or as a luxuriously colored palace, or as a combination of both.

Tiphareth is like that palace of the French kings, Versailles, complete with fleur-de-lis. It is bright, with large windows, and the sky, pointed toward Chesed, is always blue.

Geburah is a citadel, but comfortable.

Chesed is often an enormous religious building or a castle with a large temple enclosed in it.

Binah is often experienced as a pyramid or massive temple with a single spire. Hokmah and Kether exist beyond the imagery of the psyche. At best one could say Hokmah would be an experience of spacelessness—or everything in creation existing in the same place—and Kether as a single point. Clearly these two are closely related and are really aspects of the same thing—the unity that exits at that level. Malkooth of course is our physical world with all of the earth being its temple.

Contacts with Hod were especially encouraged to strengthen alchemical knowledge and technique. However, Dubuis said that only in Tiphareth do we receive back our magical powers that we renounced during our descent into matter, as well as contact with our interior master, or Holy Guardian Angel.[2] The alchemical tinctures suggested for these spheres were Caraway Seed (Mercury) and Eyebright (Sun).

With the above description in mind, it is important to strive to first develop memory in the dream and astral states. Second, it is important to strive to develop abilities, be they corporeal, such as movement, or intellectual, like the ability to read, perform mathematics, or perform abstract reasoning. By bringing our material skills into our astral life, we awaken within ourselves the ability to live fully and completely on two or more planes. Often it is believed that we are in need of only our Higher Self and that because our Higher Self is perfect, it has no need of "us," or the ego, the individualized life. But it is only through the individualized life, through the developed ego, that the totality of consciousness can be experienced or have a reference point. Unity is known *because* of separation; good is known *because* of evil; death is known *because* of life.

This is important, because whereas lucid dreaming is concerned with becoming aware of the subjective state one is experiencing, astral projection is concerned with developing a complete synthetic awareness and mastery of that state, then progressively moving on to the next level of integration. Each level of the Tree is unique, discreet, and distinct, but also contains all of the levels that proceeded it and thereby mastery of them.

Methods of Projection

Exteriorization Within the Aura

Projection Using a Pentagram, Aleph, or Shin

Project Using a Tarot Card

Projection Using Rising on the Planes

Each of the following methods of projection offers the student an opportunity to find the methods that works best for them. It is advisable to pick one method and practice it faithfully for two weeks, note your results, and then move on to the next. Lunar cycles may play a part in the results and should be carefully noted, full- and new-moon phases of the lunar cycle being the most beneficial. However, it is our goal to be able to project not only wherever, but also whenever we want, and only persistence will give us that skill. The environment should be a quiet one, free from sudden noises or distractions. If you are lying down, cover yourself with a light blanket, even if the room temperature is warm, as you may experience a chill as a result of the exercise. Some researchers suggest that a soft blue, violet (black light), or amber electric bulb will assist in creating the proper psychic conditions for projection. It is known that these colors can assist making the aura more visible, and amber in particular is helpful for viewing apparitions and ambient psychic energy. Blue is favored among certain Rosicrucian and Martinist groups. For safety, please do not leave any candles unattended, or use some form of protective device such as votive candles or glass hurricane protectors to prevent any accidents while you are in a deep state of relaxation during these practices.

Exercise: Exteriorization Within the Aura

Preparation

Sit comfortably with your back straight, feet flat on the floor, palms of your hands flat on your thighs close to your hips (to reduce stress on your shoulders and elbows), and chin slightly tucked. Breathe deeply several times, holding your in breath for as long as is comfortable, exhaling slowly, and holding out your breath out for as long as is comfortable. Feel yourself relax mentally, emotionally, and physically as you do this. Say the following prayer (or something similar): "I invoke the presence of my Holy Guardian Angel to assist me in this work of astral projection and to awaken me to the innermost depths of by being."

Affirmations or prayers to our inner self, our Holy Guardian Angel, such as the above, are powerful tools for jump-starting and maintaining our practice and success.

Explanation

This practice is fundamental to all projection exercises. While projection during its performance is rare for many beginning students, the activation of the astral body is greatly enhanced, and spontaneous projection during sleep after the practice is a common occurrence. A sense of dizziness, pressure from the left pushing forward, or even expansiveness near the left temple or side of head is a sign of the aura being expanded as a result of this or similar practices.

Type of Practice

This is a core practice designed to specifically facilitate the projection of consciousness. It can also be done alone in the evening or prior to sleep.

Method

1. While sitting in a chair or lying in bed, imagine that you are surrounded by a large sphere of light that extends out about six feet on either side of you. It is slightly violet on the edges and very solid to the touch. Develop this sphere very clearly and concretely, as it will be your primary area of working with projection.

2. Breathe deeply, imagining brilliant light entering into your nostrils and "awakening" the astral counterpart of your left foot. Focus all of your attention on your foot, in detail, and as you exhale, imagine that a bluish white light shines from every cell and forms an etheric counterpart of your foot.

3. Inhale and repeat the same process with your right foot.

4. Continue moving up your body in a spiral fashion, from left to right, until your entire body has been visualized, and energized, in this manner.

5. Be sure to include your internal organs, bones, hair, and teeth, adding as much detail as possible to the visualization. The entire process should take no less than ten minutes and as much as a half an hour. Once competency is developed, it can be done rapidly in a sweeping fashion.

6. Once this is done, breathe deeply, imagine a brilliant sphere of light in your solar plexus, and with all of your emotional energy, "will" or "push" your consciousness out of your body.

7. You may slightly tense your body as you do this. As you relax, feel your energy flow out towards the desired spot in the room.

8. It is acceptable to fall asleep at this stage of the exercise, as projection may result at this point.

9. If you do not fall asleep or sense any projection of consciousness, breathe deeply several times, holding each inhale for as long as comfortable and exhaling slowly. Sit or stand up and record your results.

Incorporation into Daily Practice

This practice should take to fifteen to thirty minutes at most and be done once or twice a day for a month so that you can become thoroughly familiar with the technique.

Exercise: Projection Using a Pentagram, Aleph, and Shin

Preparation

Preparation is the same as in the previous exercise.

Explanation

This practice prepares the mind and psychic body of the practitioner for experiencing increased psychic and mystical states by decreasing the amount of psychic resistance that might be encountered. This practice imprints new ideas into our psychic body, as well as allows us to activate them for a greater range of function specific to astral projection.

Type of Practice

This is a core practice and can be done alone in the evening or prior to sleep.

Method

1. Perform the previous exercise up to and including step number five.

2. Visualize a brilliant pentagram before you, inside the sphere of light. For now, make it bluish white or slightly silver. Later you can experiment with the various colors associated with the Elements.

3. Once this is done, breathe deeply, imagine a brilliant sphere of light in your solar plexus, and with all of your emotional energy, "will" or "push" your consciousness out of your physical body.

4. You may slightly tense your body as you do this. As you relax, feel your energy flow out towards the desired spot in the room on the other side of the pentagram.

5. Imagine that you are stepping out of your body and moving through the pentagram to that point.

6. It is acceptable to fall asleep at this stage of the exercise, as projection may result at this point.

7. If you do not fall asleep or sense any projection of consciousness, breathe deeply several times, holding each inhale for as long as comfortable and exhaling slowly. Sit or stand up and record your results.

8. You may visualize the Hebrew letter Aleph in the center of the pentagram to assist in your projection, as it assists in harmonizing your energies on a fundamental level. Shin can also be used, although its effects will be slightly different and more dramatic. If you have experienced one of the Palaces in a dream state or spontaneous projection, you may place one of the symbols you received in the center of the pentagram, coupled with the firm intention to get back to that specific level for your practice.

Incorporation into Daily Practice

This practice should take about thirty minutes or so and be done once or twice a day for two to three weeks so that you can become thoroughly familiar with the technique.

Once you have experienced projection, you can begin to move around the sphere that you have created. Think of it as a psychic womb for the maturation of your psychic body. Later you can extend your travels to various rooms in your house or to other familiar locations. With time, projection to unfamiliar territory will occur naturally for you, and you will know how to respond to what you will encounter there.

Using the above techniques, you can also affirm as you fall asleep that you will project your consciousness to a specific location, for a specific task, and thinking no more about it, go to sleep. After a period of time, it will be quite surprising how effective a method this is.

Exercise: Projection Using a Tarot Card

Preparation

Preparation is the same as in the previous exercise.

Explanation

This exercise is designed to imprint specific symbols into the subconscious of the practitioner, as well as activate these symbols for specific use in astral projection. The following example uses tarot cards, although other symbolic images and designs may be used as well.

Type of Practice

This is core practice for those working with qabalistic pathworking or seeking to understand the tarot cards; otherwise it is optional.

Method

Perform the preparatory steps 1 through 5 of the "Exteriorization Within the Aura" exercise up to and including step number five (see page 105). Take your time, be relaxed yet attentive, feel the energy fill your body and extend beyond it. The proceed with the following.

1. Visualize before you a large, heavy curtain covering a doorway. On the mantle of the doorway, in the keystone, visualize the Hebrew letter associated with the tarot card you are using. If there is none, then visualize the key symbol of the card.

2. Imagine that the curtains are drawn back, and you see, in three dimensions, the card come to life before you.

3. Once this is done, breathe deeply, imagine a brilliant sphere of light in your solar plexus, and with all of your emotional energy, "will" or "push" your consciousness out of your body.

4. You may slightly tense your body as you do this, and as you relax, feel your energy flow out towards the desired spot in the room.

5. Imagine that you are stepping out of your body and moving through the doorway into the image of the card at a great rate of speed.

6. It is acceptable to fall asleep at this stage of the exercise, as projection may result at this point.

7. If you do not fall asleep or sense any projection of consciousness, breathe deeply several times, holding each inhale for as long as comfortable and exhaling slowly. Sit or stand up and record your results.

8. If done repeatedly prior to sleep, this exercise will influence your dreams, as well as induce lucid dreaming.

Incorporation into Daily Practice

This practice should take thirty minutes or so and be done once or twice a day. It can be done in the evening or prior to sleep. The exercise should initially be done for two to three weeks to become familiar with the technique, and then at the discretion of the practitioner.

Rising on the Planes

The method known as Rising on the Planes is used extensively within the Golden Dawn system of magic. Aleister Crowley was one of the method's greatest proponents, as was Dion Fortune. In his work *Book Four*, Crowley describes where Rising on the Planes should fit into a magician's daily regime:

1. The fortification of the Body of Light by the constant use of rituals, by the assumption of the God-forms, and by the right use of the Eucharist.

2. The purification and consecration and exaltation of the Body by the use of rituals of invocation.

3. The education of that Body by experience. It must learn to travel on every plane; to break down every obstacle which may confront it.

Further on Crowley states:

He should make it his daily practice to travel on the Astral Plane, taking in turn each of the most synthetic section, the Sepheroth and the Paths. These being understood, and an Angel in each pledged to guard or to guide him at need, he should start a new series of expeditions to explore the subordinate sections of each. He may then practice Rising on the Planes from these spheres, one after the other in rotation. When he is *thoroughly* conversant with the various methods of meeting unexpected emergencies, he may proceed to investigate the regions of the Qlippoth and the Demonic Forces. It should be his aim to obtain a comprehensive knowledge of the entire Astral Plane, with impartial love of truth for its own sake; just as a child learns the geography of the whole planet though he may have no intention of ever leaving his native land.[3]

The first point Crowley states is that the Body of Light should be fortified by constant use of ritual, Assumption of the Godform, and the magical Eucharist. Ritual is a distinct and precise means of impressing symbolic forms into the subconscious, as well as the psychic body. While ritual need not be elaborate to be effective, it is important that at least a simple means of starting and ending specific periods of occult work be formulated, and several of the techniques in this book will qualify for this suggestion. Assumption of the Godform is another powerful method of visualization that facilitates our psychic attunement to specific ideas and astral experiences. More will be said on itin chapter eight. The magical Eucharist is a specific form of talismanic magic that all may not be inclined to participate in, and spagyric or alchemical tinctures would be a very viable substitute for cleansing the psychic channels. Various French schools also encourage regularly receiving Holy Communion as a means of spiritual purification and fortification.

The second point Crowley emphasizes the importance of invocation, which as we will discuss in the next chapter is a form of positive suggestion, an affirmation of the state of one's being, which thereby increases psychic attunement to the chosen ideal.

Finally, in the third point, Crowley states that is imperative that each student should practice with the Body of Light until it can go anywhere and do anything. Practice is the key to success and the true source of our ultimate illumination and liberation.

From these three points it is clear that astral projection, the Body of Light, and and students should apply a distinct map to the journey instead of wandering haphazardly. Breaking down every obstacle we encounter is the means whereby we experience true self-mastery, for all of the obstacles we encounter are really projections from deep within ourselves. This technique allows us to understand that much of our life is more perception than reality, that we create that perception, and that we can just as easily replace it with another. By bringing harmony to our inner universe through Rising on the Planes, we bring greater harmony to our physical and material life, as well as unite ourselves with the cosmos.

That being said, there are slightly different views on when one should begin practicing Rising on the Planes. Some suggest that it be undertaken after one has accomplished a complete study of the Tree of Life and the paths. Others suggest that just the paths up to Tiphareth should first be undertaken. Some say it can be done at anytime, but, of course, depending on one's level of experience, the results will vary.

There are several initial variations of the method, although they differ only slightly, the most important difference being whether or not to end the journey at Tiphareth. There seems to be general agreement that a clear and functional experience of Tiphareth is the goal of Rising on the Planes, but that pushing towards Kether is implied. There is also a second variation on the theme, and that is to undertake a direct "rising" to any sphere of choice at anytime or place without invoking the paths or intermediary spheres prior to it. Should one want to have a direct experience of the sphere of Chesed, one would go directly to Chesed and not traverse by way of the paths.

Should one desire to undertake this second method, a complete working of the Tree of Life should be undertaken first, along with the paths of the Tree up to at least the sphere one is seeking to contact.

Among the most unusual experiences of Rising on the Planes is the sense of elevation that accompanies it at various times. It has been reported that even actual levitation can be a result of regular practice—that is, one can get the sense that he or she is floating, along with a profound sense of elation and expansion. The symbols themselves are also peculiar in that of the five primary symbols, the three pertaining to the spheres are consciously visualized, while the two pertaining to the paths should spring into consciousness spontaneously. However, it is also common for many magicians to visualize them, as well to jump-start the process.

The choice of symbols is fairly standard, although it is clear that some variation exists due to the variety of symbols in each sphere and path. The key, however, is simplicity and consistency. The goal is direct experience based upon a sincere and firm aspiration (intention) to attain to Tiphareth, and therein have Knowledge and Conversation with one's

Holy Guardian Angel, or Higher Self. It is critical to remember that this is not a complex meditation, nor should it be allowed to be contorted into one. Rising on the Planes is simple, powerful, and direct. With practice, it will become one of the main pillars upon which your daily work is built. It is the foundation stone for all real inner development in the Golden Dawn and related systems. Once experience has been developed and the fundamental process have been understood, the simplicity of the practice of Rising on the Planes is transferable to others spheres, paths, meditations, forms of astral projection, skrying, and clairvoyance.

Initially when Rising on the Planes is performed, it is done as a meditative technique as described here. Once you achieve familiarity with it, you can do it using the Body of Light. Rising on the Planes constitutes, in many ways, the single most important technique there is in operative magic.

Exercise: Projection Using Rising on the Planes

Preparation

Sit comfortably with your back straight, feet flat on the floor, palms of your hands flat on your thighs close to your hips (to reduce stress on your shoulders and elbows), and chin slightly tucked. Breathe deeply several times, holding your breath in for as long as is comfortable, exhaling slowly, and holding your breath out for as long as is comfortable. Feel yourself relax mentally, emotionally, and physically as you do this. Say the following prayer (or something similar): "I invoke the presence of my Holy Guardian Angel to assist me in this work of Rising on the Planes and to awaken me to the innermost depths of my being."

Affirmations or prayers to our inner self, our Holy Guardian Angel, such as the above, are powerful tools for jump-starting and maintaining our practice and success.

Explanation

Rising on the Planes imprints and activates spontaneous responses to specific qabalistic formulas associated with the Middle Pillar on the Tree of Life, and assists us in having direct experience of Knowledge and Conversation with our Holy Guardian Angel. Communication between our various levels of Self, intuition, lucid dreaming, astral projection, and fortification of the Body of Light are all greatly enhanced by it.

Type of Practice

This is a core practice for those on a qabalistic path and should be done as often as possible.

Method

1. Perform steps one through five of the Exteriorization Within the Aura exercise.

2. Imagine that the floor beneath you is a black and white checkerboard pattern. Herein the forces of light and dark, active and passive, are equilibriated. Spend some time on this concept and what it feels like. Intone the divine name *Adonai H'Aretz* (pronounced *Ah-doh-ny Ha-ar-etz*), meaning "Lord of the Earth."

3. Visualize the Greek letter *tau*, which looks like the English capital *T*, with a drop of red blood at the center. After a minute or two, proceed to the next step.

4. Visualize an upward-pointing equilateral triangle colored silver or misty blue. It is supporting an upward curved crescent moon, like a chalice. The moon is also sometimes imagined inside the triangle. Intone the divine name *Shaddi El Chi* (pronounced *Shah-dee Ehl ch-eye*), meaning "Strength of the Living God." Hold the visualized image for two or three minutes, and then proceed on to the next step.

5. Visualize an arrow, with blue highlights on its edges, flying at great speed upwards. Hold this image for a moment or two.

6. Imagine a hexagram before you, composed of red and blue triangles. The red triangle is uppermost, and they are intertwined. Intone the divine name *Yahweh Eloha Va-Daath* (pronounced *Yah-weh El-ohah va-Daath*), meaning "Knowledge of God." The divine name *IAO* (pronounced ee-aah-ooh) can be used as a substitute. Hold this image and allow yourself to become immersed in it.

7. After a few minutes, or whenever your feel ready, reverse the symbols, without intoning the divine names, until you have returned to the checkerboard sequence.

8. Breathe deeply, open your eyes, and record your results.

As you progress in this technique, the second and fourth images of the tau/cross and arrow in flight, will spontaneously occur before you. Until then, visualize them to progress through the sequence.

Incorporation into Daily Practice

This practice should take twenty to thirty minutes and should be done three to six times a week, if possible.

Key Points

- The main difference between astral projection and skrying is that in astral projection several or all of the senses may be engaged, making communication with anyone in the room difficult, if not impossible.

- The Body of Light is the simplest and most direct method for achieving well-rounded psychic development and the ability to perform astral projection.

- Esoteric initiation is structured around a series of *progressive interior experiences*. Astral projection used in conjunction with a cosmological symbol set, such as the Tree of Life, can allow us the means to genuine self-initiation.

- Rising on the Planes, either as a meditation or using the Body of Light, should form the central part of a student's practice, as it can bring greater degrees of clarity and communication between our Higher, Lower, and Middle Selves.

• Each of the spheres of the Tree of Life will have a distinct quality to it when experienced.

• As our clarity of consciousness increases, we develop an actual "second life" in the astral, similar to our material life in that we communicate with other beings, are able to experience a synthetic existence, and remember our experiences.

• Contacts with the various levels of the Tree of Life confer specific energy, knowledge, and abilities as a result of a harmonic resonance occurring between the cosmic archetypes we encounter and their counterparts within our psyche and physical body.

• Full and conscious astral projection is rare. There almost always seems to be a period of "black out" just prior to realizing you is out of your physical body.

• Even when attempts at projection appear to fail, they are extremely beneficial in that in attempting projection the student creates a condition wherein lucid dreaming and spontaneous projection are much more common.

• The Body of Light should be worked with daily; using the Tree of Life, or an other suitable map of the cosmos, the student should travel to all planes, encounter all beings, and develop their will and awareness until all aspects of nature are known to him or her. This is part of the Great Work.

Assignments for Chapter Five

1. Select two of the books on qabala from the Reading List and create a list of the symbols relevant to each of the spheres of the Tree of Life.

2. Draw a simple copy of the Tree of Life and place it in your oratory or place of work.

3. Practice each of the methods in this chapter for two weeks. You may take a week off between exercises, but you should

practice them all diligently for no less than two weeks (a month is preferred) to allow for the full lunar cycle to equally affect your results.

4. Select one of the methods you like the best and incorporate it into your weekly practice.

5. Perform Rising on the Planes as a meditation daily for at least one month, preferably three, to saturate yourself with its symbolism and strengthen the connection between your various Selves.

CHAPTER 6

Astral Projection in Alchemy

Spagyrics and Purification

In traditional Indian, Chinese, Tibetan, and European alchemy the use of specially prepared medicines using plants and minerals forms the basis for purifying the physical, etheric, and astral bodies, as well as for the formation of the Body of Light.[1] Often, these medicines were (and in some areas still are) made by highly skilled technicians, who, after years of training, are able to safely handle the highly toxic components, such as antimony, mercury, mercury sulphide, sulphur, cinnabar, and other ingredients. In some instances, purely herbal products have been used. These products, produced through the process known as *spagyrics* in European alchemy, are often easy to make and do not involve toxic ingredients.[2] However, it is the mineral products, known as the White Stone and the Red Stone (better known as the Philosopher's Stone), that in their production give ever-increasing access to the various astral levels while bringing greater power, density, and expansion to the Body of Light.

The White and the Red Stone

In the early decades of the seventeenth century, the synthesis of the three legs of the hermetic arts and sciences—alchemy, astrology, and qabala—was completed. Here, a seamless path of theory, method, and means of assessing results was firmly established within the predominantly Christian culture of Europe. In doing so, hermeticism provided a means of taking exoteric religion and *interpreting, as well as experiencing*, it in a framework that included the acquired wisdom of the great Mediterranean civilizations. Greek philosophy, Egyptian mysteries, Roman pantheons, Jewish mysticism, Arabic science, and numerous small, but no less important ideas were amalgamated into a working practical philosophy whose goal was to unite heaven and earth. This union would be achieved through the person of the magus, or the adept of occult arts, who in his or her role as a veritable incarnation of Thoth, the Egyptian god of wisdom and magic, would be the living expression of hermetic wisdom, power, and practicality. While the heavens were to be traveled and known, it was their power, expressed through the planets and captured in talismans for the betterment of human life, that would identify the magus. The mysteries of nature and the physical world were an open book to the alchemist, who, in turn, could create medicines to cure illness, bring happiness, extend life and beauty, and, in some instances, it was said, even make one immortal (at least by human standards). The Elixir of Life was the panacea that cured all, and the Stone of the Wise, or the Philosopher's Stone, was the means whereby the rejuvenated body was made indistinguishable from the spiritual body, and the hidden energies of the earth could be manipulated to turn lead or quicksilver into gold.

The secret lay in that, for the alchemist, Mercury—the life force—was androgynous. It was the great power of life and death itself, and it united the visible and invisible realms. However, the alchemist's mercury was not common mercury—crude, dirty, and toxic. Instead it was philosophic Mercury, or the dense mineral life exalted and brought to a level of purity, potency, and perfection wherein it could be used to regenerate both metals and physical bodies and to unite human consciousness with the Divine.

The process of creating these magnificent alchemical products occurred in stages, and each successful stage led to the next in a spiral fashion. The method did not vary, only the substances used did, as in the

Flamel Path, where various lesser amalgams allow aspiring adepts to perfect their method, while exposing them to ever-increasing degrees of energy, illumination, and integration. The first major work in mineral work is the creation of the White Stone, or an alchemical product that allows for the transmutation of metals into silver, the healing of many illnesses, and the mastery over the lunar world, or astral plane. It is this stone that allows for the creation of the Body of Light.

The second creation is made in the same manner as the first, only it is of a more elevated and rarefied power. Broader in reach and scope than the White Stone, the Red Stone, or Philosopher's Stone, brings one to full adepthood; the ability to enter into any dimension of consciousness, energy, or matter; and the ability to be immortal (or nearly so by human standards). However, even here, after the completion of the Red Stone, the Great Work is not complete. The Red Stone must be "multiplied" twice more to perfection. Even here, there is a *third* and final stone to be made, of which little is spoken. Presumably it gives access to the highest spiritual dimensions, or what in qabala is known as "Crossing the Abyss."

Each alchemical product is a solidification of pure energy into a pure matter, which allows for a perfect expression of awareness. In doing this, the underlying unity of the universe is consciously expressed, and the Work of Nature brought to its logical and natural conclusion.

The fundamental philosophy in alchemy is found in the Emerald Tablet, discussed in chapter one. In the Emerald Tablet, the basis of all occult operations is expressed as, "That which comes from above, comes from below; that which comes from below, comes from above." What we do on the level of the mind is a reflection of physical experiences and has the potential to affect the physical world. What we do in the physical world is a reflection of inner experiences and has the potential to affect the invisible world. The two are not separate, but united and inseparable reflections of one another.

While it is still difficult to find exact locations, it has become an open secret, that the planets and the zodiac of the sun as well as of the moon are centered in or around the brain, the spine, the glands and diverse plexus. Also that these organs are more or less in constant and intense communication with the circumambient aether. Consequently, the seven circulations and following imbibitions, by which the white and red elixir are produced, mean in plain English but the circulation of our vital energy, our fixed power, through the different plexus and glands, also brain and spine, as well as the reinforcement of this energy by imbibitions from the circumambient aether, our volatile mercury, which by the operation is drawn in, becomes assimilated, coagulated and fixed in our organism.[3]

This doctrine of microcosm and macrocosm is taken even further and applied to all physical manifestation. Every plant, mineral, and animal has its complete and corresponding relationship to an invisible energy or collection of energies with which it is continually in connection. Physical matter is the dense expression of those energies, like a glass ball on the end of a glassblower's tube. Death is simply the systematic withdrawal of energy back to its corresponding source.

This operation of life, death, and rebirth gives rise to the second important principal in alchemy: *solve et coagula*, or "separate and recombine" (or solidify). Here, the alchemists separates out the energy of the plant, mineral, or themselves, and recombines it with the refined physical body from which it came. In matter, energy is limited and cannot accumulate without first releasing what is already present. In an energetic state, the basic life force acts endotrophically—that is, it expands and accumulates energy. If the energy that sustains it is not released or at least reduced, the physical body is too rigid or fixed to allow for toxic accumulations to be discarded to transmuted. The body, if unpurified, even to the slightest degree, would be unable to absorb the additional energy it receives when the life force is brought back into it. When the two are brought back together again, or when the increased energy is brought into a new body, it brings life, health, vitality, and awareness to the physical form. The same process that occurs in working with plants or minerals also occurs with the human body.

In alchemy, everything is seen as having three basic parts: Salt (body), Sulphur (consciousness or soul), and Mercury (life force). Just as

V.I.T.R.I.O.L

mineral work utilizes actual mineral sulphur and mercury at various points in making the White and Red Stones, plants and animals are viewed as utilizing their own equivalents of sulphur, mercury, and salt. In the plant realm, the physical plant body is the Salt, the alcohol it forms as it decomposes is the Mercury, and its essential oils, fats, and other distinguishing chemical characteristics are the Sulphur. In humans or any animal, the physical body is the Salt, its blood the Mercury, and the consciousness, or sense of self, its Sulphur. Together Sulphur, Mercury, and Salt are referred to as the Three Essentials. Only through astral projection and the formation of the Body of Light can we safely work upon the human body as a form of alchemy, as all alchemical operations require the "death" (or here the state of deep relaxation and sleep) of the physical body.

It is important to remember that despite all of the breathing exercises, visualizations, or even alchemical products one may take, the Body of Light is literally built out of the energy resident in the flesh of the operator and specifically the mineral elements that compose it. Ingesting homeopathic salts to equilibrate the mineral content of the body's blood would be beneficial. The blood is the most direct way to change consciousness, as well as etheric and physical make-up of the body. It is stated by some schools (particularly Indian, Tibetan, Chinese, and some descendents of Egyptian systems) that in making the Body of Light, over time we literally transform our physical body into light. However, the body is also over 90 percent water, and to affect the cells we need to affect the energetic state of their water content. Energy is transferred only when in a liquid state, and water is the body's most plentiful and easily affected liquid, making it the easiest to work with directly when it comes to assisting in expanding the aura, modifying the environment, and aiding in building the Body of the Light.

Sulfur   *Mercury*   *Salt*

Body of Light Exercises

Universal Mercury: Absorbing the Essence

In alchemy the universal life force is often referred to as the Universal Mercury. This life force, which emanates from the sun in our solar system, hits the earth and creates the atmosphere. This coloring (known as tincting) of the life force to our planet and its unique ability to support life as we know it, creates the Anima Mundi, or Soul of the World. It is from this soul that we unconsciously derive our life essences and to which we seek to consciously awaken. When we breathe in the life energy of the atmosphere (often called Niter in chemical work), we, in turn, color it, or turn it from impersonal energy to personal energy. This coloring comes from our degree of conscious awakening, an awakening that occurs at the level of the heart.

The energy then goes forth from our lungs into the heart and is distributed to every cell in our body, thereby giving each of them a greater or lesser harmony and awakening in direct relationship to our own state of cardiac awakening. For the ancient Egyptians, the heart is the organ of consciousness and seat of spiritual power, and, as we have seen in qabala, the heart is the only spiritual organ that can function on all planes.

The following exercise helps us better understand the power of our breath and why some degree of mastery of it is essential if we are to understand and direct our inner organization better, for the creation of a body that can travel in the subtle spiritual domains—often referred to as aetherial.

While it appears simple, this exercise is critical in stimulating the primitive areas of the brain and nervous system associated with psychic phenomena, and it demonstrates clearly the role of specialized odors in stimulating the body-mind-soul connection.

Exercise: The Universal Mercury, Absorbing the Essence

Preparation

Facing geographic east, sit or stand comfortably with your back straight, feet flat on the floor, palms of your hands flat on your thighs and close to your hips (to take stress of your shoulders and elbows), and chin slightly tucked. Breathe deeply several times, holding your breath in for as long as is comfortable, exhaling slowly, holding your breath out for as long as is comfortable. Feel yourself relax mentally, emotionally, and physically as you do this. Say the following prayer (or something similar): "Divine Mind, source of all, assist me in this work of thought, word, and deed, so that I will awaken and strengthen the powers of my body's energies and its connection to my Higher Self, my Holy Guardian Angel, to create the immortal Body of Light."

Explanation

This practice prepares the mind and psychic body of the practitioner for experiencing increased psychic energy directly related to the formation of the Body of Light. It also is a preliminary practice for use prior to meditation, prayer, or healing work.

Type of Practice

This is a preliminary practice designed to be performed prior to meditation, prayer, astral projection, or healing interventions. It is best done in the morning upon awakening, facing east, with bare feet on the grass or ground if possible. Fresh air is essential to this and all breathing practices. In the evening or after sundown, it can be done facing geographic north, thereby drawing on the denser energies of the day.

Method

Proceed as follows:[4]
1. Inhale deeply through your nostrils, filling your lungs and abdomen with air. Relax your shoulders and imagine that the air is vitalizing and charging your blood with energy. Feel as though you are inhaling the life energy of the planet and the sun and making it a part of yourself.
2. Feel a distinct and increased harmony within yourself, focused around your heart and being absorbed into your blood. See it glow bright red with a subtle golden violet hue.
3. As this energy moves through your body, feel your cells absorb it and vibrate in a greater, luminous harmony. Start with your feet and work your way up until you complete the top of your head. Include your hair, teeth, bones, and all organs.
4. Do this for at least seven minutes, preferably twenty-one minutes, as doing it for this long will give three complete circulations of the blood to your body.
5. Imagine that your body is hollow, that your flesh is light, and that you are in a sphere of brilliant luminous light, with a

slight violet-gold tinge on the edges. Rest in this image for a few minutes.

Incorporation into Daily Practice

This practice should take ten to fifteen minutes at most and be done once or twice a day for a month to get some grounded experience in the importance of this practice and to make it a habit in all spiritual work. Afterwards it can be done for three to five minutes prior to other practices. The best time of year to do it is immediately following spring and into late summer and early fall, although it can be done across the year.

After you have become familiar with the practice, perform it when evaporating some essential oils of frankincense, myrrh, and eucalyptus in equal proportion or in a 3:2:1 proportion. Stand close to the evaporating dish so that you can deeply inhale the scent as it wafts upwards and feel its energies enter into your physical and etheric bodies at the heart. This is a very fine blend of scents, specifically designed to balance and harmonize the energies being stimulated, as well as to aid in their absorption by the etheric body. While stick or cone incense can be substituted, using pure-quality essential oils is preferred. Actual frankincense tears, grains of myrrh, and leaves of eucalyptus can also be used. This is an extremely important formula and should not be overlooked.

Exercise: Sulphur as the Key of Awakening

Preparation

Sit comfortably with your back straight, feet flat on the floor, palms of your hands flat on your thighs and close to your hips (to reduce stress on your shoulders and elbows), and chin slightly tucked. Breathe deeply several times, holding your breath in for as long as is comfortable, exhaling slowly, and holding your breath out for as long as is comfortable. Feel yourself relax mentally, emotionally, and physically as you do this. Say the following prayer (or something similar): "Divine Mind, source of all, assist me in this work of thought, word, and deed, so that I will awaken the innermost powers of my astral body and create the immortal Body of Light."

Explanation

This practice activates the nervous system via the solar plexus, using its function as the psychic tuning fork of our various bodies to transmute any residual resistance between them into greater harmony, thereby allowing us a direct experience of our psychic body, the power of the Word, and our essential energetic nature.

Type of Practice

This is a preliminary practice designed to be used prior to meditation, prayer, healing, or attempts at astral projection. It is best done in the morning upon awakening, facing east, with bare feet on the grass or ground if possible. In the evening, face north, if possible.

Method

Proceed as follows:

1. Imagine that your body is hollow, empty of any solidity, and is, in fact, composed of light. Imagine within this body the psychic counterpart of your nervous system. Imagine it in perfect detail.

2. Inhale, focusing your attention on the area around your solar plexus, slightly below your heart. Imagine a brilliant sphere of red light with gold highlights present where your solar plexus is, feeling the energy enter into it as you inhale and spreading across your nervous system as you exhale.

3. Do this several times, each time seeing your light body grow brighter and, with it, your nervous system blend into the body. Be in the body; do not see it from without. Be focused in the imagined body.

4. Continue breathing. Imagine the light extending beyond the outline of your body and perfectly touching the edges of your

aura, pushing it outward in a clean, smooth, and even manner. (You may even imagine your body dissolving into the light as the central point of your solar plexus, where your consciousness is now centered, takes prominence.)

5. Vibrate the sound—"ah,"as in "father," until you can feel it in your solar plexus and vibrating across your entire body. Repeat this seven times. The Divine Name, IAO (pronounced ee-aah-ooh), may also be used.

6. Rest in this experience of light.

7. When you are done, draw the energy back into yourself and focus it in your solar plexus.

Incorporation into Daily Practice

Once learned, this exercise can be quickly applied in a variety of circumstances and with little visible preparation. It should be done at least one or twice a week as a tonic or even as a side exercise when you are not in a formal practice setting.

Projection into the Alchemical World: the Secret Garden Revisited

The well-known children's tale *The Secret Garden* by Frances Hodgson Burnett, has been a staple of entertainment since it was published in 1911. Multiple film adaptations exist because the story contains sufficient thematic ideas to allow for multiple visions while being true to the original. This is very much like alchemy. In addition, the main idea of a secret garden wherein magic and mystery come to life is a perennial alchemical theme, found in many of the woodcuts and engravings. Many gardens filled with alchemical symbolism were even built in the palace grounds of European royalty from the sixteenth through eighteenth centuries. One of Carl Jung's most significant visionary experiences was one in which he was taken to an ancient garden, and for the rest of his life, he tried to return to this secret place of mystery, wisdom, and power.

The Entrance to the Alchemical Garden from Atalanta Fugiens

After you have become comfortable in visualizing your astral double—or even better, if you have had some success in projecting your consciousness—undertake the following alchemical visualization. Pay close attention to whatever you experience and be sure to record it in your journal. If you feel that this is a pathway worth exploring, obtain one or more of the following alchemical manuscripts translated by Dr. Joscelyn Godwin and published by Phanes Press: *Splendor Solis* by Salomon Trismosin, *Atalanta Fugiens* by Michael Maier, *The Chemical Wedding of Christian Rosenkreutz* and begin a systematic journey of its plates. You will find that the images start out as imagined but after a period of time become quite "real," and dialogue with the characters is possible. Once again, all of these images exist in microcosm, or within your psyche, and in the macrocosm, or the collective consciousness. In some ways it may be difficult to assess if they exist as semi-independent beings (as ourselves) in their own space-time dimension. That, however, is one of the great mysteries that alchemy helps us to progressively and systematically unfold.

Exercise: The Secret Garden

Preparation

Sit comfortably with your back straight, feet flat on the floor, palms of your hands flat on your thighs and close to your hips (to reduce stress on your shoulders and elbows), and chin slightly tucked. Breathe deeply several times, holding in your breath for as long as is comfortable, exhaling slowly, and holding your breath out for as long as is comfortable. Feel yourself relax mentally, emotionally, and physically as you do this. Say the following prayer (or something similar): "Divine Mind, source of all, assist me in this work of thought, word, and deed, that I will awaken to the power of the natural world that is present in the innermost depths of my being, with my body, and all around me, so that I may create the immortal Body of Light."

Explanation

This exercise imprints the subconscious and psychic body of the practitioner with ideas specific to entering into communication with the astral dimensions of nature as presented in various alchemical ideas and manuscripts. This may trigger a direct experience in the form of an out-of-body or lucid dream state. Pay careful attention to dreams that occur while performing this exercise.

Type of Practice

This is a core practice for those on an alchemical path.

Method

Proceed as follows:
1. Imagine that you are standing on a path and directly in front of you is the gateway to a large garden, which is surrounded by a large red brick wall covered in ivy. The iron gate is old and creeks slightly as you open it inward.

2. Inside the garden you see a marvelous array of statues of the ancient Greek and Roman gods and goddesses, bubbling fountains, and even a maze formed of tall green hedges.

3. There are also strange creatures. Some you recognize, like a unicorn and a sleeping dragon, and others you are familiar with—such as a rabbit, a doe, and a stag. Birds chirp in the trees and fly about you.

4. Take your time to explore the garden and its secrets.

5. If you meet the gardener, talk to him or her, and listen to what is said.

6. After a few minutes, leave the garden and record your experiences in your notebook.

Incorporation into Daily Practice

After you are familiar with this exercise, perform it outside in a park or other natural area where you will not be easily disturbed. Perform it during both the day and at night. If possible, find a secret earthly garden of your own, where you can begin to experience the forces of nature as they exist around and within you. Allow them to communicate through this exercise and in your dreams.

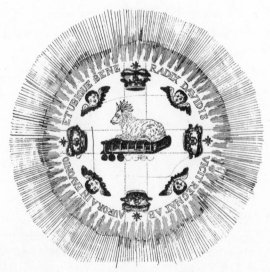

The Sealed Book of the Apocalypse as Illustrated in Secret Symbols of the Rosecrucians

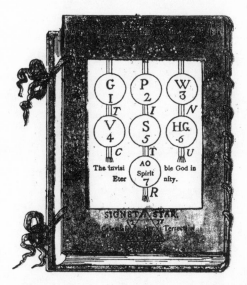

Apocalyps XIII, from Secret Symbols of the Rosecrucians

The Power of the Book

Alchemy depends heavily upon images, metaphors, poetry, and mythological descriptions to veil the obvious and reveal the hidden. The principal means of preserving and transmitting this wisdom is in books and, to a lesser degree, architecture. The alchemical garden is an extension of architecture in that it is three-dimensional and is a designed and sculpted location wherein the energies of nature are used to demonstrate the inherent power of that specific place, as well as the more general themes of universal truths and human evolution. The famous twentieth-century French alchemist Fulcanelli wrote two major works on alchemical symbolism in architecture: *The Mystery of the Cathedrals* and *The Dwellings of the Philosophers.* In *Mystery* Fulcannelli details how the practical methods of laboratory alchemy and its twin practice of spiritual alchemy were preserved in the stonework and stained glass of France's great medieval cathedrals. In *Dwellings* he describes similar designs in historical French houses and villas.

One of the most well-known images from these two volumes is of the West Porch of Notre Dame of Paris. Here we see an image of a man, presumably Christ, seated on a throne with a ladder reaching up to him. He holds an open book in his right hand and a scepter with his left. Here is an important teaching: with effort, struggle, and will we can open the book and rule with the wisdom and mercy it bestows. To do so is to sit squarely and firmly in the influence of the Higher Self, wherein the highest forces of the Middle Self are stabilized and used to ascend and descend the planes of consciousness like a sliding scale.

This image on the West Porch demonstrates many things, but the most important is the fact that the ladder of knowledge reaches to the book that the man is holding— the Book of Nature. It is the work of the alchemist to read the open Book of Nature and in doing so understand the mysteries of creation on all levels. This open book is the inner teacher, the true Book of Revelation.[5] The often-shown sealed book of the Lamb, with its seven seals, is the Book of Nature, which we must open within ourselves and, in doing so, be transformed as John of Patmos was—into a "living white Stone," a Body of Light.

We ascend the ladder by "reading" a chapter from the Book of Nature, and, in turn, the book reveals to us secrets kept with the astral memory, or the Archives of Nature. This archive is the sum of all things and has many levels, each offering us various possibilities. In general there are seven levels, just as there are seven seals on the Book of the Apocalypse, or inner revelation. The lamb, the symbol of spiritual nature, our Holy Guardian Angel, sits on the book and is its guardian. The lamb is also the Christian symbol for the new year, or Aries, and demonstrates that only through a conscious effort on our part can the seals be broken, the book open, and the mysteries of nature revealed to us. Herein is the paradox. Just as we must make the conscious effort, at some point we must also step out of our own way and let the Higher Self take over. This is the meaning of the "blood of the lamb." The very forces that initiate our undertaking on the Path of Return must be sacrificed, let go of, if we are to achieve success.

These seven seals correspond to the seven metals, planets, lower spheres of the Tree of Life, as well as seven churches, candlesticks, and letters to the churches contained within the Book of Revelation. To get any meaning out of this or any symbolic book, we must approach it from the symbolic viewpoint, rather than reading it as a rational or historical document—this is what is meant by the "letter of the law kills, but the spirit brings life."

When working with any occult text, it is important to treat it with respect and as if were a living document—that is, as if its very letters and symbols were living beings trying to communicate with us, for as we have seen with the Hebrew alphabet, the letters themselves are seen as living, burning embers of God and not abstract symbols. Cultivate this relation to your chosen texts.

Texts live because of the energy of their users. This combined energy is called an egregore and has a powerful effect across time and space. Books and manuscripts that have been handed down from generation to generation accumulate a charge from their use and the devotion given to them in the same way a talisman does. This energy also exists on another level for people who are working with the same material but who are not together because of time and space. Through their combined devotion and work, the archetype of the book is strengthened; that archetype is shared by all who possess the book and its symbols and are working with the material it contains. If laid on an altar, it should be placed on the left side because it is the material representation of the divine light revealed through material existence.

One of the main ways to connect to this egregoric energy is to copy all or part of the text by hand into your own notebook and have it present when doing any specific work. In alchemy it is not uncommon to hand color manuscripts or copies of them, and in doing so attune their message, inducing visions, dreams, and even astral projection. It is important to note that Nicholas Flamel had his vision of an angel handing him the famed hieroglyphic book of *Abraham the Jew* prior to actually receiving it in material form. Christian Rosenkreutz was buried with the *Book M* and was visited by an angel, his higher self, prior to receiving his "invitation" to the alchemical wedding.

Key Points

- Alchemy uses specially prepared medicines, known as tinctures and elixirs, to purify the physical and psychic bodies. The medicines are made from nontoxic, as well as toxic, plants and minerals.

- The main products of mineral alchemy are the creation of the White and Red Stones and the Elixir of Life. The White Stone confers mastery of the lunar world, while the Red Stone confers initiation on the solar or archetypal world. The Elixir of Life heals illness and prolongs life so that the Great Work can be completed.

- In the early seventeenth century the synthesis of the three legs of the hermetic arts and science—alchemy, astrology, and qabala—was completed, giving a seamless theory and practice in the occult arts of the time.

- The Three Essentials of alchemy are known as Sulphur, Mercury, and Salt.

- Sulphur is the consciousness or essence of a thing; Mercury its life force; and Salt the physical and etheric matrix. Everything in existence can be viewed as possessing varying degrees of the Three Essentials.

- Alchemical products can be seen as the solidification of pure energy into pure matter, so that the energy can be transferred or made usable for initiatic or healing purposes.

- The fundamental philosophy in alchemy is found in the Emerald Tablet, attributed to Hermes, which, in summary, states, "That which comes from above, comes from below; that which comes from below, comes from above."

- The Body of Light provides access to the various alchemical realms, as well as access to the hidden side of nature. The alchemist is the handmaiden of nature, and only through a complete experiencing and understanding of nature's laws can the Great Work be completed.

- The symbolism of the Book of Nature is important in alchemy, as well as in qabala and even Christian esotericism.

- Nature is the book that the alchemist seeks to read.
- During the sixteenth and seventeenth centuries, alchemical symbolism was brought to life in the gardens of many royal households.
- The alchemical garden provides us a means of moving into the secret side of nature and seeing its importance in our daily life.

Assignments for Chapter Six

1. Perform each of the exercises in this chapter once a day for two weeks.

2. Research the importance of the symbolism of the Book of Nature. Begin to think of your notebook as your "sacred text" and treat it accordingly.

3. Find an alchemical book whose images appeal to you and make its study a progressive part of your Work.

CHAPTER 7

The Body of Light: Its Creation and Use

Western esoteric literature is replete with the doctrine of the Body of Light. Unfortunately, while many references are made to the concept, little information is supplied regarding its origin (or formation), stages of growth, and applications. This chapter will provide qabalistic and alchemical students with a workable esoteric theory and practical technique, regarding this often obscure and neglected subject.

Theoretical and Historical Background

The idea of the Body of Light is seen in Gnostic literature as early as the first century, but extensive documentation and theory existed in Chinese, Mongolian, Tibetan, and Indian literature and practices as well and may herald from an earlier date. Practices under the general heading of chi kung, or Chinese internal alchemy, are designed to create and mature a body of subtle astral and etheric energy that is capable of existence independent of material consciousness. This body is also thought to be capable of infusing the material body with sufficient energy to allow it to become more subtle and "etherial." This "etherialization" is said to make the physical body, under the direction of the adept, capable of dematerialization at the time of death. Enoch, Ezekiel, Jesus, his mother Mary, and even Mohammed with his horse are examples in Western spiritual literature of people who utilized this form of dematerialization.

Unfortunately, while Eastern systems have maintained a working technical tradition of the theory and its application to achieve this goal, little information of a similar nature remains in the West. The idea of the *simulacrum* is the closest we have and may very well be the starting point of experimentation with these concepts. From the Eastern literature available, it can be seen that the idea of the Body of Light, often called the Rainbow or Diamond Body, is the perfection of a vehicle for the exteriorization (projection) *and* continuation of consciousness beyond material reality. Based on written documents, history and mythology, and contemporary anecdotes from the alchemical community, it is known that this body can be achieved through existing practices and that the stages of its growth correspond to total realization on the lunar (*Yetzirah*), solar (*Briah*), and saturnian (*Daath*) planes of consciousness as described earlier.

Dolores Ashcroft-Nowicki states:

When working in this way [traditional pathworking] you are using the astral body, and you know already about your Magical Personality which has been quietly growing in strength with each month's work.[1] But there is another form used by some magicians, the Body of Light. Some think that it is the same as the astral body, but it is in fact quite different. The astral is an etheric form common to everyone, a Magical Personality is acquired through practice and concentration. The Body of Light is deliberately built for a purpose, another term for it is "cowan." It is not easily formed, some people never manage it, or at least not fully, and once it *is* formed it can be troublesome, and requires firm handling.[2]

Ashcroft-Nowicki further states that the Body of Light can acquire a kind of self-consciousness after a period of development. This idea is also stated in Tibetan and Chinese literature. The small "child of light" is often compared to a fetus in the astral womb of the practitioner's aura and temple. It must be matured, fed, educated, and grown to proper strength so that it can be a help to the magician and not a hindrance, or even potential danger. However, in all occult activity, dangers come more often from rushing through preliminary work instead of allowing

it to proceed in a healthy and natural pace, than from the exercises themselves actually being psychically dangerous. Ashcroft-Nowicki goes on to
say that few Western magicians have ever been able to master the technique fully, although she gives no reasons.

When we attempt esoteric exercises and a return to primal unity, we
must pierce the first veil, or the veil of the *Gate of Life and Death*. It is so
called, because few people pierce it except during near-death experiences
(NDEs), out-of-body experiences (OOBEs), or physical death itself.

The astral body has access to three levels of consciousness, and then
it must be shed or encounter "the Second Death" in order to penetrate
the veil, or *Paroketh*, to the next three levels. However, precautions must
be undertaken to avoid the destruction of the astral body if the Second
Death is to be avoided. If this is not done, then the astral body must be
reconstructed with a new birth.

To be clear, the astral body is an emotional construct we form during physical life. It dies but the I or self that created it survives to some
degree. The degree of survival is a matter of consciousness. If the self
can survive the Second Death with full awareness then it can also reincarnate with awareness of the invisible worlds and past lives. The astral
body is vehicle that is separate from its driver and a clear distinction
must be made between the two. Above the solar world, the resurrection
body is established, and it is the body or expression of consciousness used
for reintegration to unity.[3]

It is possible that just as there is confusion among some students
regarding the Body of Light as being the astral body, there may also be
confusion regarding its actual purpose—that of extended consciousness,
or "surviving the Second Death." When the function of the Body of
Light is clearly understood, then greater attempts can be made to realize
its full potential.

Mead and the Subtle Body

G. R. S. Mead wrote a booklet around the turn of the nineteenth century
titled *The Doctrine of the Subtle Body in the Western Tradition*. It very well

may be one of the few available books dedicated to this subject, and while it is full of scholarly research regarding the theories and beliefs pertaining to the subtle body, it lacks any description of the techniques used to experience it. The material quoted is almost exclusively Gnostic-Christian in origin.

For Mead, the doctrine of the subtle body achieved its highest expression in India, although he may have been unaware of other Oriental teachings, and that notions of the subtle body developed along with those of alchemy and astrology. This is true in both the East and West and is seen in the techniques often suggested for use by the student. As this astrology has nothing to do with "vulgar horoscopy, philosophic astral theory set up [as] a ladder of ascent from the earth to the light world."[4] Mead states:

> But even as there was a deeper, more vital, side of astrology, a subtler phase intimately bound up with the highest themes of sidereal religion, so there was a supra-physical, vital and psychic side to alchemy— a scale of ascent leading finally to man's perfection in spiritual reality.[5]

According to Mead, Zosimus states categorically that the Rites of Mithras were identical in purpose to the practices of alchemy, that the only complete ritual of the Mithrian cult has survived to present time, and that the ritual's theurgical practices are similar to those of Indian yoga.[6] The ritual also states clearly that it is the method whereby spiritual perfection and birth of the subtle body are attained. A close reading of the *Sepher Yetzirah* and its methods for creating the *golem*, in this light, would suggest that this is also another means of creating the Body of Light.[7]

Three Levels of Light

The three basic ideas around the subtle body are that it progresses though the levels of the spheres, increases in power and purity, and is made of light and/or fire. It is described as the *spirit body*, the *radiant body*, and the *resurrection body*, depending on its degree of purity.

Mead points out that there is the possibility of extreme confusion when reading the ancient literature and the vocabulary used to describe the spiritual body. Despite appearances to the contrary, Mead asserts that the spiritual body is essentially one and that the sidereal body has nothing to do with today's astral body. The spirit-body, or *to soma pheumatikon*, is the force closely aligned to the physical body and is similar to the *nefesh*, or vegetative-animal soul, in Jewish qabala. The radiant body, allows us to experience the Vision of Beauty Triumphant, as it is referred to modern qabalistic schools, and is therefore the astral body:

> Tiphareth translates to Beauty. It is located on the Pillar of Balance which is the Pillar of consciousness and corresponds, we are told, to the highest state in which a man incarnate on this earth can live, that is, a man *"of flesh and blood."* This does not mean that he cannot receive the influences of the higher sepheroth (higher according to the Tree), perceive or live something of their nature and mode of action. This means that a man capable of remaining in Tiphareth has *"spiritualized"* his matter, has formed his glorious body and has obtained the power to go beyond incarnation.[8]

There was a time when we could behold Beauty in all its brilliance, when, together with the rest of the Blessed Company—we [philosophers] in the train of Zeus, and other [ranks of souls] in the train of the Gods—they both beheld the beatific spectacle and [divine] vision, and were initiated into that mystery, which may be called the holiest of all, in which we joyed in mystic ecstasy.[9]

Proclus states, "Moreover, the radiant vehicle (*augoeides ochema*) [corresponds] with heaven, and this mortal [frame] with the sublunary [region]."

The Christian doctrine of the resurrection of the flesh was hotly contested during its developmental stages, and the flesh lovers, as they were called, won out over those believing in a purely spiritual resurrection. Mead points out that the belief in physical resurrection was not universally accepted by the Jews of Jesus' day, yet there was a strong biblical and Midrashic tradition of an individual increases in grades of purity, allowing for ascension and resurrection to take place.

The descriptions of the ascensions of Elijah and Jesus suggest that the bodies they inhabited were the same and yet not the same. They were tangible, yet could overcome material limitations, such as when Jesus' body passed through the locked door. Elijah, unlike Jesus, however, did not die, but was taken into heaven bodily in a chariot of fire.

These "bodies," in fact, are not really separate bodies, but increasingly purified expressions of the personality, the individual and unique expression of God we all carry within us. As one "body" or expression is purified and "dies," another takes its place. What makes the resurrection body different is that while it can and does exist within the material world, it is free from material constraints. This perfect body was, or is, essentially a quintessence. It is differentiated into subtle and simple elements, whereas the physical body is contaminated by the grosser elements. Unlike some of its Christian cousins, Orthodox Christianity is quite clear in its teaching that all parts of a person, flesh included, are a sacred creation, and, as such, all aspects of the person can be used in worship. The doctrine of *theosis*, or that one can be deified while in the flesh, is expounded upon at length in relation to the lives of many mystics and ascetics of the Orthodox tradition. The Mithriac initiation states, "O Primal Origin of my origination; Thou Primal Substance of my substance; First Breath of breath, the breath that is in me; First Fire, God-given for the Blending of the blendings in me; First Fire of fire in me; First Water of my water, the water in me; Primal Earth-essence of the earthly essence in me; Thou Perfect Body of me!"[10]

The Technique

The technique given by Ashcroft-Nowicki is the simplest and most direct. However, while no specific rituals are employed, it is suggested that the ritual be performed in a consecrated temple to prevent the simulacrum from wandering. Ashcroft-Nowicki also states that when the Body of Light is sufficiently developed to begin to desire acting on its own, that it should be given firm discipline.

With the constant implanting of consciousness, even the tiny amount used here, the *cowan* [Body of Light] will eventually gain a half conscious mind of its own. You will in fact have partially ensouled it. At this point, it will almost certainly make a bid for freedom. Something you cannot allow for it has no protection against the darker forces who will take it over and use it against you and even against those with whom you are involved. They will think it is you and trust the appearance. Therefore the moment it feels as if the cowan is getting above itself, give it a good psychic shake, and in no uncertain terms remind it who is boss.

She then suggests withdrawing all contact with the cowan for a lunar month and feeling no sympathy for this self-created and projected aspect of ourselves. To do otherwise, she warns, is to court disaster. This would, in fact, be tantamount to "the Fall" in our own personal microcosm.

Yet despite these warnings and problems, creating the Body of Light, even partially, can be a very rewarding psychic and spiritual experience. It offers many avenues for psychological cleansing, as we shall see, and psychic enhancement.

These four directives—going slow, performing in a sacred space or enclosure, preventing the Body of Light from wandering, and reminding it who is boss—are common to Eastern and Western methods.

What is missing in the modern Western accounts, but clearly stated in the Oriental ones, is that the Body of Light is a superior being to the physical world *and can be directed to have effects on the physical body*, if they are desired. It is these effects that allow for the etherialization of the physical body, increased health and longevity, and possibly even a kind of psychic mutation that allows for increased psychic activity along family lines. The Western schools are silent about the implications of the hermetic axiom "the subtle rules the dense" and how it might apply here.

Despite the projective imagery, the genuine sense of the simulacrum being "other" (and the unconscious, often violent imagery that can be dredged up from instinctual and subconscious realms that do not want to be integrated into the workings of the higher mental-spiritual functions), the Body of Light is still a part of us. By disciplining it, giving it function and purpose, and guiding it with a firm hand, we are, in reality, giving those things to our self. The simulacrum, however, shows us in no uncertain terms that these forces and ideas within us, left unregenerated, will seek to manifest and to take on self-consciousness when given the opportunity. In magical work, we see this tendency for the simulacrum to take on its own will and consciousness clearly in the creation of the Body of Light; in psychology, it manifests in neurotic and schizophrenic behavior and even in severe forms of psychosis. Esoteric work allows us to address these diverse aspects of our being, to integrate them, and, in doing so, to prevent psychic ruptures that might otherwise manifest in modern terms as mental illness.

The following method can be performed by anyone regardless of his or her level of experience. Ideally, however, it would be best if it were practiced after a year or two of qabalistic study. The reason is simple: the more experience you have in psychic and occult matters, the easier it will be to achieve noticeable success. However, as we have seen, the Body of Light is easy to begin working with and for all practical purposes can be worked with at the beginning of one's esoteric training.

It should be noted that within the Hermetic Order of the Golden Dawn, the first three to five years are usually spent learning very basic magical procedures, coupled with the memorization and intellectual comprehension of a vast amount of qabalistic, alchemical, and astrological knowledge. The techniques given by Regardie in *The Golden Dawn*, such as the Supreme Rituals of the Pentagram and Hexagram and the Rose Cross Ritual, are not generally taught until the 5=6 Grade, or Adeptus Minor. On occasion, these rituals may be given in the preliminary section, known as the Portal Grade. All magical tools are also constructed after being received into the Second Order, or Adeptus Minor grade. Only after this period are planetary rituals, talismans, and related techniques as seen in Regardie's work undertaken.[11]

For those who do not belong to any formal course of study, it is generally suggested that the first year of activity be spent learning Elemental and pentagram work, the second year be spent doing planetary work, and the third year spent integrating the two. The fourth year often focuses on zodiacal magic and the completion of any pathworking. Pathworking can be started anywhere from the first year on and requires about one and a half years to fully do all of the thirty-two paths of the Tree of Life. Since each path is often done more than once, it is best to allow two to three years for this *additional* aspect of magical training. pathworking, particularly paths 32 through 24, are critical for psychological health and should be done two or three times before doing the second set of paths (23 through 19).[12] Of course, the speed at which one works is not important. It is better to go slowly and diligently and make real progress, than to rush through and simply do the work haphazardly.[13]

The most complete method available for creating the Body of Light is in the ritual called "The Magician" in *Mysteria Magica: Fundamental Techniques of High Magick* (Book 3 of *The Magical Philosophy*) by Melita Denning and Osborne Phillips.[14] The material belongs to the curriculum of the *Aurlem Solis Sacra Verbum*. The practice that follows is based upon the methods given therein, but has been sufficiently broadened to be useful to those not familiar with that particular system or who are more inclined to the Golden Dawn symbolism. All key areas have remained unchanged, and additional commentary has been included.

The ritual is divided into five main sections, composed of fourteen distinct parts in total. A note belonging to the title suggests that the ritual is considered most effective when performed at the beginning of the day, presumably during the first planetary hour ruling the day.

Among the most important points in Gnostic and Platonic literature is the need to separate the subtle body from the physical body for its purification. This imagined, and eventually real, separation forms the core of the technique. Only by freeing the psychic self from the constraints of material life can we experience the full degree of good and evil in our psyche. The methodical and militant purification of our psyche and integration of its diverse aspects constitutes the most difficult, and rewarding, psycho-spiritual practices known.

Exercise: Creating the Body of Light

Preparation

The temple area should be set as usual, with altar in the middle or slightly east of center. If possible, wear a consecrated Rose Cross pendant

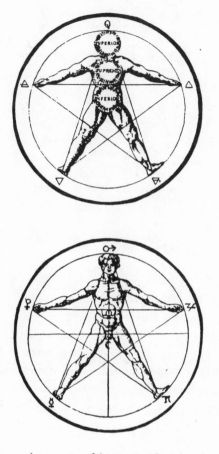

Note the Location of the "Sun" in the Solar Plexus

and place a pentacle for Earth on the altar.[15] Perform the Banishing Ritual of the Lesser or Supreme Pentagram or a similar ritual of preparation. If a pentacle for Earth is not available or used, you may substitute a holy book or anything that represents a material expression of divine law and harmony. If you are unfamiliar with any banishing rituals, use your skill of visualization create a firm and distinct sphere of light around yourself and area of work. This sphere should be approximately nine feet in diameter. A single white candle, representing the Absolute, should be present and lit upon the altar prior to the actual practice.

Explanation

This exercise draws upon our instinctual and etheric energies for the creation of a Body of Light. In addition, it harmonizes those energies with our various levels of consciousness—specifically our Self and directing will, and our sense of a Higher Self, or Holy Guardian Angel.

Type of Practice

This is a core practice for the creation of the Body of Light.

Method

Higher Self

1. Place your left hand, the hand of mercy, upon the Earth pentacle. Invoke the presence of your Higher Self. Imagine in brilliant phosphorescence a flaming sphere, or flaming Yod if you are a qabalist, touching your crown and uniting you with the cosmos. Stand in the posture of the Adeptus Minor, like that of a Tau cross, arms outstretched from your sides, palms down.

2. Lower your arms and meditate on the significance of your Higher Self, this flame of Creation within you, this cosmic seed.

3. Perform the Middle Pillar exercise, if you know it, or simply spend a few minutes energizing your psychic body through deep breathing, as previously taught.

4. Affirm your intentions for performing this exercise, and express appreciation for consciousness and the opportunity to develop in awareness and service. Ask that light, life, and love be expressed in every cell, thought, and action of your being.

The Lower Self

1. Turning clockwise, face the west of the temple. Pause and imagine the great streams of energy circulating through your physical and psychic bodies. Energize your heart center, feeling

a stream of energy running from your crown to your heart to your feet and back up again.

2. Affirm your position of authority over your Lower Self and physical body in a loving, but firm manner. Be thankful that they are present to serve you, but that they are at the service of the development of Self and are not independent beings.

3. Stand with your arms outstretched at your sides, palms facing the ground, and imagine yourself growing to a vast and immense size. Maintain or reformulate your flaming crown center. Feeling most of your consciousness operating from inside of it.

4. Send thoughts of blessing, love, good health, and well-being to your Lower Self and guph. Pause for a few moments as the feeling of vastness disappears and you return to normal awareness of the temple.

5. Turn to the east and ask that the powers of the Higher Self be present and fully utilized for this operation and at all times forward.

6. Move to the eastern quarter and face the west again.

7. Perform the Middle Pillar exercise a second time, if needed.

8. Project the simulacrum from the solar plexus, the upper abdomen region. Have the simulacrum facing east, or toward you, with the silvery bluish cord visible between it and your abdomen or solar plexus.

Exhortation and Instruction

1. In the name of your Higher Self, firmly and lovingly tell the image before you that it is to give you full assistance in the Great Work. If any particular instruction, assistance, or additional work is needed, interject it here.

2. Give blessing to your Nefesh, in the name of the Most High, and thank it for its participation in this ritual.

3. Energize and imagine the simulacrum attaining a high degree of integration.

Completion

1. Reabsorb the simulacrum and the silver cord by imaging it turning into a cloud or mist of bright bluish gray or silver psychic protoplasm and collapsing backward along the cord, returning into your body at the level it was projected from (bringing the cord with it). Close down firmly.

2. Feel the energy move throughout your body and sink deep into your muscles, bones, and marrow, and envelop you in a shell of light, just below the surface of the skin.

3. Rejoice in the success of the operation.

Incorporation into Daily Practice

This exercise should be done daily for two to three weeks to gain familiarity with the technique. Afterwards, it should be done daily by those seeking to create a Body of Light, or once or twice a week by practitioners engaged in other esoteric practices but still wishing to benefit from its secondary effects on lucid dreaming and astral projection.

Methods of Instructing the Simulacrum

After two or three weeks of successful projection and reabsorbing of the simulacrum, you can begin imprinting and activating specific ideas into it. This can be done in several ways depending on your personal preference and level of experience. Here are some suggestions.

1. Use a general plan of associating the simulacrum with the planets by imagining them along the simulacrum's spinal column, from Saturn at the base to Luna and Sol at the head. Imagine them in bright white light or according to their planetary colors.

2. After the colors, symbols, and sounds of the planets have been inculcated into the simulacrum, charge it with the various virtues and qualities of those planets. This can be done by

focusing on one planet for one week, the next planet for the next week, and so on.

3. Imagine counterparts of physical organs inside the simulacrum and having the colors and sounds of their planetary counterparts, filling the whole image with the light and sense and virtues of that planet.

4. Most of our work is on the lunar or astral purification of the simulacrum, so that it can be rightly called a silver body, as it will be influenced by and influential upon the lunar and astral worlds as a whole. At some point you can then begin to educate it further, that it might become a solar, or golden, radiant body, influenced by the Briactic Worlds. Beyond this, it would find perfection in the diamond, or resurrection, body, under the influence of the sphere of Saturn.

5. Practice performing the Middle Pillar exercise inside the simulacrum, after it has been projected.

Remember, always reabsorb the energy, either as a mist or a shadow image fusing itself into your earthly body. This energy is part and parcel of your actual physical body, as has been amply demonstrated in Spiritualist circles, particularly by that rare class of practitioner known as a *materializing medium*. Early research on ectoplasm, the basic essence of spiritualist phenomena demonstrates that ectoplasm is real and the basis for psychic phenomena.

Ectoplasm and the Body of Light

The term *ectoplasm* was coined by Professor Charles Richet from the Greek and literally means "exteriorized substance." Richet was a Nobel Prize winner, a professor of physiology at the Sorbonne, and member of the Institute de France. His studies demonstrated that in its primary phase, ectoplasm is invisible and intangible to the naked eye, but can still be photographed under infrared light and weighed, after which it becomes more solid, liquid, or gaseous and has an odor similar to ozone. In its third and final stage, ectoplasm can be seen and felt by the human hand, but has the texture of cobwebs and the physical appearance of muslin. Richet noted that on occasion it was dry and solid, sometimes moist and cold, and that the average temperature of ectoplasm was forty degrees Fah-renheit. His final conclusion was that there was sufficient proof of the actual materialization of ectoplasm to rank it as a demonstrable scientific fact.

Baron Albert Von Schrenck-Notzing, a Munich physician, demonstrated that ectoplasm is composed of white or colorless blood cells, called leukocytes, and epithelial cells and is taken from the protective tissues of the medium's body—and any sitters that may be present— during materializations. The baron's analysis of hair cut from a materialized spirit-form indicated that it was different from the medium's hair. He also noted that when ectoplasm was burned it smelled like burning animal horn, and the ash that was left behind contained sodium chloride (table salt) and calcium phosphate (an antacid). Professor W. J. Crawford of Queen's University, Belfast, conducted extensive studies of ectoplasm and recorded his findings in three books: *The Reality of Psychic Phenomena* (1916), *Experiments in Psychic Science* (1919), and *The Psychic Structures in the Goligher Circle* (1921). Crawford noted that during materializations the body weight of his medium dropped between fifteen and forty pounds.[16]

It is interesting to note that mediums, yogis, and others involved in esoteric practices tend towards being overweight—and even obese. Several factors support this obesity: the sedentary nature of the practices, a certain detachment from material concerns that often (and unfortunately) accompanies occult studies, and even the natural aging process. In addition, however, there is a certain peculiarity towards alcoholism and food addictions, with emphasis on sweets and fats—in essence, feel-good foods. While ignorance can be bliss, dealing with the transient nature of physical life and attempting to relieve human suffering can create emotional strains on people that they are unable to bear. Even the grandfather of Western alchemy, Paracelsus, was well known for his drinking to excess, despite having confected the Philosopher's Stone. While this may sound like a contradiction, it is important to remember that even though we experience broader and more expansive fields of consciousness, integrating their profound abstractions, insights, and clarity into a world that can seem as if it is filled with ignorance, fear, and delusion can be at times a nigh impossible task. We read repeatedly in the Gospels that Jesus would go off to be alone and that he would often weep over the suffering of humanity. It is one thing to know God—it is another to do so and still be human. In qabala, the spleen is associated with the astrological sign of Pisces, a sign well known for its tendency towards escapism, self-pity, alcoholism, and addictions of all sorts. It is also the last sign of development and the "end of the road" for those few addressing its inner revelations, regardless of their natural birth sign.

The spleen is an organ often listed as one of the major psychic centers and responsible for the formation of etheric energy in the body and its circulation to the entire body through the bloodstream. It is sometimes listed in place of the sexual center, although more recently it has also been exchanged with the solar plexus-naval center. Most often it is listed as a separate psychic center. During the days when Spiritualist phenomena were investigated by various societies for psychic research, as well as debunkers, it was not uncommon to see ectoplasm oozing out from the naval, stomach, and pores of the body as well as the spleen. In fact, all natural openings of the body have been used to produce ectoplasm, including the pores on the top of the head. Physiologically, the spleen has a major role in immune function, cleaning both the red and white blood cells and removing old cells so that new ones can take their place; it is the largest organ associated with the lymphatic system. The spleen also acts as a reservoir for blood in the body—the human Mercury—making it a critical organ in alchemical transmutation. The Lower Self, or Nefesh, is linked to the blood as long as we live, thereby giving the spleen an important role in the purification of the energies of the body and instinctual aspects of the psyche.

For practical purposes, we can view the spleen as a link between the sexual and naval centers, as well as the source of psychic energy we use—regardless of where we project it from—in creating the simulacrum of the Body of Light.

Ectoplasm is not limited to nineteenth- and twentieth-century Spiritualism. Emanual Swedenborg, one of the seminal influences on the philosophical development of Louise Claude de St. Martin and source of several Masonic rites that bear his name, reported seeing a haze rise up before him, or as if from the pores of his body, during some of his trance states. The alchemist Thomas Vaughn described a similar substance that is drawn from the body and referred to it as the First Matter, or Mercury.[17]

Crowley and the Body of Light

Regardless of what one thinks about Aleister Crowley's initiatic status as a genuine adept or as a role model for aspiring esotericists, there is no doubt that he is among the most influential authorities in twentieth-century occultism. This authority is derived from several factors.

1. Crowley studied and systematically employed every occult practice, teaching, or device available to him.

2. Crowley meticulously recorded his results, analyzed them, and organized a method or process he believed others could follow in order to obtain similar results.

3. Crowley published extensively on the practical aspects of magic and was a tireless promoter of his occult views.

It is not necessary to enter into an analysis of Crowley the man, with all his warts and failings, to recognize that he made significant contributions to the world in the form of methodical and practical occult teachings (although these teachings are at times muddled by his recourse to sarcasm and outright disinformation, inserted just for the fun of it).

The following points are taken exclusively from *Magick, Book 4, Parts I-IV*, but can be found wholly or in part in other books, including *The Equinox*, Regardie's *The Complete Golden Dawn System of Magic*, and modern commentaries on Crowley, particularly Lon Milo DuQuette's *The Magick of Aleister Crowley*, and various Internet sources.

According to Crowley, developing the Body of Light is the primary focus of magic.

The essential magical work, apart from any particular operation, is in the proper formation of the Magical Being or Body of Light . . . We will assume that the Magician has succeeded in developing his Body of Light until it is able to go anywhere and do anything. There will, however, be a certain limitation to his work, because he has formed his magical body of his own constitution. Therefore, although he may be able to penetrate the utmost recesses of the heavens, or conduct vigorous combats with the most unpronounceable demons of the pit, it may be impossible for him to do as much as knock a vase from a mantelpiece. His magical body is composed of matter too tenuous to affect directly the gross matter of which illusions such as tables and chairs are made.[18]

Now, then, conceive of this magical body as a creative force, seeking manifestation; as a God, seeking incarnation.[19]

The Body of Light offers the magician unlimited access to information, ideas, and experiences, making it the premier magical practice. This practice has three phases:

1. Separation of the Body of Light from the physical body;
2. Development of the powers of the astral body, which correspond to the brain and the physical senses of sight, hearing, speech, sensation, movement, and cognition;
3. Unification of the physical and astral bodies without muddling their distinct and specific functions.

Creating and developing the Body of Light is closely related to the psychic function normally classed under telepathy, clairvoyance, precognition, and so on, but it is by far a simpler, more satisfying, and worthwhile practice for developing those skills known as psychic abilities. The Body of Light possesses all of the senses of the physical body, but on the psychic level. Therefore, there is no need to partially disengage the psychic body as the clairvoyant does or to be a passive observer of psychic images. The Body of Light allows full consciousness, control, and mastery of the domain in which it lives and for greater accuracy and freedom, as it is an active experience and not a passive one.

As Crowley says:

It is of the utmost importance to the "clairvoyant" or "traveler in the fine body" to be able to find his way to any desired plane, and operate therein as its ruler. [20]

Crowley does not distinguish between the astral body and the Body of Light, using the terms interchangeably, and he does not distinguish between etheric and astral projection, but recognizes that the phenomenon associated with the former as more difficult to obtain.

Crowley also taught the following:

- The astral body must be made to push through the mirage of the astral and enter into the highest realms of consciousness to the face of God. Even if human consciousness is not aware of the experience, the psychic body may achieve this on its own (presumably during sleep or deep meditation in which there is a temporary loss of consciousness, but profound sense of refreshment and enthusiasm upon waking). This alone ensures the spiritual progress of the student and allows for future success in more conscious efforts to reach higher dimensions of experience.

- The gods are enemies of humanity. Man must overcome his own ignorance and the limits imposed by nature if he is to be a ruler in his kingdom.

The true God is Man. In Man are all things hidden. Of these the Gods, Nature, Time, all the powers of the Universe are rebellious slaves. It is these that men must fight and conquer in the power and in the name of the Beast that hath availed them, the Titan, the Magus, the Man whose number is six hundred and three score six.[21]

He said:

- After progressive traveling into the various dimensions and worlds, the magus will find that it is no longer necessary to take the long route, but can directly travel to whatever dimension desired.

- The Body of Light is key to successful practice of Rising on the Planes. Herein, one is capable of exploring all regions of the visible and invisible universe and achieving Knowledge and Conversation with their Holy Guardian Angel.

Thus, it is necessary that the technique of Magick should be perfected. The Body of Light must be rendered capable of going everywhere and doing everything. It is, therefore, always the question of drill which is of importance. You have got to go out Rising on the Planes every day of your life, year after year. You are not to be disheartened by failure, or too much encouraged by success, on any one set of practices. What you are doing is what will be of real value to you in the end, and that is developing a character, creating a *karma*, which will give you the power to do your Will.[22]

The technique of Magick is just as important as that of Mysticism, but here we have a very much more difficult problem, because the original unit of Magick, the Body of Light, is already something unfamiliar to the ordinary person. Nevertheless, this Body must be developed and trained with exactly the same rigid discipline as the brain in the case of Mysticism. The essence of the technique of Magick is the development of the Body of Light, which must be extended to include all members of the organism, and indeed the Cosmos.

The object is to possess a Body which is capable of doing easily any particular task that may lie before it. There must be no selection of special experience which appeals to one's immediate desire. One must go steadily through all the possible pylons. [23]

Crowley cleanly and simply described the process of using the Body of Light for Rising on the Planes. Note that the process here is, in fact, easier than the process outlined earlier for meditation. There is no intonation of divine names or visualization of symbols. Everything imagined is, in fact, a mirror of the world around us and the physical universe in which we live. This description is, in fact, a nearly perfect example of how simple and precise many of the most advanced methods of occult practice really are. They are more a matter of attitude and effort than organized ritual and complex correspondences. While systems can help save us time on our Path, it is through following clear instructions such as these that real inner unfolding takes place.

Liber O²⁴

V

Crowley again:

1. Let the student be at rest in one of his prescribed positions, having bathed and robed with the proper decorum. Let the Place of Working be free from all disturbances, and let the preliminary purifications, banishings and invocations be duly accomplished, and lastly, let the incense be kindled.

2. Let him imagine his own figure (preferably robed in the proper magical garment and armed with the proper Magical Weapons) as enveloping his physical body, or standing near to and in front of him.

3. Let him then transfer the seat of his consciousness to that imagined figure, so that is may seem to him that he is seeing with its eyes, and hearing with its ears. This will usually be the great difficulty in the operation.

4. Let him then cause that imagined figure to rise in the air to a great height above the earth.

5. Let him then stop and look about him. (It is sometimes difficult to open the eyes.)

6. Probably he will see figures approaching him, or become conscious of a landscape. Let him speak to such figures, and insist upon being answered, using the proper pentagrams and signs, as previously taught.

7. Let him travel about at will, either with or without guidance from such fires or figures.

8. Let him further employ such special invocations as will cause to appear the particular places he may wish to visit.

9. Let him be aware of the thousand subtle attacks and deceptions that he will experience, carefully testing the truth of all with whom he speaks.

10. Practice will make the student infinitely wary in these matters.

11. It is usually quite easy to return to the body, but should any

difficulty arise, practice (again) will make the imagination fertile. For example, one may create in thought a chariot of fire with white horses, and command the charioteer to drive earthwards. It might be dangerous to go too far, or to stay too long; for fatigue must be avoided. The danger spoken of is that of fainting, or of obsession, or loss of memory or other mental faculty.

12. Finally, let the student cause his imagined body in which he supposes himself to have been traveling to coincide with the physical, tightening his muscles, drawing in his breath, and putting his forefinger to his lips. Let him "awake" by a well-defined act of will, and soberly and accurately record his experiences. It may be added that this apparently complicated experiment is perfectly easy to perform. It is best to learn by "traveling" with a person already experienced in the matter. Two or three experiments should suffice to render the student confident and even expert.

VI

1. The previous experiment has little value, and leads to few results of importance. But it is susceptible of a development that merges into a form of dharana—concentration—and as such may lead to the very highest ends. The principal use of the practice in the last chapter is to familiarize the student with every kind of obstacle and every kind of delusion, so that he may be perfect master of every idea that may arise in his brain, to dismiss it, to transmute it, so cause it to instantly to obey his Will.

2. Let him then begin exactly as before; but with the most intense solemnity and determination.

3. Let him be very careful to cause his imaginary body to rise in a line exactly perpendicular to the earth's tangent at the point where his physical body is situated (or, to put it more simply, straight upwards).

4. Instead of stopping let him continue to rise until fatigue almost overcomes him. If he should find that he has stopped

without willing to do so, and that figures appear, let him at all costs rise above them. Yeh, though his very life tremble on his lips, let him force his way upward and onward!

5. Let him continue in this so long as the breath of life is in him. Whatever threatens, whatever allures, through it were Typhon and all his hosts loosed from the pit and leagued against him, though it were from the very Throne of God Himself that a Voice issues bidding him stay and be content, let him struggle on, ever on.

6. At last there must come a moment when his whole being is swallowed up in fatigue, overwhelmed by its own inertia. Let him sink (when no longer can he strive, though his tongue be bitten through with the effort and the blood gush from his nostrils) into the blackness of unconsciousness; and then on coming to himself, let him write down soberly and accurately a record of all that hath occurred: yeh, a record of all that hath occurred.

Notes and Advanced Practices for Working with the Body of Light

1. When venturing into the quarters of a ritual circle, use the simulacrum and tune it to the Element you seek to explore, making it a body of Fire, Air, Water, or Earth. When generally projected, it should be thought of as a body of Quintessence, or Spirit, of dynamic electric and magnetic qualities, containing within it the balanced potential for all bodies of the four Elements.

2. The simulacrum can also be projected and modified to a deific image, or godform. The effects of this are different than those of the usual methods for Assumption of the Godform. In this instance it is helpful to grow the image in size and stature to a larger-than-normal appearance after it has been created. Remember: it is important that your consciousness be projected firmly into the simulacrum during any working and that the energy be completely reabsorbed after it is over.

3. The Body of Light can be charged with Hebrew letters; engrave them according to their location and association with the physical organs as outlined in the *Sepher Yetzirah*. This can be done to the physical body as well, prior to projection of the simulacrum, and will assist in its creation and projection.[25] The letters can be done in blazing white or according to the Queen's Scale used by the Golden Dawn. The Body of Light can also be charged with the Tetragrammaton, in the normal *Y* (head) *Heh* (shoulders) *Vav* (spine) *Heh* (hips, feet) fashion. As with the Hebrew alphabet, the letters of the Tetragrammaton should be seen as existing inside the figure, glowing and strong, and not carved on the surface or projected onto it from elsewhere.

4. The purpose of the simulacrum is to create a vehicle for the purification and expression of the energies of the Middle and Lower Self. As such, it also acts as a bridge between our objective and subjective worlds and also between out emotional and physical realities. As stated, we can alter our physical appearance and health through proper and loving purification of our astral matrix. The Lower Self, which constitutes the bulk of the self that we are refining in this work, overlaps and connects the worlds of matter (guph, or the physical body) and Middle Self.

5. Working with the Body of Light will trigger psychic responses corresponding to the model of the universe we chose to work with. On the Tree of Life, this practice will have secondary effects on the twenty-fourth path and some effects on the twenty-eighth path, as this latter path governs the flow of psychic energy through our psychic centers. All of the paths below Tiphareth will be affected to some degree by this exercise. We cannot ascend and take our mistaken ideas or our exaggerated emotions with us. Both are eradicated, disciplined, or redirected by the Sword of Geburah, or an enlightened will. The lightning bolt on the tarot card the Tower, sometimes called the *House of God* (Deu) or *Fire* (Feu), shows us that the ever flowing lightning bolt of creative energy will destroy any imperfections that it comes in contact with as it travels down the Tree and as we travel upwards on the Path of Return.

Key Points

- Western esoteric literature is replete with the doctrine of the Body of Light.

- Chinese, Indian, and Tibetan schools of esotericism are in agreement with Western esotericism in saying that the creation and use of the Body of Light is critical for astral projection and occult practices related to death and after-death survival.

- The Body of Light is easy to create, but can be troubling to control, and because of this a great deal of care must be taken.

- The Body of Light draws very heavily from our instinctual nature; it is essentially etheric Nefesh in nature and will seek to express a crude form of self-consciousness. Under no circumstances can this be allowed, and to prevent it, a strict method of projection, use, and reabsorption must be utilized.

- Once created, a variety of simple methods can be utilized to train and educate the Body of Light, thereby increasing its efficiency, as well as obedience to the Middle and Higher Selves.

- There are strong similarities between the early formations of the Body of Light and ectoplasm displayed in early Spiritualist séances.

- Ectoplasm has been studied extensively by early pioneers of psychic research, including a Noble Prize winner, and authorities from various scientific disciplines.

- The spleen, sexual organs, and bloodstream play an important part in the cultivation of etheric energy.

Assignments for Chapter Seven

1. Practice the creation of the Body of Light, paying close attention to its projection and assimilation. Carefully record your experiences in your notebook, paying careful attention to the lunar phases.

2. After one month of building the Body of Light, you may begin to formulate it into a godform, as outlined in the next chapter.

3. After three months of projecting and absorbing the Body of Light, you may begin to perform Rising on the Planes with it.

CHAPTER 8

Assumption of the Godform

The technique known as Assumption of the Godform is among the most impressive, as well as challenging, techniques in practical occultism. A careful, in-depth study of a chosen pantheon is often required, along with the willingness to spend a great deal of time in extended meditation and devotion with each of the deities one uses for Assumption. In fact, it is this devotional aspect that is the key to success when applying the technique of Assumption of the Godform. If done carefully and in a progressive and step-by-step manner, Assumption of the Godform can offer tremendous insights into the depth and power of ancient cults, practices, and ideas that simply reading about them cannot confer. It becomes an initiatic practice of the highest nature.

Background on the Technique

"Think of a place and thou are there. Think of a thing, and thou are it."

—CORPUS HERMETICUM

The fundamental idea behind Assumption of the Godform is that within each of us there are powers that lie in potential for awakening. By identifying ourselves with those idealized expressions of those powers from ancient times, in the form of "gods," we can awaken through resonance similar powers and wisdom within our own psyche. The multitude of deities, gods, and heroes of ancient mythologies represent the various means of expressing the highest human ideals of that time. Surprisingly, they also seem to do the same for modern practitioners as well, because the Western world lacks a cohesive and comprehensive modern mythology to answer life's questions in the same fashion as those of Greece or Egypt do.

Modern mythologies are media creations, generated for entertainment, economic, or political purposes, and while they exert a strong influence over our collective psyche, they lack the coherent veneration, sacred status, or socio-political position of the ancient cults. Modern churches, as survivors of the Medieval and Renaissance periods, also lack any appreciation for the techniques of direct experience, although some methods have managed to survive in Roman Catholicism and some minority Protestant sects.[1] In short, if we are to have a technique that offers us direct experience of an ideal in our lives, a veritable means of incarnating an aspect of deity, we must turn our attention to the ancient cults for some guidance.[2]

Variations on the Technique

Assumption of the Godform, as a technique, exists on at least three different levels. The first level of the practice is the easiest and consists of little more than sitting in a chair and imagining that you are your chosen deity—Thoth, Ptah, Jesus, and so on. This is fundamental to success in the advanced levels, and it is suggested that this practice be undertaken until competency and familiarity with it is developed.

On the second level, it is important to study the deity you've chosen; in fact, you might want to study the entire pantheon to some degree. When picking a godform, it is not uncommon to pick one for each of the planetary powers and, when possible, have them all come from the same pantheon. In many instances, the Egyptian gods and goddesses are suggested for several reasons. First, they are still in use among esotericists and, because of this, have an inherent power that makes success easier. Second, they are abstract—neither too human, as the Greek deities are, yet not too unattainable, as others are.

When you have picked the god you wish to assume and have studied its appearance, gestures, and mannerism, you begin to build a small likeness of it in your heart. Once you feel comfortable with the image you have built, you may begin to grow the image until it almost fills your being. Stay at this level for some time.

Assumption of the Godform can create a tremendous amount of pressure on your endocrine system, presumably as it stimulates the psychic centers on a very physical level and should be undertaken slowly and with patience, so as to not create psychic or physical imbalances.[3]

In the third level, you grow the god within and allow it to expand beyond your body, growing to immense height. You may also want to sense it merging, or "clicking" with its corresponding image in the cosmos—that is, your god grows to meet or become one with its exact corresponding image in the cosmos, like two mirror images becoming one.

In *Liber O*, Crowley describes the practice of Assumption using qabalistic divine names.

After preparing your oratory ritualistically, sit in a chair in the Pharonic or Egyptian God posture, or with feet flat on the floor, palms down on thighs, and back straight. Imagine that the god you have chosen envelopes your entire being, slightly larger than you, and that you are in complete identification with it. Do not rush this part, but take your time before proceeding to the next step. Once identification is established, stand up, extend arms to your sides, and breathe in deeply through your nostrils, imagining that the name of the god is being inhaled in flaming white light. Let the name descend to your lungs, heart, solar plexus, abdomen, genitals, and feet.

When it touches your feet, quickly place your left foot forward (about one foot), while thrusting your body and hands forward (at eye level), into the posture of "the Enterer" or of the god Horus. As this is done, imagine the name ascending with force, power, and brilliance, from your feet while exhaling out of your nostrils.

Feel as though your voice carries the Name to the edges of the Universe.

Pause for a moment, and then place your left foot besides the right one, and place your left index finger on your lips, so that you find yourself in the position of Harpocrates—the god of Silence.

Success is hard to describe, but a definite sensation will be felt. If a single vocalization exhausts you, it is considered a sign that it has worked. A sensation of intense heat, onset of sweating, and possibly even trouble remaining standing will occur.

If you hear the name of the god resounding, "as if carried off by a thousand thunders"; this sound will seem to come from an enormous voice coming from the whole universe and not from him is also considered a sign of efficiency.

The more time it takes to return to normal awareness, the better the experiment.

Other modern authorities suggest inscribing the name and/or sigil of the entity in your heart prior to the vibration of its name. Then formulate the image in the East quarter of the temple area you are working in and move towards the image and into it, with your back towards the east and facing the west.[4]

The Assumption of Harpocrates

The first and most important of the godforms used in Assumption in the Golden Dawn is that of Harpocrates, the son of Osiris and Lord of Matter. Harpocrates is "the god who is the cause of all generation, of all nature, and of all the powers of the elements" and as such he "precedes all things and comprehends all things in himself."[5]

After having immersed yourself in the imagery and symbolism of Harpocrates, begin your experiment with a brief period of relaxation. You may, if you desire, prepare your working area with a ritual, such as the Lesser Ritual of the Pentagram, or simply imagine yourself surrounded by a brilliant sphere of white light.

Then imagine Harpocrates emerging from the primordial darkness on a lotus flower. When the image is real to you, step forward and assume his classical pose: the left foot about six inches in front of the right and the right forefinger to the mouth in the sign of silence. Imagine, feel, that you are becoming Harpocrates. Then vibrate his name—*Hoor-po-krat-ist*—while you imagine yourself emerging from the primordial waters of creation.

This visualization can also be made more potent by employing the following affirmation:

> Hoor-po-krat-ist, Thou Lord of the Silence. Hoor-po-krat-ist, Lord of the Sacred Lotus, O Thou Hoor-po-krat-ist (pause and contemplate the force invoked), Thou that standest in victory on the heads of the infernal dwellers of the waters wherefrom all things were created, Thee, Thee, I invoke, by the name of *Eheieh* and the power of *AGLA*.
>
> Behold! He is in me, and I in him. Mine is the lotus as I rise as Harpocrates from the firmament of waters . . . For I am Hoor-po-krat-ist, the Lotus throned Lord of Silence . . . I am Ra enshrouded, kephra unmanifest to man.[6]

If you are successful in Assumption of the Godform, you may experience a period of bliss and extreme elevation.

Divine Names

"A rose by another name. . ."

—William Shakespeare

It is often stated that the Egyptians had two names for their gods: one public and one private. It was these private names of the gods that gave the priesthood of Egypt power over them and the ability to invoke them to visible appearance in their temples. According to tradition, if you know the "name" of a god, deity, person, or thing, you can control or influence it.

Names are symbols and psychic media which convey and elicit the various units of human consciousness we call intuitions, thoughts, feelings, and vital energies. As such, Names are the true units of human consciousness, acting as streams of focused thoughts, emotions, and "bundles of energy." They are the mental lenses that focus out whole attention upon one aspect of reality, one power, or one being. Names also function as catalysts to awaken, invoke, and evoke certain energies and states of consciousness in the Psyche. **In short, they are the psychospiritual means at our disposal to invade a certain Presence and induce a certain state of consciousness by focusing our awareness.** Names are the intellectual tools by which we can recreate in ourselves an image or facsimile of that which is without, or below, or above our consciousness.[7]

Esoterically speaking, a name is the means by which we can know something, becoming its temporary channel and recreating it or allowing it to express in our consciousness and in our being.[8] This is why we have spent so much time in this book detailing the importance of the magical voice and harmonizing ourselves with the sounds of creation as expressed in the Hebrew alphabet. Through this attunement we are better able to awaken the images of the gods we are identifying with and bring them to life within us.

Exercise: Assumption of the Godform

Preparation

Perform a pentagram ritual or other such ritual to prepare your area of working. If suitable, perform an appropriate hexagram ritual. Offer an oration of your construction or a classical one, such as the *Orphic Hymns* or one from the *Egyptian Book of the Dead*. If you do not know a banishing ritual, then, using the power of visualization, create a sphere nine feet in diameter around yourself and the area of working.

Explanation

The following technique is a synthesis of several techniques and utilizes the various methods used by different exponents of the technique.

Type of Practice

This is a core practice that should be incorporated into all areas of esoteric practice.

Method

1. Imagine the deity perfectly in your heart. Cultivate a sense of personal relationship to the deity, even to the point of worship.

2. Imagine in the deity's heart its sigil or other sign that connects it to the cosmos, the totality of the godhead.

3. Imagine this image of the deity growing to match your body in size, enveloping it, masking your appearance with its own.

4. Stand upright and intone the deity's name and or the name and divine names appropriate to the godform chosen. Incorporate them into an invocation such as the following: "In the name of *YHVH Aloah Va-Daath*, I am Osiris, the Risen Lord!" If the deity doesn't fit easily into the qabalistic scheme of things, invoke it as follows: "In the name *Eheieh* and by the power of *AGLA,* I am . . ." This invocation utilizes the principal names of Spirit from the Supreme Ritual of the Pentagram and invokes their powers both general and particular. In either instance, it is important to "inhale the names," as previously described, and to exhale them with great force and visualization while positively affirming and identifying with the forces invoked.

5. Allow the image to grow to immense height, carrying you with it, for it is you.

6. Offer another oration if you like, or simply experience the results of your invocation.

7. When the moment is right, reduce the form too slightly larger than your body, then to the size of your body, and finally back into your heart. Perform the Sign of Silence by placing the left or right index finger in front of your mouth, remaining fingers closed. Absorb the energy and rest.

8. Banish, stamp your foot, and return to normal consciousness.

Incorporation into Daily Practice

This practice should be undertaken daily, preferably in conjunction with Rising on the Planes.

As one modern author states:

By way of conclusion, let the aspiring Candidate always keep present in his or her consciousness that the WORK must first be KNOWN BY THE HEAD, then FELT BY THE HEART, then CHOSEN BY THE WILL to be LIVED BY THE BODY, SO THAT ONE CAN MAKE THE "WORD BECOME FLESH" OR BECOME THE IDEAL ONE IS NUTURING.[9]

Psychological Support for the Technique

Roberto Assagioli, the founder of psychosynthesis, is one of the least known and yet most influential of modern psychotherapists. Born in Italy in 1888 (d. 1974), he was of Jewish descent, yet his mother was a devotee of Theosophy. A large portrait of Madame Helena Blavatsky is said to have hung in his house as a child. Known in Italy as the first psychoanalyst, Assagioli knew both Sigmund Freud and Carl Jung and was deeply involved in the study of human consciousness. His attempt to create a universal schematic that would allow the harmonization of a variety of psychological models and techniques became known as psychosynthesis. Convinced of the reality of the spiritual dimensions, as well as the need to make techniques universal and free of specific sectarian or academic orientations, Assagioli and his students created a comprehensive method of personal development that became, for a short period of time, one of the leading intellectual forums during the cultural awakening that took place in the 1960s and early 1970s. While psychosynthesis never became as well known in the United States as it did in Europe, several centers for study and training in psychosynthesis were established and continue to exist. For many, the depth, breadth, and practicality of its methods are what have kept this obscure system of personal integration alive and well for nearly a century.

Assagioli's "Ideal Model"

We must become aware that each of us has within himself various self-models or models of the ego, or—more exactly, using our terminology—of the personality. Such models are not only diverse in nature, origin, and vividness but this constitutes one of the major difficulties but is also one the most useful fields of application of a right psychoanalysis.[10]

Assagioli points out that there are three kinds of models that obscure and prevent our realization of what we actually are in the present moment.

1. What we believe we are, either in overevaluating or underevaluating ourselves;

2. What we would like to be, often idealized, unattainable models;

3. What *we should like to appear* to others.

Each of these three models reflects each relationship with have with others. Of course, there are also the models that are projected onto us, thereby affecting our relationships with others:

1. What others believe us to be;

2. What others would like us to be;

3. Images of ourselves, evoked by others.

Assagioli states that the rationale behind "ideal models" is in "the utilization or taking advantage of the psychological law that every image has a motor-element which tends to be translated into action—which is a rather dry, objective way of indicating the creative power of imagination . . . The model must first be static and then manifesting in motion." The stages are: first the *idea*, which if seen as desirable becomes an *ideal*, and then, ardently sought after, emerges or expresses itself in *form and function*.[11]

Assagioli further points out that ideals, or traditional "hero worship" should not be confused with modern "idol worship" such as is applied to sports players, businessmen and -women, celebrities, or those of dubious morals and character.

The ideal should be the model we chose, and the external form of the living person, or the person themselves "should be an idea, an image, introjected, and not a personal attachment to the inspirer of the model."[12]

In advanced work, an entirely new and integrated personality can be "imagined" and brought into being this way.

In his work *The Invisible Temple*, Peter Roche de Coppens describes his use of the technique of an "ideal model" and combines it with the traditional use of "Assumption of the Godform and use of Divine Names."

> Let me give you an example of how I have used (and still use) the Name of one of my teachers, who is an 85 year old woman still alive in Paris, whom I have known and been inspired by for over 25 years . . . In her presence, I have become transformed: being more myself in its higher sense, more alive, more creative, generous, and functioning at a higher level of consciousness. When I invoke her Name . . . I immediately feel her presence there and no longer feel alone, but instead connected to God, to Humanity, to Nature. All that I know about, and have experienced with her immediately returns to me and is present with me as her Spirit is connected with mine, and I become transformed again with powerful motivations and urges to become the better person I can be.[13]

In this practice, we can see the importance of a teacher in the spiritual path, as well as the significant role Assumption of the Godform plays in such systems where worshipful devotion of one's teacher is designed to produce not only union with the psyche of the teacher— guru yoga—but also with their exceptional state of consciousness, which we seek to awaken and anchor into ourselves. The godform we use is not limited to mythological or quasi-historical beings or persons, but can very well be a living being with whom we have a relationship or who has been important to us on our Path. If this person or persons belongs to a specific group or tradition, through them we can strengthen our connection to that tradition—even if it has long been dormant or we are not in a position to be physically connected to it.

Assumption

In his work *Invisibility*, Steve Richards discusses the technique of Assumption of the Godform in relationship to the practices of the Hermetic Order of the Golden Dawn and its ritual for invisibility. The godform used for this practice is the Egyptian god of Harpocrates; however, the technique is not limited just to idealized personalities or anthropomorphized archetypes. In fact, it is used in a much more practical manner: to progressively attune with the many facets of creation or to other human beings.

Any object can be used—a piece of steel, a rock, or even a pencil. All you need to do is sit quietly, still your mind, and visualize the object in front of you. Slowly increase its size until it is large enough to walk through. Then merge with this image and become one with it. Once you are successful in merging with it, become sensitive to any impressions, images, feelings, or ideas that arise.

If you are successful with this experiment, the first thing that will happen is that you will actually feel that you have, in fact, merged with whatever you are trying to merge with, if not physically then psychically. Then, as you progress with it, you will begin to have actual sensations, intuitions, and even thoughts that come to you as you do the experiment and that proceed directly from this sense of merging that you will produce.[14] After working your way up the chain from mineral to plant to animal life, you can begin to experiment with human beings.

You will now be able to merely visualize the animal or the person standing in front of you, and then, as before, imagine that you are merging with it, so that your consciousnesses are merged together and you become one with it. In this case, you may wish to visualize yourself standing directly behind the person you are assuming, then, in imagination, reach out and put your hands on the sides of the other person's head. Now, imagine that you are putting his head on, in other words, that you are slipping his head over yours, just as you would a ski mask. After you have done this, try to see with his eyes, hear with his ears, and think with his brain. His thoughts will become your thoughts, and your thoughts will become his. Using this method you can communicate with another person telepathically and implant thoughts in his mind without him being consciously aware where they came from.[15]

The amazing flexibility of this method lends itself to any number of ingenious applications, and it can be said to be the apex of psychic development. Devoid of ritualistic constructs and based exclusively on direct psychic perception, the entire universe can become an open book.

Alchemical Applications

The theory and practice behind Assumption is in no way limited to qabalists and their myriad of pantheons and mythologies. Practicing alchemists use it, even if unconsciously, when working with laboratory materials and their enigmatic picture books.

Through constant contemplation of the Work, its components, and their realizations that an energetic exchange is taking place on some level between their inner self and the outer materials, an experience of assumption is inevitable for the alchemist. This experience of oneness could even be said to be a benchmark sign of some degree of interior success or initiation in the Work at hand.

Through a conscious application of the technique, it becomes possible to have an interior awakening regarding the various manuscripts, their authors, the time and culture in which they lived—in short, to view their Work through their soul. Even if the great alchemists such as Rosenkreutz, Flamel, or Saint Germain were more legend than reality, the use of Assumption allows us to touch the archetype that they have become—to "assume" them in the same fashion the hermeticist "assumes" Thoth, Osiris, or any other deity they chose.

The advantage of this technique over many others is in its directness. When it works, we are aware of it. The knowledge and experience
we gain is often very clear and powerful. The often-confusing array of
subconscious symbols that qabalists wade through in interpreting
psychic experiences, dreams, or meditation insights is avoided.
Intuition is often the fruits of this work, signifying a more Briactic
level of experience. We get a glimpse of the powers of Tiphareth—
the powers of direct experience.

The Techniques of Western Magic

There are three fundamental techniques in Western magical-qabalistic
ritual:

1. Rituals of invocation and evocation,
2. Vibration and vocalization of divine names,
3. Identification of the operator with a chosen deific form.

The mastery of these three points leads to the mastery of ritual, in
personal practice or in a group.[16]

However, to these three points two additional ones should be added:

1. The Identification of the material world as a divine one (Vow
   of the Adeptus Exemptus),
2. Constant identification with the divine being, force, intelligence,
   and energy.

Summary

The uses of the techniques of Assumption—be it of a godform, a plant,
mineral, piece of laboratory equipment, or a mythic hero—are limitless.
When combined with a direct and real desire to perfect ourselves and to
unfold those hidden potentials buried deep within, be it through an
ideal model or a mythological character, we come closer and closer to
being a whole and holy being.

In *Book Eleven* of the *Corpus Hermetica*, the entire secret of hermetic
philosophy and practice is revealed. When examined in the light of this

chapter it is clear that all esoteric methods, techniques, practices, and meditations are but detailed commentaries designed to help us directly experience these points.

1. Consider this yourself. Command your soul to go anywhere, and it will be there quicker than your command. Bid it to go to the ocean and again it is there at once, not as if it had gone from place to place but was already there. Order it to fly up to heaven and it will need no wings, nor will anything impede it, neither the fire of the sun, nor the ether, nor the whirlwind, nor the other heavenly bodies, but cutting through them all it will soar up to the last body. And if you wish to break through all this and to contemplate what is beyond (if there is anything beyond the cosmos), it is in your power.

2. See what power you have and what speed! You can do all these things and yet God cannot? Reflect on God in this way as having all within Himself as ideas: the cosmos, Himself, the whole. If you do not make yourself equal to God you cannot understand Him. Like is understood by like. Grow to immeasurable size. Be free from every body, transcend all time. Become eternity and thus you will understand God. Suppose nothing to be impossible for yourself. Consider yourself immortal and able to understand everything: all arts, sciences and the nature of every living creature. Become higher than all heights and lower than all depths. Sense as one within yourself the entire creation: fire, water, the dry and the moist. Conceive yourself to be in all places at the same time: in the earth, the sea, in heaven; that you are not yet born, that you are within the womb, that you are young, old, dead; that you are beyond death. Conceive all things at once: time, places, actions, qualities and quantities; then you can understand God.

3. But if you lock up your soul in your body, abase it and say: "I understand nothing; I can do nothing; I am afraid of the sea; I cannot reach heaven; I do not know who I was nor who I shall be." What have you to do with God? For you cannot conceive anything beautiful or good while you are attached to the body and are evil. For the greatest evil is to ignore what belongs to

God. To be able to know and to will and to hope is the straight and easy way appropriate to each that will lead to the Supreme Good. When you take this road this Good will meet you everywhere and will be experienced everywhere, even where and when you do not expect it; when awake, asleep, in a ship, on the road, by night, by day, when speaking and when silent, for there is nothing which it is not.

4. Now do you say that God is invisible? Be careful. Who is more manifest than He? He has made all things for this reason: that through them you should see Him. This is the goodness (*to agathon*) of God; this is His excellence: that He is made manifest through all. Though you cannot see what is bodiless, *Nous* is seen in the act of contemplation, God in the act of creation. These things have been made clear to you Hermes thus far. Reflect on all other things in the same way within yourself and you will not be led astray.[17]

Key Points

- Assumption of the Godform is among the most impressive as well as challenging techniques in practical occultism.

- The fundamental premise behind Assumption of the Godform can be found in the *Corpus Hermeticum*, which states, "Think of a place and thou are there. Think of a thing, and thou are it."

- Assumption of the Godform appears in many diverse systems under different names, but its fundamental theory and practice is almost universal.

- In his work *Psychosynthesis*, Roberto Assagioli gives psychological support to the method of Assumption under the heading of the "ideal model."

- Assumption is not limited to abstract deities or even archetypal projections of living human beings; it can also be used with plants, animals, or objects.

- Assumption can be used to attune with and thereby give information to and receive information from other persons, in a manner more private and complete than telepathy.
- The exchange of self with the cosmos, as expressed in the hermetic literature, is the ultimate use of Assumption, putting us into a direct experience of the Godhead.

Assignments for Chapter Eight

1. Practice each of the methods of Assumption outlined in this chapter and integrate them into your daily practice.

2. Select a pantheon that you are comfortable with and commit yourself to working with it. Pick no more than four or five deities and, from them, choose one that you will use as your devotional deity to work with exclusively for at least one year. Note the effectiveness of your assumptions when they are focused on an integrated mythology.

3. Practice Assumption of the cosmic and Assumption with an individual as often as possible. Notice how quickly it can be done. Record your experiences in your notebook.

CHAPTER 9

Preparing for Death
and Beyond

Despite Western esotericism's focus on the invisible worlds, there is scant discussion of death and dying in its modern literature. This is presumably because past generations of students and scholars were educated in the prevailing Christian or Jewish religions of Europe and North America. Esotericism was studied to fill in the gaps created by those nagging questions that Sunday school sermons or theological seminaries could not or would not answer. Unfortunately, as we enter into the Age of Aquarius, many of these structures are collapsing and with them the social, religious, and moral understandings that held society together. With this commonality being displaced, individuals are left to their own devices, for better or worse, to fill in the gaps and often to create the needed spiritual superstructure for daily living as well. While new myths and forms of worship may be needed to assist us in this time of collective death and initiation, it is important that these be based on a working experience of the transcendent and not just wishful thinking or pleasant fictions. To be able to enter into the world of the dead and to return is critical to our growth as individuals and as a society. It is important that those who act as *psychopomps* be able to transmit this knowledge in a manner that allows continuity with the past and not seek a complete, and thereby artificial, break from it. Only death conveys immortality and adepthood. Only meditation on our personal death, and meditations that involve going through all of the stages of death and experiencing the emotional reactions that accompany each stage, can prepare us for our inevitable death and initiation (either while alive or at the moment of death) into the ranks of the adepti.

It is during our death process that we come to fully realize the importance of our esoteric experiences, of the use of the Body of Light, and the power of Assumption of the Godform, as well as the direct Assumption of the Cosmos. Then and only then can we say that we have realized anything as an esotericist. It is hoped that by now readers will have realized that the methods in this book are a seamless set of teachings and practices designed to progressively illuminate us, so that we may both live and die fully awake. Through the power of our own consciousness, of our own efforts, and of our own being, we realize that we are self-created beings.

The words of Jean Marques-Rivere state it best: "[This is] the essential teaching of Egyptian esotericism as well as that of the Greeks: the knowledge of states after death, in order that to overcome fear of this death, psychological, and human fear. The initiate had knowledge of what awaited him; what could he be afraid of?"[1]

Memory and Immortality

True death does not always happen with the end of the physical body. For many, death comes while the body still lives. The brain dies slowly and with it the traces of a life lived, or our memories. The fear of forgetting is so profound that many would prefer actual physical death to living with the knowledge that they will slowly forget who they are and what they have done on this earth. Alzheimer's disease is a perfect example of this kind of living death, and it is a painful experience for anyone who has had to witness it.

Memory is the link we have with the past, and it alone forms the continuity we call life. Without memory, it is as if something or someone never existed. In *Meditations on the Tarot: A Journey into Christian Hermeticism*, the author states that there are three kinds of memory:

mechanical, intellectual, and moral. Mechanical memory is the memory of the body and brain.[2] It is strongest in youth. Intellectual memory is developed from the ability to think and solve problems, to make connections between ideas. Moral memory is the strongest of the three and is the only one linked to the soul, in that *moral memory is the memory born of deep emotion*. The deeper we feel about an experience, person, or place, the more permanent it is for us. For this reason alone we can see the importance of artistic, devotional, and emotive forms of worship and creativity if we are to truly awaken our immortality through the use of memory.

The Egyptians erected massive monuments to their dead and developed the most intricate cult of the dead the world has ever seen. It was thought that through keeping the memory of ancestors alive not only those ancestors could guide the living, but also that they would exist in a sort of otherworldly state where their personalities would survive.

Dreams are our gateway to this other world while we still live. Through dreams, we can communicate with the gods and other beings and get a hint of what awaits us in death. Tibetan Buddhism is replete with practices under the heading of dream yoga that are designed to increase one's gradual state of lucidity and clarity in the dream state. Similar practices exist in Western esotericism and, like their Tibetan counterparts, can eventually lead to lucid dreaming, astral projection, and a complete experience of the dying process while still incarnate. Key to all of these practices is increasing the ability of the practitioners to remember their experiences, so as to be able to transfer information between the dense physical world and the subtle realms of the psychic.

Emphasis on the development of memory has always been on being able to remember what was done in a dream state upon awakening. This continuity allows for an extended state of consciousness or sense of being. This directional emphasis is a result of our being here on earth and seeking some sense of security regarding our mortal nature. Equally important is our ability to transfer information and skills from our material domain into the psychic. This allows for a continuity of consciousness and also fulfills the very reason we have taken human existence to begin with.

What Did We Come Here to Find?

It is critical that we ask ourselves the most important question there is: why live at all? According to alchemy, the answer is that the physical world exists so that we can develop our consciousness through the sequences of the experiences physical life offers. Through these experiences we develop our free will. Among the things we came here to develop is personal and direct experience of our authentic "self." Only by the experiences offered through physical incarnation—its limitations, struggles, friction, and density—can we discover it.

Our Higher Self (Binah-Hockmah-Kether) of qabala has access to all the knowledge of nature, but is unable to use it because it does not possess the necessary mental and intellectual functions possessed by the Middle Self. Individuals must acquire these functions through work and effort and give these functions to themselves as working tools for consciousness. For example, if we dream, or if during an astral projection we see a written document, we find that for a long time we are unable to read it. It is the same for numbers as simple addition or subtraction. Over time this changes, as does our awareness of the invisible worlds. The things acquired by the brain of the earth must be transmitted, as a function, to our inner self as well, and thus the faculty of reading or adding in the astral world appears. As one authority put it:

> The brain of the earth is the school teacher of the Inner Master,
> but there is from the part of the Inner Master a concern to help
> the self of the earth in this work. However, languages being dif-
> ferent, communication can only happen through one symbol or
> a series of symbols. So, progressively the transfer of the work of
> the brain of the earth allows direct conversation to become pos-
> sible and this is an important phase of the Initiation which
> authorizes us to draw from Universal Knowledge what is neces-
> sary for our Growth.[3]

Just as our Higher Self needs and wants to communicate information to our waking brain, it also needs the mechanisms of the waking brain to make use of that information. The progressive dissolving of the barriers between sleep and wakefulness is an important step in developing a powerful memory that aids in the transfer of knowledge between the instinctual energies of the soul and waking experiences of material life.

The Seeds of Life and the Seeds of Death

Qabala seeks to open the interior world through the power of symbol, ritual, and devotion. Alchemy seeks to open the invisible world through understanding the fundamental essence of the physical domain. This fundamental essence, being identical in all areas of consciousness and activity, only different in expression, is found in the hermetic axiom, "As above, so below; as below, so above." In fact, alchemists know that if they are able to achieve some kind of exceptional experience, or even a transmutation, it is only because they have achieved an inner evolution first. The outer experiences and the inner experience reinforce, support, and guide one another.[4]

The essence alchemists seek to work with in the various kingdoms (plant, mineral, and animal) is the Quintessence, or the perfect balancing of the Elements, or qualities and expressions of energy and matter. This Quintessence has within it, or more rightly can be said to be, the Seed of Life. Through this Seed of Life, all alchemical healing and transformation takes place. Counter to it is the Seed of Death. Matter is meant for a purpose, and that purpose is progressive experiences that lead to the evolution of both matter and consciousness. If death is not present, then material life would be eternal, and progress could not be made.

However, alchemy recognizes that the "normal" process of evolution used by nature takes billions of years. Through the careful study and imitation of nature, alchemy (like others systems) can speed up the terrestrial time involved in the evolution of consciousness. To do this, practices are undertaken that seek to demonstrate the ever-present powers of the Seed of Life and to transform the Seeds of Death into useful energies and tools.

Everything we eat, drink, and breathe contains a small portion of "death" within it. As these seeds accumulate, our hold on physical life eventually weakens, and we die. In practical laboratory work these "seeds" can be seen in some of the final oils that float on top of red wine when it is being distilled for use in spagyric tinctures. However, in alchemy, toxic energies, be they mineral or emotions, are not evil or bad, only very powerful and possibly chaotic. When properly understood and utilized, they can give us tremendous energy for our journey. In doing so, we transmute the Seed of Death into the Seed of Life. In this, we understand what is meant by Jesus Christ having descended into hell to preach to the demonic and fallen spirits and the apostolic statement, "I have the keys over hell and death." Peter, or *Petros*, the foundation stone of the Christian church, is seen as holding the keys to the kingdom. These keys are also found on the Hierophant tarot card, also known as the Pope, and on the papal coat of arms and flag.[5]

I am the Resurrection and the Life. Whosoever believeth in me, though he were dead, yet shall he live; and whosoever liveth and believeth in me, the same shall never die. I am the First and I am the Last. I am He that liveth and was dead—and behold! I am alive forever more, and hold the keys of hell and of death.[6]

It is interesting that Peter is the "rock" upon which Jesus said he would build his church. Esoterically this stone represents the light of inner perception (Peter said, "You are the Christ") as well as the foundation stone, or Yesod, on the Tree of Life.

Meditation, Sleep, Sex, and Death

It is stated that the clarity of mind experienced in meditation is similar, if not identical, to the clarity of mind we experience just before we fall asleep, for a split second after orgasm, and during the death process. The relationship between death and sleep is so well established that we have even used the term "eternal rest" as a euphemism for death. The relationship between sex and death is described in detail in various texts on yoga and the French term—*l'petite morte*, or "the little death," which refers to the act of orgasm. The fundamental relationship between sexual, creative, and psychic energies is well known in alchemy and qabala and is the primary reason for the development of periods of sexual restraint, and even renunciation, so that sufficient physical energy is available for ritualistic and alchemical work. The primary reason is simple: the sexual fluids are the most powerful force we have available to us. With proper nutrition and care, a single egg and sperm cell can grow to create a human body. For males, however, there is tremendous waste involved in sexual activity—an activity designed primarily to continue the existence of the human race. While only one sperm is needed to accomplish the task, millions are wasted in the process. This waste of energy is said to be slowly debilitating and depleting.[7] Here again, we see the idea that within the very Seed of Life is planted the Seed of Death so that change, evolution, and progress can continue.

Death in Qabala

In qabala, when we die the etheric body gives up its claim to the physical; in fact, the polarity that initially allowed, and even forced, the spiritual energies into matter has now been reversed. As such, the strong attraction to matter no longer exists and the spiritual energies are progressively ejected from the physical body. The body itself is a manifestation of dense energy, and eventually breaks down and returns to the energetic level. As each of the etheric Elements withdraws, their physical counterparts cease to function, and the dying process is underway. When the dissolution of the Elements is complete, only a little energy will remain in the heart area, connecting the consciousness to the body, thereby allowing a focal point of stability amidst the difficult process of physical death. This focal point in the psychic heart is what is used as the basis for all death practices. When this last remaining connection to the physical body is ejected, the actual journey into the invisible, with its choices of continuing onwards to the Nothingness or preparing for rebirth, begins.

Once this ejection occurs, the consciousness will be drawn to experience the invisible world in one of three principal ways: the Path of Air, the Path of Water, and the Path of Fire. These paths are the three lower paths leading to physical life on the Tree of Life. The Path of Air is the most common, the Path of Water the next common, and the Path of Fire the least chosen. The path we take is a reflection of our deepest held values while in life and our desire to create balance and harmony within consciousness. For someone skilled in esoteric practices there is the possibility of a choice in which path they will take.

The Path of Air

In Qabala, the thirty-second path of the Tree of Life is the pathway linking the material to the lowest levels of the psychic. Often called "the Great One of the Night of Time," it reflects the vastness of creation. The material sphere has several titles given to it that reflect the transient nature of material life, as well as the idea that to take on material consciousness, is, in some fashion, to "die" temporarily in a psychic sense. In The Mystical Qabala, Dion Fortune lists several of these titles, which include the Gate, the Gate of Tears, the Gate of the Shadow of Death, the Gate of Death, the Gate of the Garden of Eden, the Gate of Justice, and the Gate of Prayer. These titles could as easily apply to the thirty-second path, as well as the sphere, given its function as a conduit of energy and consciousness between the visible and invisible worlds.

The Path of Air is the most common path undertaken at the time of death. It is often experienced as a tunnel of gray-blue color (the color of the mineral antimony used in alchemy for purification), yet is very luminous and bright as if lit from within. The symbol of this path is the Hebrew letter Tau, also written in its most primitive form as either an X or equal-armed cross. It is for this reason that we find the symbolism of meeting points and crossroads in particular as being given psychic or occult significance. Through them it is sometimes hoped that entry into the invisible can be experienced.

For persons who has had little or no significant spiritual training, or are practitioners of one or more of the larger religious movements that encourages devotion but does not supply the tools for direct personal experience, this is the path they will choose. It will be comforting because it is filled with the thought forms they have created while alive and that are reinforced by similar thought forms of fellow believers— and in this manner is not very different from material life. It is a comforting path and good for those who want an easy transition.

It is also here that they can experience great terrors if they believe themselves to have sinned or done immoral or unethical acts in life, as their entire cosmology is present in this the sphere of illusions. They experience a complete and total projection of their deepest held subconscious beliefs, alive and present around them. Here the dying person will meet judgment, their idea of God, good and evil, or anything else that has been an important driving force while alive. In esoteric circles, this experience is also called the Guardian of the Threshold.

If one has been inwardly devoted and sincere, then the transition will be easy and they will enter their vision of heaven. If they have been an average person, they will experience some remorse, but will experience the power of forgiveness and love and move on. Others may feel that they deserve to be punished and place themselves in self-imposed exile in their vision of purgatory or hell. After a while, a time frame that has little meaning in the material world, they will move on and into the higher aspects of these self-created illusions, thereby preparing for their return to material life.

The Path of Water

The twenty-ninth path of the Tree of Life is the Path of Water. It is called "the Child of the Sons of the Mighty" and refers to the path taken by heroes into the Elysian fields in classical antiquity. This path is described as being very lush, green, and filled with natural beauty and wonders. It is a pleasant path and very enjoyable and invigorating, but the influences of Venus limit this path and make it one of a higher illusion than the Path of Air. For those who have experienced great pain and suffering in life, this path is often the one chosen. It is the reward for those who sacrificed, for the many, the paradise of the earthly delights. In this path, the memories of human life are erased, leaving only the seed ideas of lessons learned to ease the consciousness of those who travel it. In doing so, they are not burdened by painful emotions in their return journey to earth. This path requires that those who take it return to the physical world to complete unfinished business.

The Path of Fire

The thirtieth path of the Tree of Life is the Path of Fire, also called "the Last Judgment." This path is the path of the alchemist, the qabalist, or anyone who has experienced contact with their spiritual consciousness while incarnate. This path leads to the Sphere of Splendor on the Pillar of Rigor and is concerned with the nature of form and materializing energies. Whereas the Path of Water links to the energies of pleasure to ease consciousness into a state of relaxation and sleep, the Path of Fire links to energies of purification and increased wakefulness. The purifying aspects also make it a path chosen by those who have lived a lazy and debauched life and have inwardly felt unable to move towards a balanced lifestyle—or as Jesus said, "The spirit is willing but the flesh is weak." For this reason, it is often confused with the idea of hell and punishment rather than purification and balance. This way is a true occult path, and the Path of Light ("hell" is derived from the Old German word for "concealed"). It is the only path that offers us conscious memory during the after-life experiences and up to and including our rebirth. By taking this path, we can ensure that we will consciously have an opportunity to survive the Second Death, or the death of the ego.

Whereas the Path of Air is concerned with self-reflection, judgment, and evaluation after death has already been experienced, and the Path of Water is concerned with easing the emotional burdens of certain aspects of consciousness, the Path of Fire is concerned with releasing any excessive pull of matter and entering into a state of wakefulness or genuine spiritual illumination. From the perspective of qabala, this is the only path that allows for the following choices: (1) rebirth with full consciousness or (2) rejection of rebirth and movement towards the Nothingness.

The Second Death

The Second Death is mentioned in many texts, but rarely explained. In the Book of Revelation, or the Apocalypse, in the New Testament, it is said, "They shall wear a white stone upon their head, and will not taste of the second death." Just as we pass through one barrier or veil between the material and psychic worlds, we all pass through another barrier between the psychic and the world of archetypes or ideas. The third and final veil is between the world of ideas and that of pure consciousness. Each of these veils forms a kind of abyss or gulf between the two worlds it stands between, but also acts as a great synthesizer of all the previous experiences that are transferred to the world that consciousness is moving towards.

In the passing from the material to psychic world there is a progressive distillation of life experiences that takes place, thereby creating the context for one's experiences in the invisible. Just as this distillation of experiences and lessons learned happens between the physical and psychic, so does it happen again between each of the other worlds, until everything is assimilated and understood and pure consciousness alone exists. This progressive digestion of images, emotions, and experiences is what allows us to grow as Beings.

By rejecting the Second Death, we avoid the erasure of memories, as experienced in the Path of Water, and are able to make a conscious decision as to what we will do rather than an unconscious one (the unconscious choice symbolized by the Wheel of Fortune in the tarot trumps). We become the master of our destiny, of our consciousness. We are the incarnation of the paths and as such, the light bearers, awakened, illuminated, and fully responsible for ourselves and our own unfoldment.

Those who take the Path of Air or the Path of Water experience the Second Death as they enter into bliss and illumination in the Sphere of Beauty. Here, inner and outer harmony reign, and peace fills the consciousness of those who experience it. During the return to material life, this experience may be vaguely remembered and act as the seed for a spiritual life, or it may be slowly forgotten, and simply act as one's conscience, helping to guide one towards actions that are harmonious. Sometimes it may be heard as the voice of intuition, but more often as a vague feeling.

In this way our conscience is really like attuning to a radio station. When we are acting in accordance with those things that remind us of our experience in the Sphere of Beauty, we feel happy and expansive. When we act in a manner that takes us away from that distant memory of bliss, we feel disturbed. In this way, the experience between lives helps to act as an unconscious guiding force to remind us of our spiritual origins.

Qabala and the Invisible Worlds

According to qabala, upon death we leave the physical world, shedding our physical body, and our consciousness ascends into the invisible world of Yetzirah. This journey takes place in several stages. The first is identical to the alchemical path, in that the Elements that compose our body break down, and the control of the mind over the life force itself is relinquished. Earth collapses into Water; Water collapses into Air (or Fire); Air collapses into Fire; and finally, Fire dissolves into the pure energy of Spirit that unites them. This final stage is nearly identical to the one that follows it, or the withdrawal of energy into Yesod. As the energy withdraws, the consciousness accompanies it. This collapsing of the energies is the withdrawing of the vital energy of the etheric and lower astral body (Nefesh) from the physical body, so that the latter might disintegrate and return to the matter from which it was formed. This process is a slow one, and during it a variety of visual, auditory, and emotional experiences are had that are both psychic, and physical in nature.

Once freed from the material body, the consciousness of the Middle Self (Ruach) is destabilized as it enters a new environment, unless there has been significant training in meditation, lucid dreaming, astral projection, creating the Body of Light, or practices around death and dying prior to one's death. This new level of consciousness can easily be a confusing and frightening experience as well. For this reason, the spiritual seed or the Higher Self (Neshamah) will create for itself a simulacrum or projection of a spiritual being, such as an angel, god, master, or loved one, to help escort the newly deceased through the rough transition period of death. Some even suggest that the Higher Self, or an individual's Holy Guardian Angel, creates a sort of psychic shell around the newly released ego.

It is important to note that this guide is none other than the Higher Self, assisting the Middle Self back into the spiritual world. The ego unconsciously creates a variety of personalities to deal exclusively with material life, and during life these personalities can become so habitual that the ego forgets that they are a tool and not reality. It is identical to an actor who becomes so caught up in a role that he forgets that he is an actor and not the role. When these roles, personalities or subpersonalities are no longer needed, as in the invisible realms the ego feels threatened. Even if the ego is capable of transitioning into the astral dimensions without this problem, it may still have a significant enough sense of independence to keep it from fully entering into the spiritual realms. This kind of trauma is the cause of individuals becoming earth bound and the source of hauntings.

The Second Death

The Second Death, however, is tricky, in that it requires that we surrender our astral or emotional-psychic structures. If this is done, and all who take the thirty-first and twenty-ninth paths do it unconsciously, we have to rebuild them during our next incarnation.

The paths traversing the worlds of Yetzirah to Briah, specifically leading to the experience of bliss and light that Tiphareth brings, bring with them the Second Death. It must be clear that here we are talking of the sepheroth, or spheres of the Tree of Life, according to the pattern of four worlds, one Tree. If we opt to stay in the realm of Yetzirah, we find that our experience will take on a specific environment equivalent to the sepherah or level of our development. As such, we may attain to a strong Jupiter or Saturn development, but it will be specific to the world of Yetzirah.

Once in the Briactic World, our astral vehicles are destroyed, and we exist as a being of pure light. This is equivalent to the yogic doctrine of enlightenment, but not a perfect enlightenment. It is also temporary and brings a sense of balance to our being, but not a permanent readjustment in consciousness. Only through our own efforts and personal interior initiation can that be achieved.

When we leave this solar domain, we begin to take on emotional, then mental characteristics, and finally, instinctual attractions to the material realm and rebirth. We have with us specific expressions of consciousness, as illustrated in our natal chart, as well as potential expressions and areas we can best direct our attention towards. The birth chart represents the moment of birth and is limited to being a mirror of the energies present in our incarnation at that moment; it reflects and indicates future potential, but does not dictate.

Alchemy and the Stages of Dying

The alchemical Elements of Earth, Water, Air, Fire, and their absorbing into Spirit, are identical to the Elements presented in Tibetan Buddhism. In the Tibetan Book of the Dead it is said that after the dissolution of the Elements, consciousness goes through three distinct phases of white, red, and black.

Phase	Alchemy	Qabala	Tibetan Tantra	Results
Four Elements dissolving into Spirit	Black stage	Malkooth	Dissolution of the Elements	Death of the physical and etheric bodies
Awakening in the subconscious	White stage	Yesod	White stage	Death of the personality
Awakening into self-awareness	Red stage[8]	Tiphareth	Red stage	Death of the ego
Stabilizing and realization of pure Being	Multiplication of the Philosopher's Stone[9]	Daath[10]	Black stage and clear light	Illumination and new birth

The Inner Name

"Behold the servant of the Lord, I will do according to your Word."
—LUKE 1:38

This solar domain, or the experience of a centralized life force, is also the source of the energy that becomes matter for the material world. As we move away from its intense magnetic field, irregularities arise, and these form the imprint of our horoscope, or unique expression of consciousness we project. Another expression of these irregularities is in our personal Elemental balance, or ordering of the basic building blocks of creation.

This gives rise to the notion of the lost word, or inner name, that each of us carries within us and seeks to discover, for in doing so we find a direct means of expressing the centralized life force we moved away from—or, more accurately, were pushed from.

This ordering of the Elements takes its origin in the primordial being, or *Adam* (Hebrew for "man" or "first being"). When Adam "fell," he is said, in some traditions, to have fallen into pieces. Those pieces combine to form variations of the Original Being, or expressions of consciousness. The First Ordering was *Yod-Heh-Vau-Heh* and corresponds to the astrological sign of Aries, a tribe of Israel, and a disciple of Christ. These twelve archetypes form the basic personality types of all humanity. Each of us will go through each permutation of these types at least once and, as some suggest, 144 times. This, however, is a symbolic number. It is theoretically possible that one being may have perfected themselves in 12 or 144 incarnations, but it is unlikely that this is the path of the majority. This does give us some insight into how we can assess our place on the Path of Return. If we have a proper ordering of the divine names and discover our own inner name, then we can estimate how many incarnations we have left, from between one and twelve. This being said, the closer we are to the final destination, the less likely we will care about such a thing, and it is only of interest and use to us alone.

Discussing our inner name, or other esoteric names that we may receive or discover, with others is dangerous in that it inflates the ego. If this inner name or any additional name is revealed, it is best understood by working with it in meditation rather than analysis or discussion. When our name is discovered, we no longer need to act or invoke in the name of God, the angels, Christ, or some invisible beings, but instead can act in our own name, for our "name," or worldly personality, and inner name are united.

As a substitute for this inner name, esoteric students and religionists alike use the names of saints, sacred people, angels, and archangels to comfort themselves in times of distress. During death, if our inner name is not known, we may use the name of someone spiritually special to us to assist in focusing our mind for the journey.

Death and Initiation

It is this Second Death and the resurrection of the human consciousness into a more distinct and clear form that the great initiatic traditions of Freemasonry and Rosicrucianism are based on. Rooted in the Egyptian traditions, these modern and contemporary expressions of initiation share a similarity with their ancient predecessors. For this reason, some schools refer to death as the Great Initiation.

In schools of initiation of a Christian character, or that have been heavily influenced by the forms, symbols, and doctrines of the Roman Catholic Church, each of the seven sacraments is attributed to one of the spheres of the Tree of Life and, through it, a planetary influence. Death corresponds to Saturn, and the Rite of Extreme Unction or Last Rites, as they were previously called.

As an esoteric practice, we can assist the dying who have come from a Christian background or an esoteric background rooted in Christian tradition with a simple ritual, prayer, and readings of the Psalms or sections of the New Testament. This is a de facto recognition of the importance of death as the final step in our earthly journey as we travel on the Path of Return and of the profound power of faith as represented by Jesus Christ and the communion of saints, regardless of an exoteric religious significance placed on them by more doctrinal authorities.

Death Trumps Us All

The thirteenth card of the tarot's Major Arcana is Death, typically portrayed as a skeleton wielding a scythe and standing on ground spotted with the heads of nobility and peasant alike. This card has come to be associated with the sign of Scorpio, the Hebrew letter Nun, and the twenty-fourth path of the Tree of Life, which leads from Netzach to Tiphareth. It is easy to interpret this trump in a simplistic fashion, either literally as physical death or in a more abstract way as transformation, change, and the creation of new forms. A careful look at various decks shows the skeleton of death with a scythe. However, as Aleister Crowley points out in *The Book of Thoth*, Saturn has no direct relationship to the sign of Scorpio, making the symbol somewhat anachronistic according to qabalistic iconography. Long associated with Saturn, the planet of fundamental essence, the scythe points to the real purpose and power of death—the revealing of the elemental, unchanging nature of Being. Scorpio is also the second most powerful sign in the Zodiac, behind Leo, making this card "of greater importance and catholicity than would be expected from the plain Zodiacal attribution. It is even a compendium of universal energy in its most secret form."[11]

Oswald Wirth, the father of the modern tarot, states that there is a connection between the thirteenth trump and the fourth trump, or the Emperor. Wirth states that whereas the Emperor signifies alchemical Sulphur, or the power of individuation and life, Death signifies the setting free of these energies that have become not extinguished, but instead "overwhelmed by the weight of Matters increasing inertia."

Far from killing, Death revives by disassociating what can no longer live. If it were not for the intervention of Death everything would wilt, so that life finally would not be distinguishable from the common image of Death. So, it is quite right that Arcana 13 should relate to the active generator of Universal life, permanent life, of which Temperance (Arcana 14) symbolizes the moving dynamism, whereas the Devil (Arcana 15) shows its static accumulation. The profane must die to be born to the superior life which initiation confers.[12]

To know how to die is therefore the great secret of the Initiated, for by dying he frees himself from what is inferior to rise through sublimation . . . This voluntary death is demanded of the Freemason so that he can say that he is "born free" as he strikes the door of the Temple. The symbolism [is] . . . what his passage through the funeral cave, called the Room [Chamber] of Reflection, signifies.[13]

Key Points

- Meditation, lucid dreaming, and astral projection practices are to indirectly prepare us for our ultimate initiation—the death experience.

- Death has similarities to sleep and sex—similarities that allow us to use those experiences in preparing for our death.

- Only practices specifically designed to prepare us for death, however, have the directness of purpose that can allow us to deeply prepare for our death.

- By preparing ourselves for our personal death, we can learn how to assist others during—and after—their dying process.

- There are several paths open to us at the time of death. Through esoteric practices we are able to consciously chose which path we will take.

- The Second Death is the loss of self-consciousness and the dissolution of the astral body. Some schools suggest means of avoiding this experience so that the astral body does not have to be recreated.

- The stages of death in Tibetan yoga have a strong resemblance to the stages of transmutation in mineral alchemy.

- If we do not have a spiritual master or guide in life to assist us when we die, we need to rely upon our inner self, or Holy Guardian Angel. If we have not made strong contact with our inner self, we can rely on historical and inspirational teachers such as Jesus or even angels and archangels.

Assignments for Chapter Nine

1. Read one of the books from the Reading List on death from an esoteric perspective.

2. Perform each of the following exercises for at least one week until all of them have been completed. You may take one week off between exercises because of their serious nature.

3. Integrate one of the practices into your weekly practice schedule.
Pay attention to any changes within yourself, including your
attitude towards daily experiences and how it has changed
since beginning this practice. Keep track of it in your notebook.

Practices and Meditations :
Exercise One: Preparing for the Unexpected

Preparation

Prepare in any manner you deem suitable.

Explanation

Death can come at any time. Our preparedness for its arrival is important. While this doesn't mean that we should obsess about the natural
uncertainty of life, we should prepare for ourselves a certain amount of
"death insurance" within our psyche so that should we die suddenly and
without notice, we will not be caught unguarded on the other side.[14]
This process can also be done for another as a thought form, which
assists someone who is not even familiar with the process, but who, like
everyone, is in need of an afterlife game plan to aid their transition from
material to spiritual consciousness. This process is analogous to the
Middle Path, or the Path of Air.

Type of Practice

This exercise imprints specific images and ideas into our psychic body for
activation in the event of an untimely death. In addition, it can help us
transmute certain fears and anxieties we may have around the idea of our
death, thereby allowing us to be better prepared for both living and dying.

Method

1. Pick a time and place that you enjoy and imagine yourself there. This will act as a transitional "waiting room" to assist you in adjusting to your new existence. You may be as you are now, younger, or as you would like to be.

2. It is helpful to have in mind someone who is meaningful to come and greet you. This can be one person such as a spiritual teacher, a friend, parent, lover, pet, or simply someone you have never met (such as a famous figure) but who you have picked to assist you at this time of death.

3. Imagine that you take a short walk with your guide to somewhere special. This can be a house, a grove, or anywhere you would like to meet up with your friends and family who have passed on, or who are even still alive, and assisting you at the time of your death.

4. Imagine that this gathering is in honor of your having arrived on the other side, and they are welcoming you.

5. Greet each person there and proceed to go to a room or location set aside just for you. Take a rest and know that everything and everyone will be there to meet you and assist you in your transition when you are ready.

6. With the beginning and end point of your visualization firmly in place, freeze the story, and affirm to yourself that this pathworking will activate in the event of your sudden and unforeseen death.

7. When you are done, stand up, ring a small bell or stamp your foot, and become clearly present in the material world.

Incorporation into Daily Practice

Once completed, this exercise need not be repeated.

Exercise Two: Qabalistic Meditation on Personal Death

Preparation

Prepare in any manner you deem suitable.

Explanation

This exercise imprints symbols and ideas into the subconscious so that at the moment of our death we may consciously die, as well as be reborn, through the paths leading to and from the Pillar of Severity.

Type of Practice

This practice imprints and activates symbols and ideas into our psychic body and consciousness for use at the time of death. In addition, it further strengthens our understanding of the qabalistic paths proceeding from Malkuth and can assist us preparing for our personal death, as well as transmute fears and anxieties the practitioner may have around death.

Method

1. Experience the dissolution of the Elementals as your Earth center (the perineum) dissolves into your Water center (the sexual center, at the public bone). Feel your Water center dissolve into your Fire center (slightly below the heart or solar plexus). Feel your Fire center dissolve into your Air center (the throat), and finally, Air into Spirit (the crown). There is still a thin line of psychic energy connecting you to your physical body at the level of the heart. Sense the Elemental colors of red, blue, yellow, and green flashing brilliantly from your psychic heart and a deep sense of bliss and peace pervading your consciousness. You may also add their complimentary colors and white, the color of spirit, which binds them all.

2. There is momentary blackness (Black Stage) as you pass into the white light of the lunar realm. The color may transition to a blue-gray before the white. You may imagine your master, teacher, or a divine being (such as Hermes, Anubis, or Jesus) there to assist you. It is important that you realize this being is a projection of your mind created to assist you and not an objective reality. Focus on this being to the exclusion of all other images or sensations that might arise. Stabilize your consciousness.

3. Imagine that there is a path of brilliant flame before you. This fire arches up and forms a canopy. Even the ground is brilliant orange and red coals. The heat is intense and penetrates your consciousness, purifying your Body of Light.

4. Walk down the path, absorbing the heat and flame, becoming overjoyed at its intensity and the feeling of newfound strength and focus that it gives you.

5. Enter into the Temple of Splendor (Hod). This may be imagined as a simple fountain in the middle of an eight-pointed star made of two intertwined squares. The star is blue, and the tile floor it rests on is orange. The fountain is of a similar shape, and its water sparkles with luminous light. This is where the Waters of Wisdom are kept, and by drinking of them, we come to understand our reason for being. An orange priestess may hand you the cup with which you drink, or you may simply use your hand as a cup. If you are greeted, all that much better. You may pause here for a while, but do not tarry.

6. Leave the Temple of Hod and continue towards the brilliant sun. Do this by entering into the underworld. Pass into a void, or darkness, noticing that you also feel that you are not alone and that all around you is power, energy, and life. This void is both expansive and confining. You move through it, absorbing its dual nature of expansion and contraction, of pure life energy.

7. As you leave the void, you enter into the luminous Sphere of Harmony, of the Sun. You pass into the Solar Temple. This is a brilliant, luminous, white, gold, and yellow domain with a central

point that awakens within you a sympathetic resonance. These expanding heats, warmth, love, and harmony permeates your being. Rest in this feeling for a while.

8. If you have a specific time, place, and location wherein you would like to reincarnate, perform the following before returning. State your intention in a clear, simple, and declarative tone, visualizing the key point—your chosen goal or life mission—as you mentally make your affirmation. Example: "It is my desire to reincarnate in a life wherein I can most quickly, efficiently, and meaningfully express my inner creative powers as a concert pianist." If you like, you can even be more specific and name a city, state, country, or persons you would like to return with. Of course, this technique of deciding a life can also be used to further your esoteric studies as well.

9. Now, either return the way you came or, if you are an experienced qabalist, use the formula of the Rising on the Planes in its descent mode to return.

10. If you are returning by the reverse Path, re-enter the void, feeling it being impregnated with the seed thought form you created of your future life. Return to the Temple of Splendor, drink again, this time of the Well of Memory, so that you remember your expanded states while incarnate, thereby bringing the worlds closer together. Descend through the tunnel of Fire and return to your body.

11. When you are done, breathe deeply, stand up, ring a small bell or stamp your foot, and become clearly present in the material world.

Incorporation into Daily Practice

This exercise can be done daily, or weekly, as part of your regular practice program. It is important, however, that it be done regularly, as a means of consciously preparing for one's personal death.

Exercise Three: Simplified Alchemical Meditation on Personal Death

Preparation

Prepare in any manner you deem suitable.

Explanation

This practice takes you through the stages of dissolution of the Elements, as understood alchemically, and into the various phases of death as understood from an alchemical perspective. This practice is the basis for several more that follow.

Type of Practice

This practice imprints and activates symbols and ideas into our psychic body and consciousness for use at the time of death. In addition, it further strengthens our understanding of the alchemical process and can transmute fears and anxieties we may have around death.

Method

1. Experience the dissolution of the Elementals as your Earth center (the perineum) dissolves into your Water center (the sexual center, at the public bone). Feel your Water center dissolve into your Fire center (slightly below the heart or solar plexus). Feel your Fire center dissolve into your Air center (the throat), and finally, Air into Spirit (the crown). There is still a thin line of psychic energy connecting you to your physical body at the level of the heart. Sense the Elemental colors of red, blue, yellow, and green flashing brilliantly from your psychic heart and a deep sense of bliss and peace pervading your consciousness. You may also add their complimentary colors and white, the color of Spirit, which binds them all.

2. There is momentary blackness (Black Stage) as you pass into the white light of the lunar realm. The color may transition to a blue-gray before the white. You may imagine your master, teacher, or a divine being (such as Hermes, Anubis, or Jesus) there to assist you. It is important that you realize this being is a projection of your mind, created to assist you, and not an objective reality. Focus on this being to the exclusion of all other images or sensations that might arise.

3. Move through the whiteness to the Red Stage of the Solar Light. Here you join with the being and become it, and your psychic body is pervaded with a red or pinkish light.

4. Now there is a period of darkness (first multiplication) followed by a clear light of the morning sky (second multiplication, or Chesed on the Tree of Life, Jupiter, the Sky God).

5. This is followed by a sense of great bliss and peace as the remaining energies of the heart are released, and all connection to the material world is severed. Rest in this peace.

6. When the impulse moves you—often point of light (sometimes blue) appears to indicate your readiness—feel yourself feel yourself moving from the abstract to the more concrete images of the psychic world. Using a divine image and Assumption of the Godform can strengthen this stage of the practice.

7. Maintain awareness of this expanded state, its expression through the godform you've reassumed. After a period of time, feel it become concrete, in and through your physical body. Rest in that expression of illumination as you sit in meditation, aware of the room around you, and of the insight attained.

8. When you are done, breathe deeply, stand up, ring a small bell or stamp your foot, and become clearly present in the material world.

9. Leave your meditation with a renewed sense of unity and that all sense of separateness, duality, or life and death are just illusions.

Incorporation into Daily Practice

This exercise can be done daily or weekly, as part of your regular practice program. It is important, however, that it be done regularly, as a means of consciously preparing for your personal death.

Exercise Four: The Importance of the Heart in the Work and the Union of the Solar King and Lunar Queen Stages

Preparation

Prepare in any manner you deem suitable.

Explanation

In alchemy, the Philosopher's Stone is confected when we balance the Elemental energies of our psychic heart. The heart is considered the location of consciousness in Egyptian cosmology. In Tibetan Buddhism, the heart is the key to unlocking the secret or inner fire, located at the navel, and is the center most focused on at the moment of death. It contains the mechanism to experiencing pure consciousness, just as the Philosopher's Stone contains the mechanism to uniting the inner and our worlds. A common symbol used for meditation in Tibet to represent this union will not be lost on practical alchemists: the union of the moon and sun and their conjoined white light with hints of red and pink. The wedding of the Solar King and Lunar Queen is the focal point of alchemical symbolism and, as demonstrated earlier, can be utilized in purification practices. The Star of David is also used to represent this union. The following meditation is taken directly from the alchemical stages. This meditation should be practiced regularly in preparation for death, but also as a means of more deeply and personally experiencing the alchemical path of personal transformation.

Type of Practice

This practice imprints and activates symbols and ideas into our psychic body and consciousness for use at the time of death. In addition, it further strengthens our understanding of the alchemical process and can transmute fears and anxieties we may have around death.

Method

Proceed as follows:

1. Experience the dissolution of the Elementals as your Earth center (the perineum) dissolves into your Water center (the sexual center, at the public bone). Feel your Water center dissolve into your Fire center (slightly below the heart or solar plexus). Feel your Fire center dissolve into your Air center (the throat), and finally, Air into Spirit (the crown). There is still a thin line of psychic energy connecting you to your physical body at the level of the heart. Sense the Elemental colors flashing brilliantly from your psychic heart and a deep sense of bliss and peace pervading your consciousness.

2. There is momentary blackness (Black Stage) as you pass into the brilliant white light of the lunar realm. You may imagine your master, teacher, or a divine being (such as Hermes, Anubis, or Jesus) there to assist you. It is important that you realize this is a projection of your mind, created to assist you, and not an objective reality. Focus on this being to the exclusion of all other images or sensations that might arise.

3. Move through the whiteness of the lunar realm to the Red Stage of the Solar Light. Using the technique of Assumption, you join with the being and become it, and your psychic body is pervaded with a red or pinkish light.

4. Now there is a period of darkness (first multiplication) followed by a clear light of the morning sky (second multiplication, or Chesed on the Tree of Life, Jupiter, the Sky God).[15] This is followed by a sense of great bliss and peace, as the energies of the heart are released and all connection to the material world is severed. Rest in this peace.

5. When it is time to return to earth, to assist others in your new found wisdom, practice reversing the current. Imagine the clear, luminous light reversing itself in its nature, moving from the abstract and becoming concrete in the form of the divine being who assisted you earlier. Remember, you are this being; you are expressing the Divine.

6. This concrete image, or godform, stays with you and becomes dense and physical as you move from the Red Stage back into the White Stage. It is the physical expression of the abstract in divine form. You are expressing the Divine not only in your psyche, but also into the world.

7. Imagine now that you are seated in your chair as this divine form and that all of your psychic centers are open and harmonious, starting at the crown and working down to the perineum.

8. Hold this image for a while and then arise.

9. When you are done, breathe deeply, stand up, ring a small bell or stamp your foot, and become clearly present in the material world.

10. Leave meditation with a renewed sense of unity and that all sense of separateness, duality, or life and death are just illusions.

Incorporation into Daily Practice

This exercise can be done daily or weekly, as part of your regular practice program. It is important, however, that it be done regularly, as a means of consciously preparing for your personal death. This practice is the complete process of the dissolution and creation of matter-consciousness in a single practice.

The Importance of the Teacher, Guide, or Friend in the Death Stage

We need to identify with this tradition for practical reasons—to have a boat when we cross the astral waters to the shore of primordial consciousness. The important role of a spiritual teacher or friend is to help you in death even more than in life. Many people report seeing friends, relatives, spiritual figures such as Jesus or Mary, during near-death experiences (NDEs). These people appear and help them adjust to the new environment. The role of comforter is critical at this time, as our thoughts create our experiences, and fear, anger, and attachments all can make it harder to move through the invisible realms.

However, we should not play dice with our death anymore than with our life, and picking our guide ahead of time is critical. If we are fortunate enough to have a good spiritual friend, then they will be there for us. If not, we need to pick one, even if it is a symbolic figure such as a saint, Jesus, or an archangel, so that we can transition easily. Now, it is important to know that these figures, even if real people who we know, in most instances, do not meet us in the invisible, but instead are projections of our own mind. This is okay, as the entire experience is a projection of our mind, only this projection, this person, gives us a focal point so that we can avoid the waves of chaos that seek to distract us.

If we can blend with this figure, just as we do in Assumption of the Godform, during our actual death experience, we can then move forward more easily. The ideal is to die either consciously in the Assumption of the Godform or as a being of pure light—as a self-created god.

Exercise Five: Meditation on the Teacher at the Time of Death

Preparation

Prepare in any manner you deem suitable.

Explanation

Death can be frightening for many people, and through their connection with a spiritual teacher, these fears can be significantly reduced. It is important that the person you use is one you have complete trust and confidence in. It is unimportant if they are alive or dead, as it is their spiritual essence you are attuning with.

Type of Practice

This practice imprints specific ideas and images, based on a specific relationship with your spiritual teacher, into your psyche for activation at the moment of death. This relationship can be a literal one or a spiritual one, using someone who you see as your ideal teacher.

Method

1. Prepare as usual. After the dissolution of the Elements, imagine that you are exiting out the crown of your head, into a brief blackness and then into brilliant light.
2. Imagine a large figure before you. It is your spiritual teacher, chosen divinity, an ideal teacher from the past, or a brilliant sphere of white light.
3. Using the technique of Assumption, merge with this figure.
4. Move along your chosen path as this being, or simply become a point of light.

Incorporation into Daily Practice

This exercise can be done daily or weekly, as part of your regular practice program. It is important, however, that it be done regularly, as a means of consciously preparing for your personal death. This practice can be done in conjunction with exercise one, so that should you die suddenly there will be a trigger mechanism to allow you to recognize your new state and move on.

CHAPTER 10

Assisting the Dying

For the experienced ritualist, certain qabalistic pathworkings on the Tree of Life can be used to assist the dying: the thirteenth and thirty-second in particular, but also the twelfth and eleventh, depending on the circumstances. However, it is best if we understand the nature of the death process firsthand through our own meditations, and thereby directly aid the dying with the power of our spoken word, psychic constructs, confidence, and compassion.

Practicing exercise five from chapter nine, of going through the death process, will greatly enhance your ability to assist others, to recognize the dissolution of the Elements as they are occurring, and to give calm, soothing, and confident guidance in either verbal or visualized form. If you are uncertain what to do, simply stay with the dying person and visualize their spiritual teacher or friend in the air before them, brilliant and radiating, extending rays of light from the upper psychic centers to the psychic centers of the dying person.

In the Roman Catholic Church one can often see pictures of Jesus painted to show one hand over his heart, the other pointing towards heaven, and rays of blue, red, and white light radiating from his heart. These colors are identical to those used in Tibetan Vajrayanna practices and even symbolize the same ideas of thought, speech, and action, or "thought, word, and deed," as mentioned in Zoroastrian, Jewish, and

Christian scriptures. They can easily be used here, seen radiating from either the heart of the friend or one each from each of the centers: white from the crown, red from the throat, and blue from the heart.

Students familiar with ritual may want to create a sacred space around the room for the dying person. The *Practice of the Six Directions* as described in *Kabbalah for Health and Wellness* is ideal for this work. However, a simple sphere of brilliant light will suffice. What is most important is that you sincerely desire to assist the person enter the invisible *and that in doing so*, they are able to maintain a clear and focused awareness with which to make their choices. This overriding desire and singleness of purpose is more important than all the rituals, symbols, or visualizations that can be devised.

The fundamental idea that they are at peace and that all attachments to this life are cleanly and smoothly released may be used to formulate the initial meditations, and when signs of life have ceased, there can be a transition to their experiencing a clear and focused consciousness with which to enter into the invisible.

It is most critical that the environment of the dying person be free from distractions, wailing, and the sights and sounds of upset relatives. These are only distractions and obstacles for the dying and anyone assisting them.

Helping the Dead

It is possible that we may not hear of someone's passing until after the fact. However, opportunities are still present for us to assist them in their journey. Since each will travel to their own spiritual level, or "mansion," at their own pace and each will reincarnate according to their innermost desires, it is beneficial to offer prayers and visualizations for the dead for up to forty days—the traditional period of mourning—after their death.

This is particularly beneficial to those who died young, suddenly, or as a result of violence or trauma. The ability to separate from physical life may not be as strong as they would like, and, as such, they may become what is commonly called earth bound. Even if they are not earth bound, they may find it difficult adjusting to their new environment, and any assistance will be helpful to them. It is also helpful for those who may have not had a firm spiritual life, those who had feelings of hostility towards spirituality because of actual or perceived errors in common religious teachings that prevented them from picking an inner path, or even those whom we often see as evil.

It is easy to pray for the consciousness of those we love or feel pity for, but to pray for those who have injured us or others, so that they may experience a release from their state of ignorance, is beneficial for everyone. If we are successful, they are bolstered in their after-death journey and have an opportunity to see clearly what they need to do to correct their errors, and we also release and transmute the damaging energies of anger, hate, and revenge that we will have to address in our own post-death journey.

Offerings of food to the deceased are common in Eastern cultures, as well as in Egyptian practices. While this is not necessary, the symbolism of an offering such as flowers, commonly used in modern burial practices, can also be used to bring great focus to the work.

Raising the Dead: Is It Possible?

Jewish and Christian scriptures are replete with examples of the dead being raised. While it would be possible to discuss these incidents as metaphors, similar to the dismemberment and resurrection of Osiris in Egyptian mythology, some instances clearly state that physical death is what was being overcome. In addition to resurrection, we also have the statement of bodily ascension or dissolution of the physical body of Moses and Jesus. Lore also states that Jesus' mother, Mary, as well as Mohammed and his horse, ascended bodily into heaven in a cloud.

More recent stories of these phenomena include that of Paul Sedir, a leading figure in the French occult revival during the late nineteenth and early twentieth centuries, witnessing the physical resurrection of a recently deceased woman. The story is retold by Mouni Sadhu in his book *Ways to Self-Realization* and summarized here.[1]

Paul Sedir (Yvon Le Loup) was born in 1871 and was a physician by profession, Sedir's greatest passion and fame came from his involvement with the many Martinist, Rosicrucian, and Masonic bodies in existence during the French occult revivial, a period spanning nearly seventy years, but whose high point was from approximately 1880 to 1914 and paralleled that of the hermetic Order of the Golden Dawn. The First World War put an end to European occultism, as many of its members were called off to serve in the trenches. Among them was one of Sedir's close associates, Gerard Encausse, better known as Papus and author of over seventy works on occultism. Papus died in 1916 of influenza while serving as a physician in French frontlines. There was a brief revival of European occultism in the 1920s and 1930s; however economic depression and the Second World War crushed any hopes of significant activities. It was in this milieu, in Paris, at the height of French occultism and the Belle Époque, that Sedir would experience his dark night of the soul and meet his spiritual master.

In his memoirs, Sedir writes that on a cold and rainy November evening, after returning from visiting patients, he laid down to catch some rest. Suffering from tuberculosis in one lung, he was experiencing nightly fevers and was filled with an intense emptiness, causing him to be indifferent to everything—even life itself. His bookshelves were empty. He had long since disposed of his library and resigned from his numerous positions in many of the leading esoteric bodies of the day—several which he had even helped establish. As Sedir prepared to retire for the evening, his doorbell rang. He immediately assumed it was a patient too destitute to pay another physician, as his reputation of never refusing a patient was well known.

The man at his door was a low-level official whose wife was dying of the same disease that scourged Sedir himself. Knowing that her hours were numbered, the man sought relief for his wife's suffering—the slow death of suffocation as her lungs filled with fluid. Sedir put on his coat, grabbed an umbrella, and followed the man into the bitter evening, towards his house in the Parisian suburbs. Sedir himself was still suffering from fever and intense chest pains as they walked through the wind and rain.

As they passed a dim street lamp, Sedir looked up and noticed a tall man, well built, wearing expensive clothes. On close examination, he appeared in his forties, with a deep tropical tan and piercing, yet peaceful eyes. When the pair came closer, the man addressed Sedir with great dignity and politeness, even going so far as to ask him if he was a physician on his way to see a patient! When this was confirmed, the stranger asked if he could accompany Sedir, saying that he may be able to help. Thinking that it could do no harm, as the woman was going to die shortly, if was not already dead, Sedir agreed.

Upon arriving at the man's home, they received the news that his wife had passed while he was gone in search of a doctor. Grief overtook the man as he saw his wife's waxy corpse, illuminated by two candles, one on either side of her head, and her two young children kneeling at the side of her deathbed.

The stranger had been silent, but now suggested that Sedir inspect the corpse. Sedir obliged out of courtesy, knowing well that the woman was dead—all that remained was a slight warmth around the solar plexus—and said that she had been dead for about one hour. This statement caused the stranger to almost smile at Sedir's credulity as he asked the grieving husband, "Do you want your wife alive? Will you swear to me now, that you will always be good to her, if she comes back?"

Sedir writes:

The poor man was astonished and almost afraid. "It is not possible! See for yourself! Surely she is dead." The voice of the stranger went on pitilessly: "I ask you only if you want to have her back again? And will you swear that she will never again suffer from your behavior?"

The man replied that he would take an oath on the Holy Cross, only that it was too late and he could not believe in the impossible.

Then the Unknown Man went close to the bed, took the head of the dead woman gently in his hands, bent down and whispered to her; but everyone in the room could hear his words clearly.

"My dear, my daughter, come back again, return, they need you. It will be favorably counted to you, this sacrifice which you make."

When we heard that whisper, there was no doubt in us but that she must rise from the dead. There was no power which could oppose the words of the Unknown. The dead woman immediately lifted her head and opened her eyes, looking around as though from another world. "I was dreaming,'" she whispered.

The Man ordered more lamps to be brought. The old lady and her son went out like automatons, and I felt that they did not yet believe what had happened before their eyes only seconds ago.

When they came back, holding large lamps in their hands, the woman, restored to life, sat up in bed, her face pressed close to the powerful arm of the Unknown, like a child seeking a secure place. She wept.

The Man then took both lamps in his hands and directed the light onto the face of the woman. Before my eyes, the flesh began to reappear under the skin of her cheeks, neck, and shoulders, and the whole complexion returned to its natural color, instead of that of a corpse, which I had seen only seconds ago.

The stranger informed Sedir that he was leaving Paris that evening for Saigon and that Sedir could accompany him if he wished. For eight hours they shared a private compartment, the stranger revealing to him all that had happened, why, and even what the future held. Yet what is most amazing about the stranger was not his level of erudition, fluency in a dozen languages, or even clairvoyance, but that in many ways, he was very human. He ate a normal meal and even offered Sedir a cigarette. Sedir refused, stating his lung condition, to which he received the reply, "Do you really feel there is something still wrong in your chest, dear doctor? Yes, my son, you are cured of your inner faults, so how could the physical ones resist being cured?"

The stranger never revealed his name, at least not verbally. Sedir said that he received it telepathically. Oddly, upon hearing Sedir's story, two of his oldest companions said that they had also met the stranger. They had met him twice and were confident of a third visit before their deaths.

You are entitled to hope for the first time. If you follow his advice you will see him again in this life. I saw him first thirty years ago, and he was then also in his forties, as you say he is now. No one knows his birthplace or nationality: with a French-man he behaves as a Frenchman, with an Italian he behaves as an Italian, and so on. He is recognized in the most secret circles of the East and West, as a great Master. I saw many Yogis and Chinese Mandarins versed in the hidden teachings, prostrating before him without hesitation. Now he has a mission in the East and it is because of that, that he has left our country. He travels throughout the whole world.

Paul Sedir established a small circle of Christian mystics, which continues to publish his works today. He died in 1926.

Physical Immortality: Is It Possible?

The idea of physical immorality, or near immortality, is repeated throughout esoteric literature of nearly all ages and times. Chinese, Korean, Indian, Tibetan, Mongolian, and other cultures all have their stories of the perfect master who ascends bodily into heaven but who can also return. The same is true of Western alchemists, who claim that many of their great teachers are not dead and, indeed, are several hundred years old. It is difficult to say anything about these stories other than the obvious. It is easy to make such a claim and nearly impossible to prove or disprove it. Within the faery traditions of Britain and other Celtic lands there is a rich custom of those who have entered physically into the underworld only to emerge many years later with no signs of having aged. Here again , claims are one thing, proof is another. Alchemy, Celtic shamanism, chi kung, and Tibetan yoga share a great deal of beliefs and practices, as well as the underlying goal of extended life span in order to complete the work of personal transformation. Until recently, life was hard, brutal, and short in most parts of the world. It is easy to understand why someone seeking liberation from the pain of incarnating would like to live long enough to be free from the ignorance that causes suffering in this world.

Key Points

- There are qabalistic pathworkings that can be used to assist the dying.
- It is important that a dying person is free from distractions and that any assistance be given in accordance with a spiritual and cultural tradition they are familiar with.
- There are various angels in qabala that act as guides for the dead. They can be called upon during the period of transition between life and death to ease the passing.
- One of the powers attributed to highly developed beings is the ability to raise the dead back to physical life.
- Alchemy and several schools of occultism state, or hint, that physical immortality is possible for the adept. This may simply be a continuation of consciousness rather than actual physical life, or very long life spans that from the human perspective are tantamount to immortality.

Assignments for Chapter Ten

1. Read one of the books from the Reading List on death and dying.
2. Think of someone you know who has died and perform the exercise for helping someone who is not present.
3. Spend one week on each of the following practices and meditations. Because of the serious nature of the work, take one week off between each exercise. When you have completed both of them, compose your own meditation about dying, death, and the afterlife and what it would mean to the world if there was no fear of death.

Practices and Meditations
Exercise One: A Short Ritual for Helping the Dying[2]

Preparation

If possible, play a little soft, soothing music in a low, barely audible tone. Burn a little incense or, if preferable, use a diffuser with some essential oils of frankincense, myrrh, and benzoin. This should be just enough to provide an environment and not overwhelm the dying person or others present. Dispense with any unnecessary metals in the room or on your person or that of the dying.

Explanation

One of the greatest services we can give is to assist someone who is dying. This ritual provides a framework wherein we can create a psychic environment that aids another person at their moment of death, as well as in their transition into the invisible realms.

Type of Practice

This practice is designed to imprint and immediately activate symbols and ideas in the consciousness of the dying person to assist them in their journey. It can be done as a preparatory ritual in conjunction with other practices described in chapter nine.

Method

Proceed as follows:
1. Bow at the waist, head level, to the four cardinal directions, starting in the east; turning to the south, the west, and the north; and returning to the east. Say, "Hear my prayers before, O Lord, and accept this offering of incense rising to the heavens!"
2. Continuing to face east, say, "Forgive any transgressions, errors, misdeeds, or sins committed by (name of person) in

thought, word, or deed; be they done in knowledge or out of ignorance; of free will or under influence." Repeat this one, three, or seven times, bowing after each completion.

3. Say, "Direct (name of person) that they find the supreme rest of peace profound in the heavenly mansions, where there is no sickness, suffering, concerns, or death, but only infinite light, life, and love." Repeat this one, three, or seven times, bowing after each completion.

4. Say, "Welcome (name of person) into the perpetual Light of Wisdom through the mercy of (name of a person or faith of spiritual significance to the dying person) forever." Repeat this one, three, or seven times, bowing after each completion.

5. Repeat the entire sequence facing the south, west, and north.

6. Spend time in prayer, visualizing the dying person surrounded by a brilliant white light and being greeted by a person of spiritual significance to them (or simply an angel),who leads them to the heavenly realms. This visualization should be maintained for several hours after the moment of death, if possible, either in the vicinity of the corpse or elsewhere.

With this environment created, you can now proceed to read selections from holy scriptures or similar texts that are of importance to the dying person. If they are not conscious but still present, the following psalms are useful: 17, 38, and 113, and 38, 48, and 54 to overcome fear of death. (The numeration given is from the King James Bible.) Use of the Psalms for magical and healing practices is common in French, German, and American (Pennsylvania German) traditions.

Incorporation into Daily Practice

If one is working in hospice care or in a situation where death is common, this exercise can be of assistance in daily activities.

Exercise Two: Conversations with the Angel of Death

Preparation

Prepare in any manner deemed suitable. Environments wherein grieving over deaths is a common occurrence, such as a cemetery or hospital chapel, are exceptionally useful.

Explanation

This practice allows us to address death in one of its most powerful anthropomorphic forms within Western esotericism. Because it does so, it can transmute our fears, anxieties, and other concerns we have about death as a whole.

Type of Practice

This practice imprints and activates specific ideas about death, as well as transmutes them into positive experiences and emotions for our personal growth and service.

Method

Proceed as follows:
1. Prepare your oratory, lighting your candles and incense.
2. Center yourself through breath, focusing on your heart.
3. Dissolve everything into light.
4. Call upon Azrael, the Angel of Death, to bring those souls of the departed to rest and peace. Pay attention to any images of Azrael that may occur and, in the future, use them as reference points when addressing issues around death.
5. Send out thoughts of peace, well-being, and illumination to the departed. Allow these thoughts to spread to include all those who have recently died or are in the process of dying.

6. Imagine that the departed or dying are met by their spiritual teacher, an angel, or simply a brilliant sphere of light, which merges with them; brings them peace; frees them of any overwhelming emotions of attachment, sorrow, or fear; and fills them with joy and well-being, as it takes them into the brilliant light of awakening.

7. Do this practice for forty days, either as an exercise for dialoging with "Death" or for a specific person who has died, to ensure their transition to the invisible realms.

Azreal can be imagined as a brilliant angelic figure in a black robe with white trim and with massive wings that move the airs of life as they move. Black and white are the two colors associated with energy and matter in its various expressions. Azrael can be replaced by Gabriel, the angel of the moon, or even Michael or Mercury, the Psychopomp or Guide of the Souls, but if this is done, the appropriate colors should also be utilized.

Incorporation into Daily Practice

If one is working in hospice care or in a situation where death is common, this exercise can be of assistance in daily activities.

Reading List

Death and Dying

Aries, Philippe. *The Hour of Our Death*. Translated by Helen Weaver. New York: Barnes and Noble Books, 2000. The classic history of Western attitudes towards death over the last one thousand years.

Ashcroft-Nowicki, Dolores. *The New Book of the Dead*. London: Aquarian/Thorsons, 1992. A landmark work on the esoteric considerations of death.

Carlson, Lisa. *Caring For Your Own Dead*. Hinesburg, VT: Upper Access Publishers, 1987. Legal, medical, and spiritual considerations in caring for your dead.

Fortune, Dion. *Book of the Dead*. York Beach, ME: Weiser Books, 2005.

Hill, Gary Leon. *People Who Don't Know They're Dead*. York Beach, ME: Weiser Books, 2005. A very good modern look at the subject of after-life survival and communication with the reluctant dead.

Kübler-Ross, Elisabeth. *On Death and Dying*. New York: MacMillian, 1969. A classic book and essential reading for understanding the death process.

Worden, J. William and William Proctor. *PDA: Personal Death Awareness*. Englewood Cliffs, NJ: Prentice-Hall, 1976.

Western Esotericism

Faivre, Antoine. *Access to Western Esotericism*. Albany, NY: SUNY Press, 1994. This is one of the finest and most detailed introductions to the various branches of Western esotericism from one of the most respected scholars in the field, and it is essential reading for the serious student of esotericism.

Godwin, Joscelyn. *Pagan Dreams of the Renaissance*. Grand Rapids, MI: Phanes Press, 2002.

Knight, Gareth. *The History of Magic*. St. Paul, MN: Llewellyn, 1991. A really fine survey of nearly five thousand years of the development of Western esotericism in an almost study-guide fashion, complete with key words in bold. What it lacks in detail it makes up for as a survey that ties key ideas together. This book is ideal for the beginner who wants to learn key ideas and put them in context.

Merkur, Dan. *Gnosis: An Esoteric Tradition of Mystical States and Unions*. Albany, NY: SUNY Press, 1993. A detailed study of mystical and visionary states in the major disciplines of Western esotericism.

Smoley, Richard and Jay Kinney. *Hidden Wisdom: A Guide to the Western Inner Tradition*. New York: Penguin/Arkana, 1999. This book is by the former publishers of *Gnosis* magazine and is a treat to read. This should be considered essential reading for the serious student.

Alchemy

McLean, Adam. *The Alchemical Mandala: A Survey of the Mandala in the Western Esoteric Traditions*. Grand Rapids, MI: Phanes Press, 1989.

Stavish, Mark. *The Path of Alchemy: Energetic Healing and the World of Natural Magic*. Woodbury, MN: Llewellyn, 2006.

Qabala

Cicero, Chic and Sandra Tabitha. *Self-Initiation into the Golden Dawn Tradition*. St. Paul, MN: Llewellyn, 1995. This book is a fabulous source of information, terms, definitions, diagrams, concise articles, and exercises.

Even if you are not interested in working the Golden Dawn system, you will still find it of immense reference value.

Stavish, Mark. *Kabbalah for Health and Wellness*. Woodbury, MN: Llewellyn, 2007.

Astral Projection

Ophiel. *The Art and Practice of Astral Projection*. York Beach, ME: Weiser Books, 1998. A fine little book packed with information in an easy-to-read style.

Enochian Magic

Skinner, Stephen, and David Rankine. *Practical Angel Magic of Dr. John Dee's Enochian Tables*. London: Golden Hoard Press, 2004.

Stavish, Mark. *An Introduction to Enochian Magic*. Wyoming, PA: The Institute for Hermetic Studies, 2005, *www.hermeticinstitute.org* (under "Products").

Psychology

Assagioli, Roberto. *The Act of Will*. New York: Penguin Books, 1993.

———. *Psychosynthesis: A Collection of Writings*. New York: Penguin Books, 1976.

Ferrucci, Piero. *Inevitable Grace*. Los Angeles: Jeremy P. Tarcher, Inc., 1990.

———. *What We May Be: Techniques for Psychological and Spiritual Growth Through Psychosynthesis*. Los Angeles: Jeremy P. Tarcher, Inc.,1982.

Hardy, Jean. *A Psychology with a Soul: Psychosynthesis in Evolutionary Context*. New York: Penguin/Arkana, 1982.

Physical Resurrection and Incorruptibility

One of the more interesting aspects of Western esotericism is its relationship to traditional Western religious practices as born in the Middle East. While many countries and cultures have held a belief in reincarnation, it is in India, China, and Tibet where this doctrine has been most clearly elucidated and with whose teachings modern students of esotericism are familiar. Within these cultures, specific systems of philosophy developed, and along with them, practical methods of realizing the ideas presented. The majority of Eastern thought seems to look poorly upon the body, viewing it at best as a prison house for the soul, as something to be neglected, and even as outright evil. Despite this, there are schools of Indian, Chinese, and Tibetan esotericism that view the body as essential to personal development. These schools fall under the classification of Tantra and include practical experimentations in alchemy.

The common thread among these schools is their belief in the realization of the *diamond body*, or the Body of Light, while physically incarnate or at the moment of death. This diamond body is created out of the energy that forms the very material substance of the physical body. Reports of the Body of Light have occurred in Eastern (tantric) schools until recently and state that all that remains of the physical body is some hair and nails. The process of "dissolving the Elements" takes several days, and upon completion bright lights or a rainbow are reported to have been seen over the area where it took place. If the practitioner is interrupted during their practice or fails in some crucial stage, it is said that a puddle of fluid or a small, childlike, shrunken corpse is all that will remain.

As mentioned in the introduction, these reports have been taken seriously enough to warrant investigation by Father Francis Tiso, and Brother David Steindl-Rast, Roman Catholics, under the joint sponsorship of the Esalen Institute and the Institute of Noetic Sciences.

In *Three Books of Occult Philosophy* (chapter 20) Cornelius Agrippa says: In the human body there is a very small bone called Luz by the Hebrews, which is the size of a pea, and is incorruptible, also it is not capable of being damaged by fire, but always remains unhurt. According to Jewish tradition, when the dead are raised, our new bodies will sprout from it as plants do from seeds . . . However, these powers cannot be fathomed by the mind, but have to be verified empirically.

In Hebrew *luz* means "almond" and is translated as "nut," "seed," or "bone."[1] Luz is also the name for the town Beth-El, or "house of God." It was in Beth-El that Jacob wrestled with an angel, his Higher Self/Holy Guardian Angel, after which he received the name Israel ("He shall rule as God"). Jewish folklore states that Azrael, the Angel of Death, has no power in the city of Luz and that its citizens are immortal. Entrance to Luz is gained through a secret cave hidden by the trunk of an almond tree, wherein there is a hole that gives entry to the cave. The almond has come to represent the sphere of Kether, or Crown, the highest psychic center man possesses, connecting him to the absolute Nothingness (Ain Soph Aur). Staffs and wands of almond-tree wood are used in the *Tanakh* (Old Testament) when entering into the Holy of Holies. Almond is the preferred wood for constructing a wand in medieval magical systems, particularly that of *The Sacred Magic of Abramelin the Mage*.

Occult philosophers locate the *Luz* bone along the spine or in the skull at various locations. For our purposes, we will discuss the symbolism of the luz from the perspective of Agrippa. *Luz* also means "inward curving," and it is easy to see how it can refer to the base of the spine.

However, folklore and traditional Jewish law are in disagreement on what is required for resurrection. According to Jewish law, only the thighbones and skull are needed for physical resurrection. Together they form the famous pirate flag, originally the naval flag of the Knights Templar fleet. The skull and crossed thighbones are found in modern Freemasonic York Rite rituals related to the Knights Templar. It may be that the luz represents a genuine *spiritual and physical regeneration* rather than a physical resurrection from the dead, and that the latter concept is a degeneration of the former in the popular mind. In fact, it would be easy to dismiss the idea of resurrection from the dead if it were not for its widespread occurrence throughout the Jewish and Christian bibles.

Rosicrucianism and Physical Resurrection

In May 1920 the Rosicrucian Order AMORC (the Ancient and Mystical Order Rosae Crucis), then located at 1255 Market Street, San Francisco, California, published its monthly magazine under the title *The American Rosae Crucis: An Official Publication of Rosicrucian Mysticism.* Written primarily for members of the organization, it bore a cover price of thirty-five cents. *The American Rosae Crucis* in later years would change its title to *The Mystic Triangle* and finally to its current name, *The Rosicrucian Digest.*

The May 1920 issue carried an article titled "The Raising of the Dead: A Supplement to 'Jesus as a Normal Man,'" which stated that it was a continuation of the April issue. The article points out that according to the Christian Gospel, Jesus raised the dead on at least three occasions: (1) The widow's son (Luke 7:11–16), (2) Jairus's daughter (Matthew 9:18, 19), (3) Lazarus (John 11:1–46). In addition, there are references to Elijah (1 Kings 17:17–24), Elisha (2 Kings 4:18–37), Peter (Acts 9:40), and Paul (Acts 20: 9–12) raising the dead. The power to raise the dead was not limited to Jesus or his predecessors, and he instructs his disciples to do it as well (Matthew 10:8). The author of the Epistle to the Hebrews refers to this power as one of the outward signs of inner faith (Hebrews 11:35).

When analyzed, each instance gives us a clue as to the process involved. When taken synthetically, they present the method in total.

According to the author of the May 1920 article, physical death is the result of the polarity between the body and conscious breaking down and consciousness essentially becoming passive in relation to the spiritual worlds. This passivity creates a strong attraction that pulls it from the body and returns the soul, or consciousness, to the spiritual domain. Therefore, if this polarization can be maintained, so can health. If it can be restored, then (the recently) dead can be returned to physical life. For this to work, operators must have a thorough understanding of the polarization concept and be completely confident in its reality and practical application. They must also open themselves completely as a channel for the manifestation of "Vital Life Force" (as AMORC refers to it), or the Universal Mercury of the alchemists. In addition, the following steps are given in the article:

1. The operator must be motivated by a pure desire and sympathy for the deceased and surviving family and friends.

2. A pure will must be expressed, in an unwavering and overwhelming intention to restore physical life.

3. The operator must be alone with the deceased or with only those that are in harmony with the operator and the operation.

4. Verbal instruction should be given to the soul, urging it to return to physical life and presenting it with an overwhelming reason to live.

5. The operator should lie next to or on top of the deceased, *heart to heart* (italic original) and use deep and retained breath to vitalize the body.

6. Mentally, the "Lost Word" should be pronounced. This word is unique to AMORC, in that it is delivered in the Fourth Degree and further explained in the Ninth Degree. The word is *Mathra*, or *Mathrem*, and is found in the *Gathas of Zarathustra* from the *Zend-Avesta*.

7. The operator should call the soul forth by its familiar name, while taking the deceased's hand (right to left or left to right).

The author further points out that Jesus specifically commanded his disciples to raise the dead as if it is within their power, as well as their duty, and the Gospel gives record of it having been achieved. While some of these instances may have been resuscitations rather than resurrections, it is clear from some of the accounts, such as that of Lazarus, that the deceased in question were already displaying signs of decay.

Incorruptibility

A phenomenon peculiar to Roman Catholicism and certain schools of Buddhism and Vedic yoga is the notion of incorruptibility. This is clearly different from the normal process of mummification, mummification by natural means, or the practice of ingesting tar pine to mummify oneself while still alive, as done by at least one Japanese sect. Here, the bodies of those considered saints, holy people, or completely awakened beings stay in various forms of completion centuries after their deaths. There are also instances of this occurring in the twentieth century. Several Indian yogis, as well as several leaders of Tibetan sects, have been reported to be incorruptible. According to reports, their flesh was still supple and elastic despite being dead for several years and no attempts at preservation being made. While there are no reports of Western adepts outside of the Christian churches performing the same feats, there is reason to believe that these reports support the theory that genuinely spiritually minded people affect a marked and lasting change on their physical bodies.[2] This is an area that needs considerably more research from an esoteric perspective as the etheric body of these individuals is still in varying degrees of intactness. This intact nature of the etheric is vital to connecting with the astral realms and the reason why the actual flesh, organs, and bones of deceased saints are highly prized as relics. The most common of these naturally forming talismans are bone fragments; however, soft tissue and organs, such as the heart, are well-known and preferred relics. Bones will naturally last for millennia, whereas there soft tissue should completely decompose within several weeks. Clearly if it has not, there must be either a physical or supraphysical reason to explain it.

The Hebrew Letters and Their Esoteric Meanings

The following chart gives the Hebrew letters and some of the meanings given to them by modern and ancient authorities. Because of the incredible flexibility in these meanings, it is best to form a synthesis of their main idea rather than to pick one system over the others. If one closely reads what each author has to say about the letters, it becomes clear that they are in much closer agreement about function than the following chart might suggest.

References

1. Haralick, Robert M. *The Inner Meaning of the Hebrew Letters.*
2. Suares, Carlo. *The Cipher of Genesis. The Second Coming of Rabbi YHShVH.*
3. Dubuis, Jean. *Philosophers of Nature, Qabala, Lesson 4.*
4. Zalewski, Pat. *Kabbalah of the Golden Dawn.*

LETTER	HARALICK 1	SUARES
Aleph	Pulsating force	All potential and unity
Beth	Container	Containers
Gimel	Nourishment	Organic movement
Daleth	Physicality	Physicality
Heh	Power of Being	Universal life
Vau	Connection and unification	Fertilizing agent
Zain	Movement	Achieved impregnation
Cheth	Life	Energy storage at rest
Teth	Goodness	Female energy that builds
Yod	Spirituality	Projection of original energy
Kaph	Crowning achievement	Reception
Lamed	Learning, teaching, and purpose	Connection
Mem	Perfection and completion	Maternal waters
Nun	Emergence	Individual existence
Samek	Support	Female fertility agent
Ayin	Insight and consciousness	Possibilities
Peh	Speech and freedom	Endless reserve of energy
Tzaddi	Righteousness and humility	Transfigured womanhood
Qoph	Growth and holiness	Destroyer of illusions
Resh	Cosmic container	Cosmic container
Shin	Cosmic nourishment	The Holy Spirit
Tau	True law	Exaltation to the highest capacity

DUBUIS	FELKIN/D'OLIVET
Primordial air/energy	Unity, power, stability
Will/action	Interior action, virility
Inner development	Organic development
Work of the Quaternary	Physical abundance
Being	Universal life
Evolutionary force	Action, connection
Union of forces	Dazzling movement
Evolutionary field	Material life and area of labor
Silver cord	Protection, refuge, goal
Young man	Creative power both human and divine
Mold of life	Reception and assimilation
Extension	Extension, creative omnipotence
Universal femininity	Protective creative power
Potential passivity	Produced, reflected, unfolding
Link and lock to the astral	Supporting (spiral) movement
The void	Emptiness
Foundation–individualized life	Power of speech
Awakening the divine energy	Severance, solution, divine refuge
Completed work	Repression and decision
Order, the Word	Renewing movement
Universal masculinity	Movement of duration
Equilibrium, perfection	Reciprocity, exchange

The Powers of the Hebrew Letters, According to Eliphas Levi

From *Transcendental Magic*, in which Levi quotes a sixteenth-century manuscript:[1]

Hereinafter follow the powers and privileges of the man who holds in his right hand the Clavis of Solomon, and in his left hand the branch of Blossoming Almond.

Aleph—He beholds God face to face, without dying, and converses familiarly with the seven genii who command the entire celestial army.

Beth—He is above all griefs and all fears.

Gimel—He reigns with all heaven and is served by all hell.

Daleth—He rules his own health and life, and can influence equally those of others.

He—He can neither be surprised by misfortune nor overwhelmed by disasters, nor can he be conquered by his enemies.

Vau—He knows the reason of the past, present, and future.

Zain—He possesses the secret of the resurrection of the dead and the keys of immortality.

Such are the seven chief privileges, and those which rank next are these:

Cheth—To find the Philosophical Stone.

Teth—To possess the Universal Medicine.

Yod—To know the laws of perpetual motion and to prove quadrature of the Circle.

Kaph—To change into gold not only all metals but also the earth itself, and even the refuse of the earth.

Lamed—To subdue the most ferocious animals and have power to pronounce those words which paralyse and charm serpents.

Mem—To have the Ars Notoria which gives the Universal Science.

Nun—To speak learnedly on all subjects, without preparation and without study.

These, finally, are the seven least powers of the Magus:

Samek—To know at a glance the deep things of the souls of men and the mysteries of the hearts of women.

Ayin—To force Nature to make him free at his pleasure.

Peh—To foresee all future events which do not depend on a superior free will, or on a discernable cause.

Tzade—To give at once and to all the most efficacious consolations and the most wholesome counsels.

Qoph—To triumph over adversities.

Resh—To conquer love and hate.

Shin—To have the secret of wealth, to be always its master and never its slave. To enjoy even poverty and never become abject or miserable.

Tau—Let us add to these three septenaries that the wise man rules the elements, stills tempests, cures the diseased by his touch, and raises the dead!

Notes

Chapter One

1. For more information on alchemical tinctures see, *The Path of Alchemy—Energetic Healing and the World of Natural Magic* by Mark Stavish, Llewellyn Worldwide, St. Paul, MN, 2006.

2. *Corpus Hermeticum* 1.27-31, and 13.

3. *"Hermeticism"* by Antoine Faivre, *Encyclopedia of Religion*, edited by Mircea Eliade.

4. Astrology in Alexandrian Hermeticism is initiatic and represents the journey of the individual as well as collective soul on the "Path of Return" or regeneration. Since the Seventeenth Century astrology has increasingly become little more than a form of divination divorced from spiritual practices and understanding.

5. Freemasons will recognize the presence of the Sun and the Moon as two of the three Lesser Lights of the Lodge, with the Master, balancing and directing their energies, as the third of the Lesser Lights.

Chapter Two

1. Israel Regardie was a strong proponent of integrating psychotherapy into initiatic and occult training so that the personality is transformed rather than disfigured by the increase of energy and awareness that such training can bring. See his book *The Middle Pillar* for additional information.

2. Some schools will place the order as Fire, Water, Air, and Earth. Hermetic and alchemical utilize the order given in the chapter. The *Sepher Yetzirah* is clear in the order of generation: Fire, Water, Air, but also states that Air comes between Fire and Water. Both models work, remember, "The map is not the territory."

3. Sepherah is singular; Sepheroth is plural.

4. For more information on this process see: "The Portae Lucis Method of Jean Dubuis" by Mark Stavish, published in *The Stone* and available online at *www.hermeticinstitute.org* and "The Experience of Eternity—Initiatic Esotericism" by Jean Dubuis, available from Triad Publishing at *www.triad-publishing.com*.

5. These are often called the 32 Paths of Wisdom in total. Location and associations of the Paths are fairly standardized, but the Tree of Life variations exist.

6. For a detailed survey of Renaissance Magic and its impact on contemporary esotericism see: *Drawing Down the Life of Heaven—Magic in the Renaissance* by Mark Stavish, available through *www.hermeticinstitute.org*.

7. For a detailed study of Fludd's life, works, and their importance to modern esotericism see *Robert Fludd—Hermetic Philosopher and Surveyor of Two Worlds* by Joscelyn Godwin, Phanes Press, 2005.

8. *Magick* by Aleister Crowley, Weiser Books, San Francisco, 2000, p. 62.

9. For additional information see: *Spanish Christian Cabala—The Works of Luis de Leon, Santa Teresa de Jesus, and San Juan de la Cruz* by Catherine Swietlicki, University of Missouri Press, Columbia, 1986.

Chapter Three

1. For a very effective and simple approach to awakening the psychic centers see: *Wisdom of the Mystic Masters* by Joseph Weed.

2. *Kundalini, Evolution and Enlightenment*, edited by John White, Anchor Press, Doubleday, Garden City, New York, 1979, p. 83.

3. *The Sword and the Serpent,* vol. 2 of *The Magical Philosophy* by Melita Denning and Osborne Phillips. Llewellyn Publications, St. Paul, MN, 1988, pp. 188 and 189.

4. White, from *The Restored New Testament* by J. M. Pryse, p. 432.

5. *The Middle Pillar* by Israel Regardie, Llewellyn Publications, St. Paul, MN, 1991, p. 113.

6. Ibid., p. 116.

7. *A Practical Guide to Qabalistic Symbolism* by Gareth Knight. Samuel Weiser, Inc., York Beach, Maine, 1978, p.105.

8. Knight, p.111.

9. The thyroid is a secondary sexual organ.

10. *Awaken Healing Light of the Tao* by Mantak & Maneewan Chia. Healing Tao Books, Huntington, New York, 1993, pp. 223–34.

11. See *Kabbalah of the Golden Dawn* by Pat Zalewski, Llewellyn Publications, St. Paul, MN, 1993, pp. 15–36 and 187–223.

12. For more information on Tibetan Dream Yoga see *The Tibetan Yogas of Dream and Sleep* by Tenzin Wangyal Rinpoche; *Meditation, Transformation, and Dream Yoga* by Ven. Gyatrul Rinpoche; and *Sleeping, Dreaming, and Dying* by the Dalai Lama.

13. *The True Art of Healing* by Israel Regardie, edited by Marc Allen. The New World Library, San Rafael, CA, 1991, p. 32.

Chapter Four

1. *Inner Space* by Aryeh Kaplan, Moznain Publishing Corp., Brooklyn, NY, 1990, p. 22.

2. Kaplan, p. 26

3. PON Qabala Course Lesson, 61, p.1

4. Ibid., p. 3.

5. On a personal note, this writer can take any amount of criticism and editing after the initial product is finished, but will not even acknowledge a work is in progress until then.

6. PON *Fundamentals of Esoteric Knowledge Lesson 10*, p. 3.

7. PON *Qabala Course Lessons 9–11*. Please note, the various versions of the *Sepher Yetzirah* differ on the attributes. The *Gra* edition is the most common. See *Sepher Yetzirah—The Book of Creation, In Theory and Practice* by Aryeh Kaplan for a comparison of the different editions. Also see Franz Bardon's *Key to the True Kabbalah* for additional attributes of the Hebrew Letters. Please note however, that they must be transliterated back from *phonetic German* into Hebrew to be of use.

8. For more information on the continuation of phonetic qabala in folk magical practices see *Pow-Wow, Psalms, and German Magical Folklore* by Mark Stavish, M.A., in the Articles section at: *www.hermeticinstitute.org*.

9. PON *Qabala Course Lesson 61,* p. 7 and *The Golden Dawn* by Isreal Regardie, Llewellyn Publications, St. Paul, MN, 1986. "The Vibratory Mode of Pronouncing Divine Names," p. 487.

10. Students who wish to learn more about the potential uses and combinations of the Hebrew letters and their magical uses are encouraged to read Franz Bardon's *The Key to the True Kabbalah,* Merkur Publishing, Inc., Salt Lake City, UT, 1996. For a correlation between the phonetic German in the text and Hebrew see *www.abardoncompanion.com.*

11. PON *Qabala Course Lessons 8 & 9*; PON *Qabala Lesson 13.*

12. PON *Qabala Course Lesson 9,* p. 5.

13. PON *Fundamentals of Esoteric Knowledge Lesson 5,* pp. 5–6.

14. PON *Qabala Course Lesson 61,* pp. 4–5.

15. There are several variations of the spelling of Pasqualez's name, this one being the most common.

16. See *Kabbalah* by Robert Ambelain, translated by Pierce Vaughn, at: *www.moup.org.* I originally became aware of this ritual when a member of the Elu Cohen sent it to me several years ago asking for assistance in deciphering some of its meaning as well as potential uses. The expanded version in this chapter is based upon that request and additional commentary from participants in research specific to this ritual that was undertaken by the Institute for Hermetic Studies.

17. See *The Sign of the Cross* by Mark Stavish, at: *www.hermeticinstitute.org* in the Articles section.

Chapter Five

1. The difference between the 'personal' and the 'impersonal' regarding a sepherah is that the 'note' remains the same, only the 'octave' changes.

2. This is a tricky point and need to be clarified. Magical operations exist in the levels below Tiphareth, but it is only after we have had a profound and permanent change in consciousness at the level of Tiphareth are we able to perform magical operations without failure, and more or less on a level that does not require any ritual or external supports.

3. *The Complete Golden Dawn System of Magic* by Israel Regardie, New Falcon Publications, Tempe, AZ, 2003, p. 465.

Chapter Six

1. "Indians who innovated this body of theory and practices called it *tantra,* the warp (of reality)." The word has a most interesting pedigree. Its

root, tan, means "to stretch," as one would a thread on a loom (also called tantra) or, in Vedic parlance, a body (tanu) to be sacrificed on an alter within a ritual framework (tantra)."—*The Alchemical Body: Siddha Traditions in Medieval India* by David Gordon White, University of Chicago Press, Chicago, Illinois, 1998, pp. 1–2. This definition of Indian alchemy and their practices could just as easily apply to alchemists everywhere.

2. For additional information on the creation and use of spagyric products, see *The Path of Alchemy—Energetic Healing and the World of Natural Magic* by Mark Stavish, Llewellyn Publishing, St. Paul, MN, 2006.

3. Freemasons will recognize the presence of the Sun and the Moon as two of the three Lesser Lights of the Lodge, with the Master, balancing and directing their energies, as the third of the Lesser Lights.

4. This exercise is similar to what is presented in *Introduction to Magic— Rituals and Techniques for the Magus* by Julius Evola and the UR group. Inner Traditions. Rochester, VT, 2001.

5. *The Apocalypse* by Jean Dubuis, translated by Patrice Maleze, copyright 1999 Jean Dubuis. The following article appeared in the final issue of *The Stone* (Nov.–Dec. 1999), the bi-monthly publication of *The Philosophers of Nature* (PON), the American branch and successor to *Les Philosophes de la Nature* (LPN), a French Hermetic and Alchemical organization started by Jean Dubuis in the late 1970's. PON ceased operation on December 31, 1999, however the lessons in English and French, along with back issues of *The Stone*, may be obtained from Triad Publishing at *www.triad-publishing.com* or via email at *info@triad-publishing.com*.

Chapter Seven

1. The Magical Personality is defined as a self-created image of one's self that allows for greater power and presence when doing esoteric work.

2. *The Ritual Magic Workbook* by Dolores Ashcroft-Nowicki, Samuel Weiser, Inc., York Beach, Maine, 1998, p. 153.

3. See *Fundamentals of Esoteric Knowledge*, Lesson 1-3. The Philosopher's of Nature (PON), Wheaton, Ill, 1988.

4. *The Doctrine of the Subtle Body* by GS Mead, Weiser Books, York Beach, Maine. 1993, p. 9.

5. Ibid., p. 13.

6. Ibid., P. 30.

7. Ashcroft-Nowicki also suggests this possibility in her book *The Magical Use of Thoughtforms,* and gives a ritual wherein it can be created.

8. As mentioned, in the *Hermetic Order of the Golden Dawn,* the Hermetic Rose+Cross and the Pantacle of Earth are 'adept level' tools. In *The Philosophers of Nature* (PON) *Qabala Course,* they are not constructed until the very end of the six year course. However, the Supreme Pentagram and Hexagram rituals are presented in the second year.

9. Mead, p. 58.

10. Ibid., p. 102.

11. See *Self-Initiation into the Golden Dawn Tradition* by Chic and Sandra Tabatha Cicero, Llewellyn Publications, Saint Paul, MN, 1995.

12. For more information on Pathworking see: PON *Qabala Course,* Lessons 36–57. *Highways of the Mind* by Dolores Ashcroft–Nowicki and *Magical States of Consciousness* by Melita Denning and Osborne Phillips.

13. A complete outline of a four-year study plan for individuals and groups can be found at www.hermeticinstitute.org in the Articles Section.

14. Pages 359–362.

15. Use of the 'Elemental Grade Signs' or the 'Rending of the Veil' is at the performer's discretion.

16. *Encyclopedia of Occultism and Parapsychology, Vol. 1,* Edited by Gordon Melton, Gale Group, New York, 2001, pp. 469–473.

17. In one of the libraries of Brown University, Providence, Rhode Island, there are the notes of two researches into the similarity between ectoplasm and the writings of the later alchemists. This research was apparently done in the 1920's.

18. *Magick: Book Four* by Aleister Crowley, Samuel Weiser, Inc., York Beach, Maine, 2000, p. 201.

19. Ibid., p. 202.

20. Ibid., p. 246.

21. Ibid., p. 248.

22. Ibid., p. 249.

23. Ibid., pp. 248–9.

24. Ibid., p. 624.

25. One student who did this noted that the simulacrum was more vital, but also slightly more difficult to control. They also noted that when they imagined the letters within their physical body when falling asleep, that astral projection occurred rapidly, often before the fifth or sixth letter was reached.

Chapter Eight

1. For this reason it is common in some Western esoteric and initiatic organizations for their teaching, or at least members, to maintain a tie to their traditional religion. Many Martinist groups are openly Catholic in their orientation (although far from all), while many Rosicrucian, Templar, Martinist, and Masonic bodies are distinctly oriented towards an esoteric interpretation of Christian teachings.

2. Not all esotericists agree on this point or turning to the ancient cults. For an alternative point of view see *Occult Catholicism—Real Magic for Devout Catholics* by Fr. Augustinus Thaumatourgos, *www.lulu.com*, ID: 141817.

3. *The Sacred Cord Meditations* by Dolores Ashcroft-Nowicki, Aquarian Press, Wellingborough, Northhamptonshire, 1990, p. 107.

4. *The Secrets of a Golden Dawn Temple* by Chic and Sandra Cicero, Llewellyn Publishing, St. Paul, MN, 1995, p.374.

5. PON *Qabala Course Lesson 67,* p. 130

6. Ibid., p. 132.

7. Ibid., p. 84.

8. Ibid.

9. *The Invisible Temple* by Peter Roche de Coppens, Llewellyn Publications, St. Paul, MN, 1987, p. 17.

10. *Psychosynthesis—A Collection of Basic Writings* by Roberto Assangioli, Penguin Books, New York, NY, 1976, p. 166.

11. Ibid., p. 168.

12. Ibid., p. 169.

13. Roche de Coppens, p. 93.

14. *Invisibility—The Art of Vanishing* by Steve Richards, Aquarian Press, Wellingborough Northamptonshire, 1992, p. 125.

15. Richards, p. 126.

16. PON *Qabala Course Lesson 67,* p. 5.

17. Ibid., pp. 57–58.

Chapter Nine

1. *Histoire des doctrines esoteriques*

2. *Meditations on the Tarot: A Journey into Christian Hermeticism,* anonymous, Element Books, Rockport, MA, 1985, p. 346.

3. *The Philosophers of Nature Qabala Lessons* by Jean Dubuis, Triad Publishing, Wheaton, IL, 1996, Lesson 59, pp. 4–5.

4. For more information on practical alchemy, see *The Path of Alchemy—Energetic Healing and the World of Natural Magic* by Mark Stavish, Llewellyn Worldwide, St. Paul, MN, 2006.

5. Tradition states that the keys are made of lead, the metal of Saturn. Saturn is associated with Binah, "Queen of Heaven and Earth" as well as death and renewal.

6. *The One Year Manual* by Dr. Israel Regardie, Samuel Weiser, Inc. York Beach, Maine, 1981, p. 66.

7. See *The Zodiac and the Salts of Salvation—Homeopathic Remedies for the Sign Types* by Goerge Washington Carey and Inez Eudora Perry. Samuel Weiser, Inc., York Beach, Maine, 1996, p. 219.

8. Sometimes a fourth stage is inserted between White and Red, or Yellow, indicating perfect fecundity. This is a brief stage and passes quickly, and not mentioned in all sources.

9. After the creation of the Red Stone, it is multiplied twice more to perfect its power. This pushes the Stone from the level of Tiphareth, to Geburah, and finally Chesed. Beyond this is another stone, possibly the so-called Firestone, of which little is said.

10. This may be by way of the Dark and Light Angels of Geburah and Chesed, or by way of their synthesis in a direct ascent up the Middle Pillar.

11. *The Book of Thoth* by Aleister Crowley. Samuel Weiser, Inc. York Beach, Maine. 1995, p. 101

12. *The Tarot of the Magicians* by Oswald Wirth. Samuel Weiser, Inc., York Beach, Maine, 1985, p. 114.

13. See "The Chamber of Reflection" by Mark Stavish, at *www.hermeticinstitute.org*, Articles Section.

14. In her work *The Ritual Magic Workbook*, Dolores Ashcroft-Nowicki discusses the problem and solution to the possibility of 'sudden death' through "The Rite of Withdrawal." Mrs. Ashcroft-Nowicki describes the Rite as "a ritual pathworking which is then time-locked by intent, so to work at the moment of his [the magician's] death. If that death is a sudden event, it will snap into operation just before the consciousness goes, if there is time to reflect, the working can be done in full consciousness, which is the way all initiates should 'go out'."

15. The image of the sun rising in the morning, or the 'Golden Dawn,' is replete throughout alchemical literature and the writings of theosophists such as Jakob Boehme. Emphasis on the brilliant reds colors of the morning, here again, reference to the Red Lion, or the Red Stone of the Philosophers.

Chapter Ten

1. *Ways to Self-Realization* by Mouni Sadhu, Wilshire Book Company, North Hollywood, CA, 1962, pp. 226–231.

2. From *The Tarot* by Mouni Sadhu, Wilshire Book Co., North Hollywood, CA, 1973.

Notes

1. Could this be the seed Jesus referred to when he said, "If you have the faith of a mustard seed you could command the mountain to come down and it would"?

2 Christian Rosenkreutz is reported to be incorruptible, but to date CRC has not been definitively identified as a historical person, or his tomb physically located. See *Opening the Vault: Rosicrucianism for the 21st Century* by Mark Stavish at: *www.hermeticinstitute.org.*

About the Author

Mark Stavish has over a quarter-century of experience in traditional spirituality and is an internationally respected authority in the study and practical application of alchemy, qabala, and astrology. Stavish has published several hundred articles, book reviews, and interviews on the traditions of Western Esotericism, many of which have been translated into Dutch, French, Swedish, German, Turkish, Italian, Spanish, Russian, and Portuguese. He has also been a consultant to print and broadcast media, and several documentaries. In 1998 Stavish established the Institute for Hermetic Studies. In December 2001, to further the advancement of nonsectarian and academic approaches to Western Esotericism, he established The Louis Claude de St. Martin Fund, thereby creating the only widely known nonsectarian, tax-deductible, non-profit fund dedicated exclusively to advancing the study and practice of Western Esotericism. Stavish's education includes two undergraduate degrees (Theology and Communications) and a Master's degree in Counseling (Rhode Island College, Providence). He has also been a member and officer in several traditional initiatic organizations focusing on Rosicrucianism, Martinism, regular Freemasonry, including Ancient and Accepted Scottish Rite, and York Rite. He resides in Wyoming, Pennsylvania.

To Our Readers

Weiser Books, an imprint of Red Wheel/Weiser, publishes books across the entire spectrum of occult and esoteric subjects. Our mission is to publish quality books that will make a difference in people's lives without advocating any one particular path or field of study. We value the integrity, originality, and depth of knowledge of our authors.

Our readers are our most important resource, and we appreciate your input, suggestions, and ideas about what you would like to see published. Please feel free to contact us, to request our latest book catalog, or to be added to our mailing list.

Red Wheel/Weiser, LLC
500 Third Street, Suite 230
San Francisco, CA 94107
www.redwheelweiser.com